XML Weekend Crash Course™

XML Weekend Crash Course™

Kay Ethier and Alan Houser

Hungry Minds™

Best-Selling Books • Digital Downloads • e-Books • Answer Networks •
e-Newsletters • Branded Web Sites • e-Learning

Cleveland, OH • Indianapolis, IN • New York, NY

XML Weekend Crash Course™

Published by
Hungry Minds, Inc.
909 Third Avenue
New York, NY 10022
www.hungryminds.com

Copyright © 2001 Hungry Minds, Inc. All rights reserved. No part of this book, including interior design, cover design, and icons, may be reproduced or transmitted in any form, by any means (electronic, photocopying, recording, or otherwise) without the prior written permission of the publisher.

Library of Congress Control Number: 2001092747

ISBN: 0-7645-4759-3

Printed in the United States of America

10 9 8 7 6 5 4 3 2 1

1B/RQ/QZ/QR/IN

Distributed in the United States by
Hungry Minds, Inc.

Distributed by CDG Books Canada Inc. for Canada; by Transworld Publishers Limited in the United Kingdom; by IDG Norge Books for Norway; by IDG Sweden Books for Sweden; by IDG Books Australia Publishing Corporation Pty. Ltd. for Australia and New Zealand; by TransQuest Publishers Pte Ltd. for Singapore, Malaysia, Thailand, Indonesia, and Hong Kong; by Gotop Information Inc. for Taiwan; by ICG Muse, Inc. for Japan; by Intersoft for South Africa; by Eyrolles for France; by International Thomson Publishing for Germany, Austria, and Switzerland; by Distribuidora Cuspide for Argentina; by LR International for Brazil; by Galileo Libros for Chile; by Ediciones ZETA S.C.R. Ltda. for Peru; by WS Computer Publishing Corporation, Inc., for the Philippines; by Contemporanea de Ediciones for Venezuela; by Express Computer Distributors for the Caribbean and West Indies; by Micronesia Media Distributor, Inc. for Micronesia; by Chips Computadoras S.A. de C.V. for Mexico; by Editorial Norma de Panama S.A. for Panama; by American Bookshops for Finland.

For general information on Hungry Minds' products and services please contact our Customer Care department within the U.S. at 800-762-2974, outside the U.S. at 317-572-3993 or fax 317-572-4002.

For sales inquiries and reseller information, including discounts, premium and bulk quantity sales, and foreign-language translations, please contact our Customer Care department at 800-434-3422, fax 317-572-4002 or write to Hungry Minds, Inc., Attn: Customer Care Department, 10475 Crosspoint Boulevard, Indianapolis, IN 46256.

For information on licensing foreign or domestic rights, please contact our Sub-Rights Customer Care department at 212-884-5000.

For information on using Hungry Minds' products and services in the classroom or for ordering examination copies, please contact our Educational Sales department at 800-434-2086 or fax 317-572-4005.

For press review copies, author interviews, or other publicity information, please contact our Public Relations department at 317-572-3168 or fax 317-572-4168.

For authorization to photocopy items for corporate, personal, or educational use, please contact Copyright Clearance Center, 222 Rosewood Drive, Danvers, MA 01923, or fax 978-750-4470.

Trademarks: Weekend Crash Course is a trademark or registered trademark of Hungry Minds, Inc. All other trademarks are property of their respective owners. Hungry Minds, Inc. is not associated with any product or vendor mentioned in this book.

Hungry Minds™ is a trademark of Hungry Minds, Inc.

About the Authors

Kay Ethier is manager of new business with Bright Path Solutions of Research Triangle Park, North Carolina. Kay is an accomplished writer and regular contributor to *IT: Information Technology for Professionals*, for which she writes on a variety of technology topics. She instructs technical courses on such topics as FrameMaker, FrameMaker+SGML, XML, HTML, and Adobe Acrobat. In addition to teaching, Kay works with clients on paper and electronic publishing projects, manages internal corporate publishing projects, and lectures at national seminars and conferences.

Alan Houser is co-founder and principal partner of Group Wellesley, a Pittsburgh, Pennsylvania–based company that provides technical documentation and information management services to technology-based companies and organizations. Having more than 12 years of experience in the software industry, Alan enjoys developing solutions to support information management and information re-use, and he has designed enterprise-wide processes for writing, maintaining, and publishing technical documentation. He has presented on publishing solutions, including XML and SGML, at local and national conferences, and he provides classroom training to corporate audiences in XML and FrameMaker+SGML.

Credits

Acquisitions Editor
Grace Buechlein

Project Editor
Neil Romanosky

Technical Editor
Ken Cox

Copy Editor
Jeremy Zucker

Editorial Manager
Colleen Totz

Project Coordinator
Maridee Ennis

Graphics and Production Specialists
Joyce Haughey, Betty Schulte,
Kendra Span, Erin Zeltner

Quality Control Technicians
David Faust, Carl Pierce

Permissions Editor
Laura Moss

Media Development Specialist
Angela Denny

Media Development Coordinator
Marisa Pearman

Proofreading and Indexing
TECHBOOKS Production Services

To Candace, Mom, and Dad.
Thanks for encouraging me.
— Kay Ethier

To my mother. I know
you are always with me.
— Alan Houser

Preface

Welcome to *XML Weekend Crash Course*™. The Weekend Crash Course book series is designed to provide you with quick overviews of technical topics. In this book you will find what you need to get started using XML and to begin organizing and creating XML documents and sample projects. So let's get started!

Who Should Read This Book

XML Weekend Crash Course is designed to walk you through short, easy lessons that help you pick up the concepts you need in the span of one weekend. The book is created for:

- Those who need to learn XML quickly. Whether you need to start a project at work or pass muster at a job interview, this book is for you. This book is designed for beginners and assumes little if any programming background. Even if you are unfamiliar with programming, we will not leave you hanging.
- Those who are working with HTML and need to transition to XML. Many of the exercises in this book reference HTML features and compare them with XML's. This should help you make the move to XML painlessly and quickly.

To get the most from this Weekend Crash Course, you should already have some familiarity with creating text files on your PC and using a Web browser. Some knowledge of HTML will be helpful but is not mandatory.

What You Need to Have

To make the most of *XML Weekend Crash Course*, you should have a computer set up with:

- Microsoft Internet Explorer 5.0 or later, included on this book's CD-ROM
- A text-editing tool (Windows Notepad will suffice)
- The desire to work through the exercises and learn about XML

There isn't a minimum computer speed required for this book. Any machine that runs Microsoft Windows (including Windows 95, Windows 98, Windows NT, Windows ME, or Windows 2000) should do the trick. Your XML documents are going to be small, text-based documents that do not require today's ultra-fast PC processors.

What Results You Can Expect

You can expect to pick up the main points of XML this weekend. You will gain an understanding of XML documents and what it takes to create working, viewable XML. You will also learn about several related XML technologies you may have heard of: XSLT, XLink, XML schemas, and more.

This Weekend Crash Course is just that: a quick trip through the important points of XML. It's not a complete reference guide, but it will give you what you need to know to get started creating XML documents.

Features and Layout of This Book

This book, like all books in the Weekend Crash Course series, is designed for optimum readability and hands-on practice. We urge you to follow the suggestions for timing and breaks — be sure to rest between major sections.

This book is arranged in 30 sessions, each of which should take approximately 30 minutes to complete. You'll find five questions at the end of each session to help you review what you've learned, and at the end of each of the book's six parts is a longer Part Review. Answering the Part Reviews gives you an opportunity to review the major points of each session — and we even provide you with the answers (in Appendix A).

Again, be sure to take breaks between parts. This series is designed to be an effective learning experience, so following the suggested time schedule should maximize your learning experience and help you gain a solid foundation with XML.

The following sections break down the book's six parts.

Part I: Friday Evening

On Friday evening, you will learn about the concept of *structured* documents, and why XML makes it easier to exchange, process, and reuse your information. You will create your first XML documents and learn about how XML documents can drive Web-based and other applications.

Part II: Saturday Morning

On Saturday morning, you will learn the nuts and bolts of XML — the syntax that defines XML. You will learn the components of XML, and how these work together to create rich, structured documents. You will also learn about XML Document Type Definitions (DTDs), the blueprints for creating valid XML documents.

Part III: Saturday Afternoon

On Saturday afternoon, you will explore XML DTDs in much more detail. You will learn all that you need to create your own XML markup language and formalize that language in an XML DTD. You will also get an introduction to processing XML documents with the XML transformation language, XSLT.

Part IV: Saturday Evening

You will spend Saturday evening learning more about XML transformations. You will learn to select and sort components of XML documents. This section provides the grounding you need to begin manipulating, reusing, and publishing your XML documents.

Part V: Sunday Morning

Sunday morning is about formatting and displaying your XML documents on the World Wide Web. You will learn the two major mechanisms to do this — cascading style sheets (CSS) and the XML transformation language (XSLT). You will also get an introduction to creating dynamic, scripted XML documents and learn about XHTML, a version of HTML that conforms to XML syntax.

Part VI: Sunday Afternoon

Sunday afternoon you will learn about XML schemas, a relatively recent addition to the XML family. XML schemas provide an alternative to XML DTDs for serving as the blueprints for your XML documents. You will also get a tour of some industry-standard XML vocabularies, like the Wireless Markup Language (WML) and Scalable Vector Graphics Language (SVG). Finally, you will be introduced to the XML standards for linking and referencing external documents, which promise to revolutionize the plain old hypertext of today.

Weekend Crash Course icons

As you go through each session, watch for the following status icons. These will give you hints about your progress through each session.

**30 Min.
To Go**

This book also contains icons that highlight important comments from the authors, which are represented by the following icons:

Other conventions

Three other conventions appearing in this series are important for you to know.

- To indicate menu choices, we use the ⇨ symbol.
- To indicate code or a Web site address within body text, we use a `code-type` font, as illustrated in this sentence.
- To indicate programming examples, we use all code. Thus,

```
This is code not within the line of text.
```

Accompanying CD-ROM

XML Weekend Crash Course includes a CD-ROM inside the back cover. This CD-ROM contains a self-assessment test, source code for session examples, software that you may install, and links to other useful software. For a description of the CD-ROM items, refer to Appendix B.

Reach Out

Hungry Minds, Inc., and the authors want your feedback. After you have had a chance to use this book, send any feedback to my2cents@hungryminds.com. Please include the book's ISBN and/or title in the subject line so that your comments reach the right people. If the book worked for you, if you found typos, or if you want to let us know what you thought, feel free to e-mail the authors at:

```
kethier@travelthepath.com
arh@groupwellesley.com
```

You are now ready to begin. Make sure you that you have set aside time for the weekend, that you have snacks close at hand, and that your computer is poised and ready. Good luck with your *XML Weekend Crash Course!*

Acknowledgments

I want to thank my children — Joseph, Riley, and Nadia — for allowing me to take the time to write this book. It was time away from them and I appreciate their understanding. Also, thanks to my Mom and Dad for providing me with the backup I needed to make my deadlines. I could not have written this book without their help. And thanks to my husband, Denis, for keeping the house in order.

I'd also like to thank the folks at Computer News Group in Raleigh for publishing some of my first technology articles. Also, thanks to David, Eduardo, Leatta, Leslie, and Pam for their encouragement. Finally, thanks to my students for giving me such positive feedback through the years, making me love my job.

Most of all, thanks to my co-author, Alan Houser, for writing this book with me and sharing the fun and the stress. It has been a pleasure, Alan.

— *Kay Ethier*

I want to thank David Mundie, who founded and leads the Pittsburgh Markup Language Users Group (http://www.pittmark.org). David and his organization have helped me to go from using markup languages like XML and SGML to really "getting my head around them."

I want to thank my dear wife, Mary, for her encouragement and support while she endured a stressed and grumpy spouse for many weeks. Thanks also to my small children, Samuel and James, for their loss of "Daddy time" during the course of this project. I hope to make it up to them by taking them to see lots of "tall buildings!", "real trains!", and all sorts of other sights that young children (and adults like myself) find so fascinating.

Thanks to my co-author, Kay Ethier, for bringing me into this project. She endured the idiosyncrasies of my work habits and writing style like a champ. I have always wanted to write a general-press book — now that life's dream is accomplished. What's next?

— *Alan Houser*

Contents at a Glance

Contents

XML Weekend Crash Course™

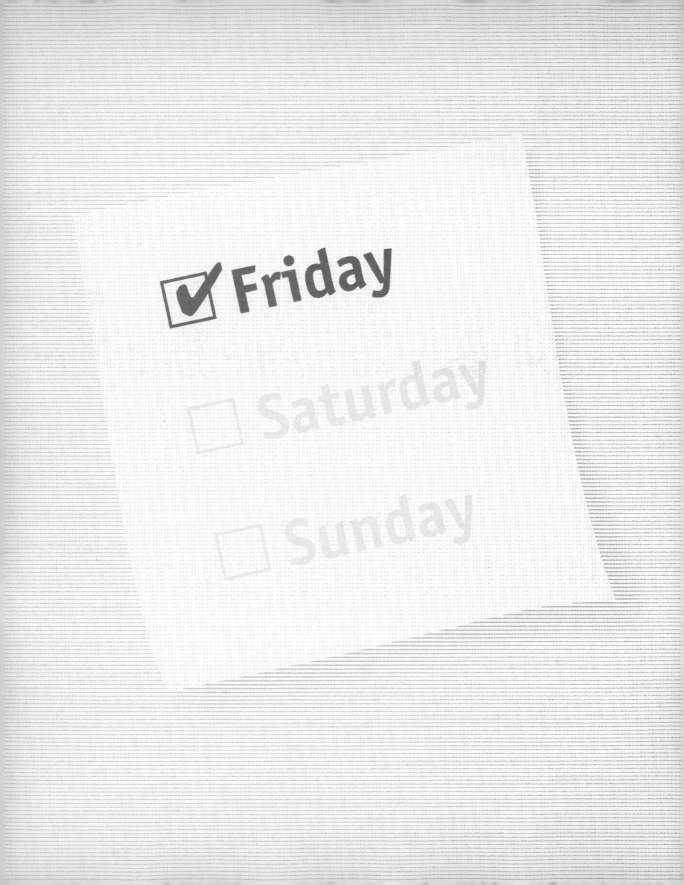

Part I — Friday Evening

PART

I

Friday
Evening

Introduction to Structured Documents

Session Checklist

✔ Introducing structured documents

✔ Learning how documents are changing as the Web evolves

✔ Considering XML capabilities for reusability

Getting Started with Structured Documents

**30 Min.
To Go**

In general, we demand much more from our documents than we used to. We print documents and we display them in Web browsers, personal digital assistant (PDA) screens, and cell phone screens. We integrate them with databases. We create customized documents for specific applications. The days of simply writing and printing documents are over.

Not only are we reusing information, we're exchanging information more and more. The sheer volume of the information we need to exchange is greater than ever before, and it can't be tied to proprietary platforms or vendors. Just as Java provided a platform-independent programming language, we needed a platform-independent means of exchanging information. Extensible Markup Language (XML) is that means.

Before we dive into XML, we're going to look at the concept of structured documents. This will lay the groundwork for you to understand the concepts behind XML, as well as specifics of XML syntax.

A simple document may be loosely structured. If you understand that most documents have a structure — loose or rigid — it's not a far leap for you to understand XML documents. Two examples of loose document structure are:

- **An HTML Page:** Within an HTML page, you may have a heading (marked by the heading tag `<H1>`) followed by a paragraph (marked by the paragraph tag `<P>`). Other headings occur on the page with paragraphs after them. You may have any number of paragraphs or headings.

- **A paper document:** In a printed letter, you may have a date, sender's address, recipient's address, a salutation, the letter body, and a close.

In the HTML and paper document examples, there is a very loose structure. There are not, however, any steadfast rules governing the order of items on the page or the number of paragraphs (neither a minimum nor a maximum) in the document.

In this book, when we refer to structured documents we may refer both to documents that have this loose structure and to documents that have rigid structure controlled by document rules.

XML documents are structured documents. They may follow a strict structure, where certain parts occur in a particular order with predefined frequency, or they may be loosely structured. XML documents with a strict structure receive their structure from a set of structure rules that are assigned to the document.

Document structure explored

Most documents have some structure even if they don't have rules to guide the structure. The following figures show the simple documents mentioned earlier in this session.

First, we will look at a document that has loose structure. Figure 1-1 shows an HTML page in Internet Explorer.

The document in Figure 1-1 displays in the browser and is readable. It has a structure, in that the text consists of headings followed by paragraphs. No rules limit the document and we could just as easily have used inappropriate heading sizes, as shown in Figure 1-2.

Figure 1-1
A loosely structured Web page, no rules

Figure 1-2
An inappropriately formatted structured Web page, no rules

Next, we will review a paper document that has a loose structure. In Figure 1-3, you see a basic letter. The letter begins with the sender's address, followed by the date. Next come the recipient's address, subject, salutation, and body. At the bottom are the closing, signature, and cc line. No rules are associated with this letter's structure, so we could easily have forgotten one of these components or put them in the wrong order (date at the top, for example).

If we were to create this letter in XML, we would define the components (address, date, and so on) and apply rules. These rules could be used to do many things, including but not limited to: ensuring pieces are not left out, ensuring pieces occur in the correct order, and limiting the number of paragraphs in the letter body.

Rigid structure with rules

Rules for a document may describe the order in which the pieces can occur, how often they are allowed to occur, or both. As we move forward with XML, we provide examples for loosely structuring a document. A statement describing such a document might be: "This document shall have first- and second-level headings plus paragraphs."

We will also look at applying rules to form a rigidly structured document. The statement describing this document could be: "If this document has a first-level heading, it must be followed by at least two second-level headings, with at least one paragraph between the second-level headings and at least one paragraph beneath."

In Figure 1-2, we viewed a document that — for lack of rules — had text marked with incorrect heading levels. The headings "Generation X" and "Next Generation" should be the same size. But "Next Generation" was marked as a first-level heading and appears larger. A simple document rule, perhaps something like "any first-level heading must have at least two second-level headings," would have alerted us that something was wrong with the document.

We discuss structure rules in much more detail later, when you learn about formalizing these rules with document type definitions (DTDs) in Session 9.

Big Powerful Corporation
6 River Plaza, Suite 101
Pittsburgh, PA 15699
412.555.1212
Fax 412.555.2222

April 15, 2001

Anon E. Mouse
Steel City Corporation
6 River Plaza, Suite 102
Pittsburgh, PA 15699

Subject: Meeting Confirmation

Dear Anon:

This letter confirms our meeting Thursday, April 19. Please arrive promptly so we may begin the meeting at 10:00a.m.

Our HR Manager will also attend the meeting. I have informed her of the issue of your anonymity--since your current employer is right next door. Per your request, we are willing to interview you for the IT opening even if you wear a bag over your head.

I look forward to meeting you Thursday.

Sincerely,

S.C. Kahuna
IT Manager

cc: P.C. Orrek

Big Powerful Corporation

Figure 1-3
Letter with simple structure

Comparison of digital document types

If you use Microsoft Word, Adobe FrameMaker, or other advanced software tools, your documents are saving to a proprietary file format. Each file contains text you type, images you place, and hidden processing information the program uses to display your file. These data are *binary*, or stored in a proprietary file format of ones and zeros, which limits them in several ways:

- Normally, they can only be read with a proprietary software tool.
- Formatting information is embedded with the content. You can't easily (in other words, on the fly) change the format of a propriety file format for display to a different device (like a PDA screen). Nor can you easily extract only the content.
- They are in danger of being lost over time as the software tool is revised and becomes unable to access previous-version files.

Even when using the same tool, a file may become inaccessible if archived through multiple version changes. A file saved in Word 6, for example, may be inaccessible by future Word releases due to backwards-incompatible software changes. The program will fail to understand the file's information in whole or in part.

Some formats are binary, but less proprietary. Documents saved as TIFF, for example, are binary files but are easily accessible by a variety of tools.

ASCII (or plain-text) files, on the other hand, do not have underlying processing information. The files are text files without proprietary data. Your saved files may be opened by hundreds of software applications and text editors. You may even access a text file through a database or write a small program or script to perform an action on it.

With either binary or text files, you may display and read the information somehow. With advanced tools, you can manipulate your file contents. But your file contents are not designed for reuse or reorganization. This is where XML and similar documents are the exception. XML documents are saved in text format and follow an open standard, designed by the World Wide Web Consortium. We discuss this in Session 2.

With XML, you don't need to worry about having the right proprietary software, being on the right platform, or dealing with the right vendor to be able to exchange and manage your information. XML is easily readable by computers — not to mention by people. This is part of what makes it so useful for today's information management needs.

**10 Min.
To Go**

The challenging demands for reusing information

Organizations in the twenty-first century need to manage more information in more types of media (paper, Web, CD, digital devices) than ever before. Examples of the types of data a company might be publishing to these media are:

- Customer databases
- Product catalogs
- Products and services data
- Web sites
- Marketing materials
- Personnel information
- Informational CD-ROMs
- Messages

There may be overlap among these items. Or, there may be data in one format (for example, a database) that the company would like to push into another format (like an online catalog) or perhaps even several formats.

Customization of deliverables

Customization of data to send to clients is possible with advanced software tools. Tools on the market now allow you to manipulate a deliverable to include a customer's name, purchase specifications (basic service plan, premium service plan, and so on), and related contact information — even custom pricing or discount information for each client's deliverable.

But if the customization of deliverables is not fully automated, there is more room for error and you must spend extra time checking and reviewing the final deliverable. If, however, a system is fully automated, there is little chance of errors and multiple outputs for multiple clients become easy. XML provides the ability to fully automate this information by combining publishing and scripting capabilities with database connectivity.

Data republishing/repurposing

Republishing information in multiple formats is sometimes difficult, depending on the tool selected. In fact, tools like Adobe FrameMaker are gaining popularity because of their ability to output from one document type into several media formats.

This is why one of the greatest benefits of XML is the "X" — *extensible* is the key. XML may be written to fit a specific need, attached to databases, and outputted from documentation systems. In addition, it can be expanded without breaking because of its extensibility!

Done!

REVIEW

- Most documents have a structure, albeit a simple one.
- XML documents have structure, and may or may not have rules to go with the structure.
- XML files are ASCII text files and thus have a long shelf life.
- XML allows information reuse.
- Many software tools can interact with XML.
- Databases may be used with XML, or XML files may be used as databases.

QUIZ YOURSELF

1. Does an e-mail message have structure? (See "Getting Started with Structured Documents.")

2. True or False: An XML document may have structure rules assigned to it. (See "Getting Started with Structured Documents.")

3. When no document rules exist, what prevents you from erroneously tagging your information? (See "Document structure explored.")

4. What are some of the limitations of binary files? (See "Comparison of digital document types.")

5. Can XML be used to publish a piece of information to several formats? (See "Data republishing/repurposing.")

Why XML?

Session Checklist

✔ Understanding the limitations of HTML

✔ Learning about XML documents

✔ Discussing XML possibilities

**30 Min.
To Go**

In this session, we take a look at where XML has come from and its purpose. XML came to be because of shortcomings in available technologies. Read on for a little history and some comparisons with HTML.

The W3C and Setting Open Standards

The World Wide Web Consortium (W3C) is an organization that develops standards for a variety of Internet-related technologies, such as HTML and Cascading Style Sheets (CSS). The W3C also supports initiatives and standards for increasing the accessibility of the World Wide Web to people with disabilities.

The W3C refers to their standards as *recommendations*. Among these is the XML recommendation. XML, like HTML and CSS, is an open standard. An open standard is shared and available to all. A proprietary standard, on the other hand, is not shared and is held as a secret.

Other organizations, such as the Institute for Electrical and Electronics Engineers (IEEE), American National Standards Institute (ANSI), and International Standards Organization (ISO), develop open standards, but the W3C focuses on Web standards.

The W3C devised HTML's specifications and issued revised specifications as more functionality was requested for the Internet. The Web started out plain and the HTML (not surprisingly) was simple. Early Web pages did not have graphics or complex layouts. To provide graphics capabilities, the W3C expanded HTML's tag set. New tags allowed graphics to be referenced by HTML documents and viewed in Web browsers. When the Web expanded even more, requests for form capabilities led the W3C to add HTML tags for forms.

By setting these open standards, the W3C makes it possible for many companies to access their recommendations and start at the same point. This ensures files created for the Web will work with different tools — such as multiple Web browsers and HTML authoring tools. When more tools are available, more people have the ability to access information and create it. These standards made it possible for the Web to grow so rapidly and expansively.

The W3C's XML recommendations give us XML as an open standard. Because access to the information is open, many XML authoring tools have come into the market, along with a few Web browsers.

Microsoft, Netscape, and other companies implement the W3C's recommendations in Web browsers and other applications and interact with the W3C to develop new recommendations.

XML Documents as Data

XML documents can stand alone or be used with other XML documents. They may interact with other files, be referenced by other XML documents, or be referenced by programs.

Instead of ending up with an HTML document that can only be viewed in an HTML browser and that cannot be easily transformed into a printable document, you end up with an XML document that can be acted upon as a whole or as individual parts. This is because of XML's extensibility — new tags are added for new types of information.

A database, for example, is made up of fields, as shown in Figure 2-1. The fields usually have names that describe their content.

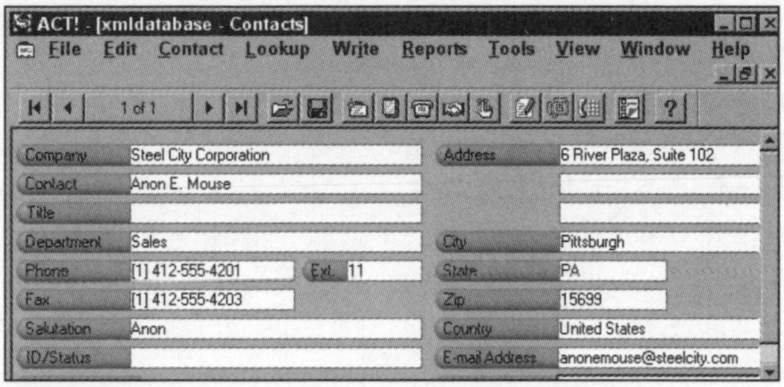

Figure 2-1
A database view using Symantec's ACT! software

In the preceding graphic, we see the field names — Company, Contact, and many more — followed by space for the field content to be typed. XML mimics database capability by turning your documents into sorting, reusable, and optional *fields*. XML does this by allowing you to give the parts of your document names or *tags*. These tags represent *metadata* — literally, data about the data within your document. You get to decide what these tags are, which we discuss in Session 3.

These document names offer descriptive information about the XML document's content, which allows software to utilize the file in whole or in part. Instead of having HTML's limited choices:

```
<P>
<H2>
<TITLE>
<BLOCKQUOTE>
```

you set up the tags that you need:

```
<price>
<firstname>
<state>
<heading>
<userprefs>
<editor>
```

Because you are able to add the tags that you need, you are able to define many separate "containers" for your information. Since XML is oriented toward documents as data — HTML is more oriented to formatting — we need these extra tags to differentiate pieces of information.

This flexibility enables you to use XML as you see fit, with the information following your specifications. You may find this to be easier for you to work with than HTML's restricted tag set is.

XML allows you to use lowercase, uppercase, or mixed case. But within an XML document or among multiple interacting XML documents, you must be consistent. If you use `<state>` in one part of the XML document and later add lines containing `<State>`, it will not consider the tags to be the same. Pick your case preference and use it consistently for all tags in all documents.

Here's an example of a possible HTML snippet:

```
<BODY>
<H1>Workplan</H1>
<P>This project begins April 16, 2001 and ends on June 18,
2001.</P>
<P>Costs of this proposal are expected to be $150 - $200,000</P>
</BODY>
```

This same snippet in XML could be very descriptive. Note in the following code that the XML tags provide metadata about the content of the document:

```
<proposal>
<scope><head>Workplan</head>
<schedule>This project begins <startdate>April 16,
2001</startdate> and ends on <enddate>June 18,
2001</enddate>.</schedule>
<fees>Costs of this proposal are expected to be <range>$150 -
$200,000</range></fees>
</scope>
</proposal>
```

Even without special software, you can view the XML document and understand the information in it. And as we will show you later, you can share this information to and from a database because of its structure.

XML Advantages

**20 Min.
To Go**

In the next sections, we explore HTML limitations and XML strengths. It is important for you to understand the "why" of XML so that you move comfortably forward using it. You need to know some of the great things XML now makes available for you.

Overcoming HTML limitations

XML was devised to advance the Web beyond what was possible with HTML and HTML-related technologies (JavaScript, ASP, and others). HTML has limitations that XML is able to overcome for the Web, other electronic distribution methods, and information management. HTML limitations include:

- Inability to sort data on the fly
- Little ability to separate portions of a document's content
- No capabilities for advanced formatting (equations and chemical symbols)
- Little ability to specify the meaning of information
- Inefficiencies and bloating caused by adding hundred of tags over the years

You may create documents that look all right and display quickly; your readers may even understand and use them. But they are static documents with the limitations we mentioned previously. As shown in Figure 2-2, you can view the text but you can't reuse it easily to other (non-HTML) formats.

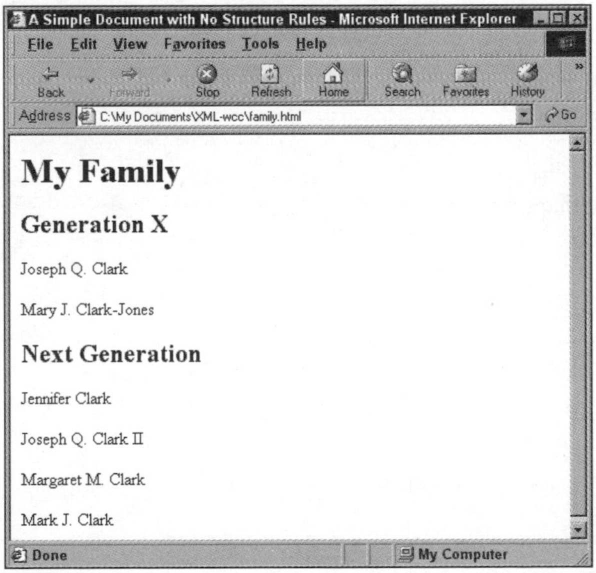

Figure 2-2
An HTML document displayed in Internet Explorer

XML, on the other hand, isn't restricted by the same limitations as HTML. XML documents don't need to be static; they can behave dynamically. With XML documents, for example, you can:

- Sort information in the browser (no server or database connectivity required)
- Separate parts of a document or pull parts of a document from external sources
- Specify the meaning of as many or as few pieces of information as you like
- Add tags as you need them (no bloat)

HTML was designed — or defined — to be easy. It was meant for Web publishing by anyone using minimal tool sets. To ensure easy implementation, many browsers were built to be forgiving — to overlook user coding errors. HTML's simplicity and browser "best effort" displaying together allowed anyone to publish their data to the Web for others to view. That was all well and good, but it has allowed for poor document setup and inefficiencies. XML prevents these inefficiencies because it is less forgiving and requires content to follow a structure. It does force you to be more careful and disciplined, but the payoff for this extra care is that XML allows you to:

- Sort information easily
- Reuse information (create once, use many times)
- Reformat information easily
- Separate parts of documents from the rest

Allowing easy processing

Companies looking to build e-commerce Web sites can use XML to tie databases of product information to their Web sites. XML can interact with databases and be used to do many things, such as:

- Create shopping carts (the Web variety)
- Mimic active server pages
- Create matching paper, Web, and PDA outputs
- Compare information (more accurate search engine hits)
- Manipulate more easily, with common tools and programming interfaces

Here's further contrast between HTML and XML: HTML consists of a fixed set of tags. Tags such as <B>, <EM>, and <H1> are more about how to format the text in a Web browser than they are about the content of the text.

XML allows this formatting, which we will discuss later, but XML separates the formatting from the content. This enables you to focus on your content (data) first. Additionally, the separation of formatting and data makes it easier to change the output's look at a high level and have the look inherited to the lower level. It also means that you can publish your data to the Web one minute, then transform specific summary data for transmission as a cell phone message in the next minute.

Publishing information easily

**10 Min.
To Go**

You can find more than a few software tools on the market that provide a user interface for producing XML documents. You can create XML documents in a text editor, such as Microsoft Notepad, or in an XML editor, such as Microsoft's freely distributed XML Notepad.

> **You may wish to install XML Notepad to assist you with the coming examples. In some instances we refer you to an editing package and you may wish to experiment with this tool. Microsoft provides a free download at** http://msdn.microsoft.com/
> xml/notepad/download.asp.

Creating an XML document is as easy as typing a document in a word processor. Well, almost that easy. If you have an idea of the text you want to include and what the important pieces of information are, you can create an XML document.

Take a second look at the XML document example given earlier in this chapter.

```
<proposal>
<scope><head>Workplan</head>
<schedule>This project begins <startdate>April 16,
2001</startdate> and ends on <enddate>June 18,
2001</enddate>.</schedule>
<fees>Costs of this proposal are expected to be <range>$150 -
$200,000</range></fees>
</scope>
</proposal>
```

Each piece of the document is typed as it would be in a word processor. Then markup is put before and after the text to describe it — similar to database fields, as mentioned earlier. The tags are what you call them and there can be as many or few as you decide.

If you are familiar with HTML, you could create this document by starting with what you know (<H1>, <H2>, <P>) and putting in the more complex markup later.

In the next chapter, we'll review XML documents and their components. We'll use an example of XML for a family tree to show you how to create a loosely structured XML document.

Done!

REVIEW

- The W3C develops XML recommendations, which provides us with XML as an open standard.
- XML documents are more flexible than HTML documents because they include content within user-defined tags.
- XML allows publishing to multiple media without re-authoring due to the accessibility of each piece of data, due to the descriptive tag names.

QUIZ YOURSELF

1. What does the W3C provide for the Web? (See "The W3C and Setting Open Standards.")
2. What is an advantage of having an open standard instead of a proprietary system? (See "The W3C and Setting Open Standards.")
3. What do I gain by being able to name tags for my XML documents? (See "XML Documents as Data.")
4. Which type of document is most like a database: XML or HTML? (See "XML Documents as Data.")
5. Can HTML provide descriptive tags the way XML can? (See "Allowing easy processing.")

A Simple XML Document

Session Checklist

✔ Using tags to label XML content

✔ Creating a simple XML document

✔ Viewing an XML document in a Web browser

**30 Min.
To Go**

The best way to start using XML is with a single, small project. In this book, you're going to start small, troubleshoot as you go, and build your project slowly. This will give you a feel for what does and does not work, without weeding through large amounts of information.

The exercises in this book walk you through creation of XML documents. Over the course of the book, you build on the earlier exercises and see your entire project come together in small, logical chunks.

As we described in Session 1, XML documents are made of information (content) inside tags, with the tags nested in a hierarchical and consistent structure. The example in this session serves two purposes: to clarify the relationship of tags and to have you create a simple XML document with recognizable information. We use family tree information for this sample. If you have a family or know anyone who has a family, you will easily grasp the structure of the example document.

Beginning Your XML Document

On the first line of your XML document, you type an XML *declaration*. The declaration tells your Web browser (or other computer application) that this is an XML document. The browser reads this declaration and processes the document accordingly. The declaration may contain other information, but a simple declaration looks like this:

```
<?xml version="1.0"?>
```

In some cases, the XML declaration is optional. It's a good idea, however, to always begin your XML documents with an XML declaration.

Creating Tags

Unlike HTML, in which the tags are provided, XML allows you to create the tags that you need. You create and use tags depending on the type of document that you are creating and what you plan to do with it. A document may have as few or as many tags as you like.

After the XML declaration, your XML document must begin and end with a single tag, referred to as the *root* tag. It's best to pick a name for this tag, because it describes the XML document that you are creating. Each XML document must have a single root tag that begins and ends the document. A family tree document, for example, may use the root tag <family>, as in the following code:

```
<?xml version="1.0"?>
<family>
[...rest of XML document...]
</family>
```

Just like HTML, the end tag includes the tag name plus a forward slash. You can pick any name you like for the root tag, but the name you choose should probably be descriptive of the XML document. The following tag name, for example, is legal:

```
<xyz>
</xyz>
```

But this tag is not descriptive and will not be very useful. You will want a more descriptive tag name. For example, the following may be typical root tag names: `<invoice>`, `<manuscript>`, `<chapter>`, `<purchaseOrder>`.

Nesting Tags

The relationships between tags are sometimes referred to as *nesting*. Nesting implies that one tag is contained inside another. Tags nest in a particular order, with nested tags residing completely inside the tag that contains them. This is similar to mathematical expressions. If you think in terms of a simple math problem, the following is a properly nested expression:

```
( X + [ Z - X ] )
```

The parentheses must begin and end appropriately to work. With XML tags, nesting must occur the same mathematical way. Later in this book, we will clarify nesting of elements within elements, in which pieces of your XML documents wrap in a manner similar to the equation above.

A Family Tree XML Document

Figure 3-1 shows a graphical view of a family tree. This figure makes it easy for you to determine the relationship between family members. It's clear that Mark is the child of Joseph and Mary. Mark has two sisters, Jennifer and Margaret, and a brother, Joseph.

Although the meaning of this figure is clear to most people, the information in this figure is difficult for a computer program to reuse. If you want to change the format of this family tree, you must redraw the graphic. If you want to show only a portion of the family tree, you must redraw the graphic. There's nothing that you can use to automatically reformat the graphic or extract specific information. If instead we created this graphic using XML, we could adjust the view by adjusting the XML. This is discussed briefly in Session 29.

To avoid the hassle of redrawing a figure every time you want to change the family tree, you can instead write your family tree as an HTML document (see Listing 3-1). Information in a text file is easier to reuse, but nothing in this file tells the reader (or a computer application that processes this document) the role of each name in the HTML file. In other words, if you want to figure out the names of the Clark children based only on the contents of this document, you're out of luck.

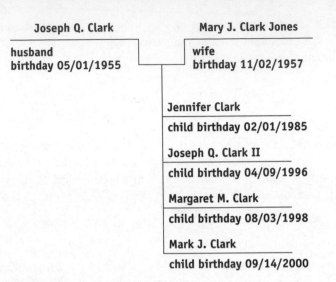

Joseph Q. Clark	Mary J. Clark Jones
husband birthday 05/01/1955	wife birthday 11/02/1957

Jennifer Clark

child birthday 02/01/1985

Joseph Q. Clark II

child birthday 04/09/1996

Margaret M. Clark

child birthday 08/03/1998

Mark J. Clark

child birthday 09/14/2000

Figure 3-1
Graphic representation of a family tree

Listing 3-1
HTML view of the family tree

```
<table>
<tr>
   <td>Joseph Q. Clark</td>
   <td>Mary J. Clark</td>
   <td>Jennifer Clark</td>
   <td>Joseph Q. Clark II</td>
   <td>Margaret M. Clark</td>
   <td>Mark J. Clark</td>
</tr>
</table>
```

To produce a simple family tree document as an XML document (see Listing 3-2), you must type your text inside tags that describe the text:

Listing 3-2
XML view of the family tree

```
<family>
<father>Joseph Q. Clark</father>
```

```
<mother>Mary J. Clark</mother>
<offspring>
    <child>Jennifer Clark</child>
    <child>Joseph Q. Clark II</child>
    <child>Margaret M. Clark</child>
    <child>Mark J. Clark</child>
</offspring>
</family>
```

Listing 3-2 is the code for your first XML document, which you will create in the next section. Not only does this XML document include the name of each family member, it includes the role of each member of the family. The XML tags describe the content, whereas the HTML tags are all the same and only determine how the names appear.

**20 Min.
To Go**

Creating and Viewing Your First XML Document

Now let's create and view your XML document by using the sample text in Listing 3-2. Create a folder (directory) on your workstation and name it **XML-wcc**. Be sure to create this folder in a location that you know you can easily find throughout the exercises. If you're on Windows, for example, we suggest that you make the folder as a subfolder of C:\My Documents.

Creating your XML document

Open your favorite text editor, such as Microsoft Notepad. For simplicity, these examples stay with one editor — Notepad — but you can use any text editor on any hardware platform. If your view does not match our screenshots, it may be because you're using a different editor.

In your text editor, you will create your family tree document. Then you will save it with a special XML filename extension. Type the document as shown in Listing 3-3. This is basically the text from Figure 3-2 with an XML declaration above it. You may edit and expand the document later, so don't be concerned by its simplicity.

Listing 3-3
Family tree with XML declaration added

```
<?xml version="1.0"?>
<family>
<father>Joseph Q. Clark</father>
<mother>Mary J. Clark</mother>
<offspring>
    <child>Jennifer Clark</child>
    <child>Joseph Q. Clark II</child>
    <child>Margaret M. Clark</child>
    <child>Mark J. Clark</child>
</offspring>
</family>
```

To save time, you may open the listing from the CD instead of typing it — though the typing is good practice. This listing is available on the book's CD in the Session3 folder. It is saved as `family.xml`.

Use your Enter key to separate the text into logical chunks so that you can edit them more easily. When viewing your XML document, you will not see these dividing linespaces; the browser ignores them the same way browsers ignore linespaces in HTML. (Browsers also ignore any spaces beyond one. This is why you are able to use spaces to indent code for easier editing without affecting display.)

Unlike HTML, XML requires that every begin tag has a matching end tag. The exception in XML is empty tags, which have a special syntax and are discussed later.

Now save this file as `family.xml`. If your operating system version adds the extension `.txt` to the filename, you may need to enclose the file name in quotes to save it properly, as shown in Figure 3-2.

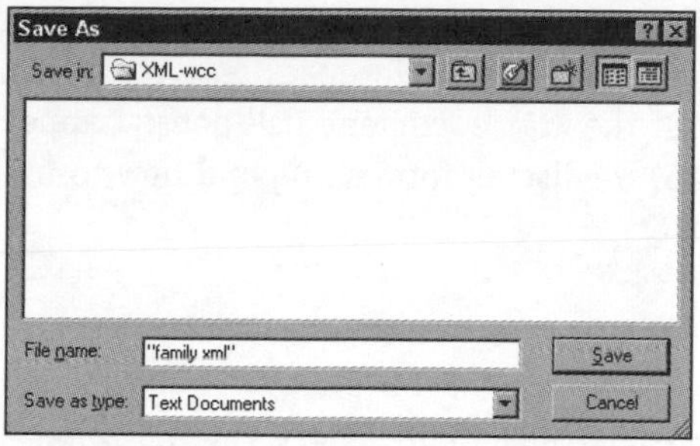

Figure 3-2
Saving an XML document in Notepad

Viewing your XML document

After creating a simple XML document, you should view it in your browser. If it's
not already open, launch Microsoft Internet Explorer 5 (or higher). If you don't
have Internet Explorer 5 or higher, you will need to install it from this book's companion CD-ROM. (Previous versions cannot display XML documents.)

After launching Internet Explorer, choose File ⇨ Open, browse to your recently
created `family.xml` file in the `XML-wcc` folder, and double-click to open it.
Figure 3-3 shows what it should look like in your browser.

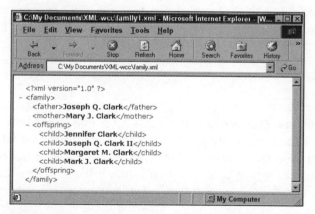

Figure 3-3
An XML document displayed in Internet Explorer

You have created and viewed an XML document! If your file does not display properly or an error appears, check your XML code in Notepad, resave your document, and redisplay it in the browser. If the XML document still doesn't appear, refer to the next section. In Session 16, we discuss formatting and how to improve the appearance of your XML document

Possible errors

If you get an error when you open your XML document, check the following:

- Is the XML declaration on the first line of the file with nothing before it?
- Are your tags properly typed?
- Does every start tag have an end tag?
- Did you save your XML document as a text file?

Expanding Your XML Document and Improving Data Accessibility

10 Min. To Go

After you create and view your first XML document, you can experiment by substituting other tags, adding new tags, or removing tags. You should only do this, however, if you're comfortable with the tags and sure that you won't become confused. In your experiments, be sure to follow three simple rules mentioned earlier:

- Use a root tag
- Nest mathematically
- End each tag you start

You may choose to add new XML tags to your document because the current XML doesn't contain enough information to support the ways you might use your information. Your current XML document doesn't include tags around the last name of each person. This would make sorting by each person's name difficult or impossible.

If you use an online address book for your family, you may recognize certain pieces of information by which you want to sort. Breaking these pieces into separate tags allows you to work with them as individual items. We discuss actions you can perform on them on Saturday Evening (Part IV), when we discuss manipulating XML documents.

To expand your document with additional tags containing smaller pieces of information, modify your family.xml document as shown in the following code listing.

To save time typing this file, feel free to open the listing from the CD. The filename is `family-surname.xml` **and it is in the Session3 folder.**

```
<?xml version="1.0"?>
<family>
<father>Joseph Q. <surname>Clark</surname></father>
<mother>Mary J.
<surname>Clark</surname><maiden>Jones</maiden></mother>
<offspring>
    <child>Jennifer <surname>Clark</surname></child>
    <child>Joseph Q. <surname>Clark</surname> II</child>
    <child>Margaret M. <surname>Clark</surname></child>
    <child>Mark J. <surname>Clark</surname></child>
</offspring>
</family>
```

Save this modified file as `family.xml`. Display the `family.xml` file in your browser and compare the result to Figure 3-3. Notice the expansion because of the new tags that you added.

Once you progress further in this book and create more XML document examples, you will see that there are many other variations you can use to present the same information. Select the tags that you use based on how you may want to format or even reuse and sort data later. You could, for example, just as easily set up your document as shown in Figure 3-4.

Figure 3-4
A family tree document with alternative tags

The fact that this same small document could be created in several ways should not discourage you. XML's flexibility (extensibility) means that you can decide which pieces of information are important, what tags should be called, and how data should be put together. This makes it easier for you, not harder.

Done!

REVIEW

- XML does not have a predefined set of tags.
- A root tag is required at the start and end of your document.
- All tags must have a begin tag and an end tag.
- All tags must be properly nested.
- Tags can be added at any point because XML is extensible.

QUIZ YOURSELF

1. Is an XML declaration optional or required? (See "Beginning Your XML Document.")
2. How many tags can you have in an XML document? (See "Creating Tags.")
3. When must you stop adding tags to your tag set? (See "Creating Tags.")
4. Do all XML tags require an end tag? (See "Nesting Tags.")
5. What happens when you try to view an XML document whose tags are not properly nested? (See "Nesting Tags.")

Using XML on the Web

Session Checklist

✔ Exploring the differences between HTML and XML

✔ Formatting XML documents for display in a Web browser

✔ Delivering XML content to Web browsers

✔ Building applications around XML documents

**30 Min.
To Go**

In this session, you take your first look at publishing XML documents on the World Wide Web. We introduce ways to format XML documents in Web browsers as well as the concept of an XML-based application — using XML as an integral part of an information-management solution.

Using XML for Web Publishing

We've already talked about how XML embeds metadata — information about your document — within your document. An XML document looks like any other text document, but with the addition of XML tags, it looks like this:

```
<invoice></invoice>
<chapter></chapter>
<image source="graphics/flow.gif" height="3.5 in" width="5 in"/>
```

HTML (HyperText Markup Language) documents also look like this, for good reason. Both have similar syntax rules and both are derived from the same parent, the Standard Generalized Markup Language (SGML). But there is one critical difference between HTML and XML documents: HTML provides a specific set of tags that are used in every HTML document, while XML provides a syntax for creating your own sets of tags — your own XML vocabularies based on the needs of your documents.

HTML is a specific vocabulary — the set of legal HTML tags defined by the HTML specification. Because HTML is a specific vocabulary, Web browsers can be designed to "do the right thing" when processing HTML documents. A Web browser knows, for example, that an <H1> tag in an HTML document denotes a primary-level heading. The browser has built-in style rules to make the header text stand out from the body text.

XML, however, is not a specific vocabulary. XML provides the syntax for creating vocabularies. An XML document contains the tags of your choosing. The XML tags you use should reflect the contents of your documents and should serve to identify portions of that content. The XML vocabulary you use in your family tree example (Session 3) includes tags like <father>, <mother>, and <child>.

Web browsers know how to display text within an <H1> tag because the <H1> tag is part of the HTML specification. But how should a browser display the contents of a <father> tag? How about a <child> tag? Browser designers could not anticipate these XML tags, so browsers don't have built-in rules for displaying them.

Because the browser doesn't know how to display these tags, you need to tell the browser how they should be displayed. You must give the browser information about how to display the contents of a <father> tag.

Rendering XML in the Browser

How do you tell the browser how to render the contents of a particular XML element? Figure 4-1 shows how Internet Explorer version 5.5 displays the <father> element in your family tree without any formatting information.

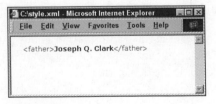

Figure 4-1
XML document fragment displayed in Internet Explorer

Figure 4-1 probably isn't what most people have in mind for displaying information in a Web browser. To tell the browser to display the contents of the `<father>` element in bold, 20-point Arial type, you have two choices:

- Use a cascading style sheet to specify formatting information for each XML element
- Transform XML elements to HTML for display in a Web browser

**20 Min.
To Go**

Cascading style sheets and XML

Cascading style sheets were developed as a way to override the browser's default formatting of HTML elements. Cascading style sheets allow you to specify formatting attributes such as font size, color, and family; text placement; and background colors. You specify these attributes for individual HTML tags. Code from a cascading style sheet that specifies the format of an HTML `<H1>` tag might look like this:

```
H1 {font-weight: bold; font-size:20; font-family: Arial}
```

Because cascading style sheets allow you to specify the format of an HTML element, it is logical to extend them to allow you to format XML elements. Browsers that support formatting XML documents with cascading style sheets allow you to do just that. Your XML `<father>` element in your XML document may appear as:

```
<father>Joseph Q. Clark</father>
```

An accompanying cascading style sheet (either in an external style sheet file or within the same XML document) for the same element might look like this:

```
father {font-weight: bold; font-size:20; font-family: Arial}
```

Transforming XML to HTML

You can also transform an XML element to HTML for display in a Web browser. The resulting HTML code can be displayed properly by modern browsers:

```
<div style="font-weight: bold; font-size:20; font-family: Arial ">
Joseph Q. Clark
</div>
```

You can perform this transformation by using a new language called XSLT (XML Stylesheet Language: Transformations). XSLT enables you to sort, select, and manipulate the content of XML documents, as well as transform your XML documents to HTML for Web publishing. Here's an example block of XSLT code that will transform your <father> element to HTML:

```
<xsl:template match="father">
<div style="font-weight: bold; font-size:20; font-family: Arial ">
<xsl:apply-templates/>
</div>
</xsl:template>
```

You may notice that XSLT looks a lot like an XML document. XSLT style sheets are legal XML documents. An XSLT program is commonly called a style sheet. The XSLT style sheet consists of a series of templates that match XML elements and provide a transformation to HTML. We cover XSLT in more detail in Session 16.

Viewing the results

With a browser that understands how to handle XML and cascading style sheets, both the cascading style sheets and XSLT methods for displaying XML will yield the same result. In the listing below, Figure 4-2, notice how the <father> element appears in Internet Explorer version 5.5, given either of the previous two formatting statements.

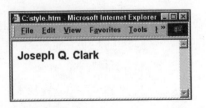

Figure 4-2
Formatted XML document fragment displayed in Internet Explorer

We haven't given you all of the code that you need to do this yourself now, but we will later in the book, when we discuss cascading style sheets and XML transformations in detail. For now, remember that XML tags tend to provide information about the content of a document, and that formatting information is typically separated from the content. This allows you to easily reformat XML information according to the constraints of any particular display device. You'll probably want, for example, to format a document differently in print, on a Web browser, or on the display screen of a personal digital assistant (PDA). Of course, you need applications that know how to apply formatting information to XML documents. The next two sections cover your options for formatting XML documents.

Processing XML on the Client

HTML has been around for more than 10 years. XML, however, has been a finalized recommendation for only three years. That's a significant difference, and relative levels of support for XML in popular Web browsers reflect this. As of this writing, few popular Web browsers support the rendering of XML documents by the browser. Fortunately, the popular Internet Explorer version 5.5 supports rendering XML via cascading style sheets, or transforming XML to HTML at the browser. We will use Internet Explorer version 5.5 to demonstrate several exercises later in this book.

If you do not currently have Internet Explorer 5 or higher on your system, we suggest you take the time to install Internet Explorer 5.5 from this book's CD-ROM.

Processing XML on the Server

Until browser technology catches up with XML, perhaps the best way to render and display XML documents on the Web is to transform XML to HTML on the Web server, thereby delivering HTML to the client browsers. This publishing scheme has several advantages:

- Browser-independence is preserved. Because you're delivering HTML to the Web browsers, any browser can read your Web pages.

- You can still leverage the capabilities of XML to generate customized documents by doing this work on your Web server.

- Most popular Web servers support XML. See your Web server's documentation for more information.

Unless you know that all of your users will be viewing your XML documents with Internet Explorer version 5.5, the safest way to publish XML on the Web is to transform your XML documents to HTML on the server, and deliver HTML to your client browsers for viewing.

XML Document-Based Applications

XML is not just about publishing documents (and it's especially not just about publishing Web documents). XML facilitates the development of a whole new category of computer programs — the document-based application. Not only can you reuse your information more than ever before, you can expect more from that information. Let's look at an example application that you can build around the content of documents.

Background information

10 Min.
To Go

Acme Industries sells and services a large assortment of technical equipment. Acme has discovered that they are rewriting much of their information several times. They produce a printed manual to send to each customer, a database of troubleshooting procedures for the telephone support staff, and a Web-based interface to an online documentation set. Now the field-service people are asking for online documentation that they can access on their wireless digital devices. "By the way," say the field-service folks, "It would be really nice if we could order parts and prepare invoices by clicking part numbers in the repair procedures."

Consider how Acme Industries created and published this information:

- Acme's Technical Publishing department created a printed user manual that shipped with each product.

- The telephone support staff identified troubleshooting information manually in the user manuals and re-key that information into a database. When Technical Publishing updated the user manual, the telephone support staff had to update the database manually.

- Acme's Web master created a Web-based version of the user manual with a special Web-publishing tool. The Web site maintainer had to update the online information manually each time the user manual was updated.

- The field support people carried dog-eared copies of the user manual. They couldn't even find the information they needed, let alone order parts automatically!

Forward-thinking solution

Acme Industries' process was time consuming, inefficient, expensive, and prone to errors. Creating structured XML documents with tags that identify the content of those documents can simplify Acme Industries' information management problems. To solve this problem by using XML, Acme Industries can do the following:

- Create a set of XML tags (an XML vocabulary) for their documentation. Use XML markup to denote troubleshooting information, repair procedures, and general user information. Also use XML markup to denote parts and part numbers.

- Print all the XML content to create the user manual for each product.

- Populate the customer service database with the troubleshooting information.

- Create a small-screen version of repair procedures for the field service personnel.

- Link part numbers in the repair procedures to a wireless ordering and invoice creation system.

Figure 4-3 shows a block diagram of Acme Industries new information management system. The system has several advantages over Acme's old system:

- Information is written only once.

- Appropriate information is automatically delivered to the people who need it.

- Information is formatted for the appropriate display device — hard copy printing, Web browser, wireless device screen, or even database input/output.

- Information is updated quickly throughout the system. Field support people who carried hard copy manuals, which could not be updated easily, now get fresh information on their portable wireless devices.

- The information now supports business applications — like allowing field support people to order parts and automatically generate invoices by clicking part numbers in the documentation.

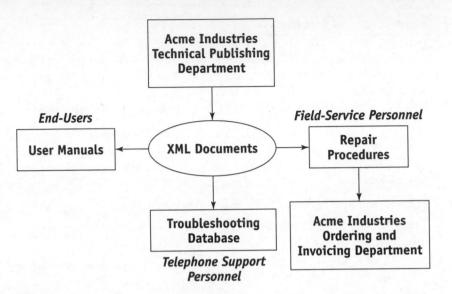

Figure 4-3
Flow-chart of Acme Industries XML-based product information delivery system

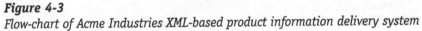

Done!

REVIEW

- XML documents contain metadata, in the form of XML tags, which provide information about the contents of the document.

- HTML is a vocabulary of a fixed set of tags; XML provides syntax for defining your own tags.

- XML documents typically separate content and format information. You must specify how your XML document should be formatted. Two ways to do this are by using cascading style sheets or XSLT.

- Some browsers support XML, but it is safest to transform XML to a publishable form (such as HTML) on the server.

QUIZ YOURSELF

1. True or False: Like HTML, XML provides an explicit set of tags for Web publishing. (See "Using XML for Web Publishing.")

2. Why is it necessary to provide separate formatting information for publishing XML documents? (See "Using XML for Web Publishing.")

3. What is the risk of sending XML to a Web browser? (See "Processing XML on the Client.")

4. What are the two ways to format XML documents on a Web browser? (See "Rendering XML in the Browser.")

5. True or False: Companies and organizations can design their own XML tag sets to support their particular needs for information management and re-use. (See "XML Document-Based Applications.")

PART

I

Friday Evening

1. What does the acronym XML stand for?

2. Are XML documents structured documents?

3. What type of file is in greater danger of becoming inaccessible over time, binary or ASCII?

4. Name two online publishing issues that XML addresses better than HTML.

5. True or False: Database information may be combined with XML documents.

6. What body or organization sets the standards for most Web-related technologies?

7. True or False: HTML documents, not XML documents, are designed with an emphasis on data rather than formatting.

8. What limits does XML have on the number of tags that you can create?

9. Name two limitations of HTML that XML does not face.

10. Is the following fragment representative of HTML or XML?

    ```
    <scope><topic>Workplan</topic></scope>
    ```

11. When getting started with XML, does this book recommend starting with a large, technical project or with a small, manageable pilot?

12. In an XML document, where should the XML declaration appear?

13. Is the following snippet showing proper or improper nesting? Explain.

    ```
    <b><i>This is an HTML sentence.</b></i>
    ```

14. True or False: Microsoft Notepad allows editing of XML documents.

15. What three simple rules should you follow as you create an XML document?

16. What is metadata?

17. True or False: All Web browsers know how to display the `<child>` tag.

18. Can cascading style sheets be used with XML?

19. True or False: XML documents that are transformed to HTML may be viewed within a browser.

20. Name three potential applications of XML.

PART

II

Saturday Morning

5

Creating XML Documents

Session Checklist

✔ Understanding how XML documents are processed

✔ Learning several ways to create XML documents

**30 Min.
To Go**

I n this session, we discuss how XML documents are processed. We also look at several ways that you can create XML documents. Before we begin, you must first understand some basic terms:

- **Syntax:** A set of rules that specify how words, symbols, and other characters must be combined for a program or document to be understood by other programs. All computer programs must conform to the syntax of the target computer language.

- **Transform:** To convert an object or thing from one form to another form.

- **Compile:** To transform a document or computer program into a form that the computer can use.

Processing XML Documents

People who have been writing computer programs for years are very much aware of the strict syntax of computer programming languages. Computers are extremely picky about their input; if a computer cannot understand its input, the computer cannot act on it. A C program that's missing a single semicolon, for example, won't compile, let alone run. For a computer to understand higher level languages and transform those languages into compiled versions, computers require that programs and other input strictly adhere to programming syntax.

The developers of XML wanted to create a platform- and vendor-independent means of representing and exchanging information. You can better understand what a complex task this is if you visualize the available computer systems, display devices, and media types. Consider, for example, the inconsistencies between systems in different companies and organizations. Any recipient of an XML document from a different company or organization must be able to process that document with freely available, non-proprietary tools.

To support processing of XML documents on a variety of platforms and tools, XML syntax is, by definition, very strict. Like a program with a missing semicolon, an XML document with a single error is not a legal XML document.

The XML processor

The XML recommendation defines a software module called an XML *processor*. An XML processor reads an XML document, verifies that the document meets applicable syntax rules and, if provided, verifies the XML document against a set of externally defined structure rules. If the document passes these tests, the XML processor provides an internal representation of the content and structure of the XML document for use by an XML application.

 A document's rules are defined in an XML DTD or XML schema. A DTD is a document type definition, which lists the available tags and the structure rules relating to each tag. A schema is similar, as it is a set of rules, but schemas are more complex and are written as XML documents. Both are discussed in detail later in this book.

The XML application

An XML application is any application that processes an XML document, putting the document through the steps outlined in the preceding section. Examples of XML applications include publishing systems, database integration systems, business-to-business e-commerce exchanges, and any other application or system that uses XML as an information exchange format. In every case, the XML processor reports an error to the XML application if it attempts to process an XML document that contains syntax errors.

Creating XML Documents

By now, you're probably wondering how you create an XML document. You have several options:

- Using a text editor
- Using an XML editor
- Outputting from computer applications (software tools)
- Drawing from other XML documents
- Using a database
- Drawing from other applications

The following sections examine the pros and cons of each of these options.

Creating XML documents with a text editor

20 Min. To Go

An XML document is just a text document with a special syntax defined by the XML recommendation. Because it's just a text document, you can use any text editor to create your XML documents. Figure 5-1 shows an example XML document created in a simple text editor, Microsoft Notepad.

Using a text editor to create XML documents has several advantages:

- Text editors are ubiquitous; there are many text editors to choose from, and text editors are available on virtually all computing platforms.
- Text editors are easy to use. Most people are familiar with how to use text-editing applications.
- Many text editors are free.

What's the disadvantage of using a text editor to create XML documents? Most text editors don't help you to conform to XML syntax. Remember that XML processors are very picky about XML syntax. Just as a C program won't compile if it's missing a semicolon, an XML document won't pass the processor's tests if it contains an XML syntax error. If you create XML documents in a text editor, you must use an external XML processor to verify that your XML document is legal.

Figure 5-1
An XML document viewed in a text editor, Microsoft Notepad

Creating XML documents with an XML editor

A goal of the people who created XML was for XML documents to be human read-able. Although XML syntax is relatively simple — especially compared to languages that preceded XML — humans frequently need help creating documents that con-form to XML syntax.

 Don't worry about knowing syntax yet. You learn the details of XML syntax later in this book. For now, be aware that XML editors can help you to create legal XML documents — documents that conform to the rules of the XML recommendation.

Figure 5-2 shows a simple XML document that was created in Microsoft XML Notepad, a free XML editor that is available through the Microsoft Web site (`http://msdn.microsoft.com/xml/`).

Take a moment and compare Figure 5-1, the text editor view, with Figure 5-2, the XML editor view. The XML editor view provides error checking, tag viewing, and easy editing. Other available XML editors provide development environments for XML programming, or text editing functionality for creating XML documents. We mention Microsoft XML Notepad here because it's free and relatively easy to learn.

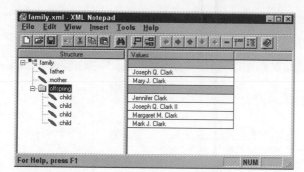

Figure 5-2
An XML document viewed in Microsoft XML Notepad, an XML editor

Creating XML documents from other applications

**10 Min.
To Go**

We've talked about how XML syntax reflects the structure of a document, and how even non-XML documents have an implicit structure. It makes sense that computer applications could save their own XML representation of a document's structure. A user, therefore, doesn't need to know XML to create an XML document.

Options that enable you to save files as XML are becoming more widely available on common desktop applications, such as publishing programs, word processors, and spreadsheets. This option saves a structured representation of a document as an XML file. You can then process the XML file as you would any other XML document. The example shown in Figure 5-3 is an XML document created by a publishing package called Adobe FrameMaker+SGML, which has a "Save As XML" option.

If you save a computer application file as XML, you can still review the saved XML file in a text editor or XML editor.

As XML becomes more prominent for publishing to the Web and other output devices, you will see more computer software manufacturers adding XML functionality. Expect to see more XML editors, XML output options, and XML management tools.

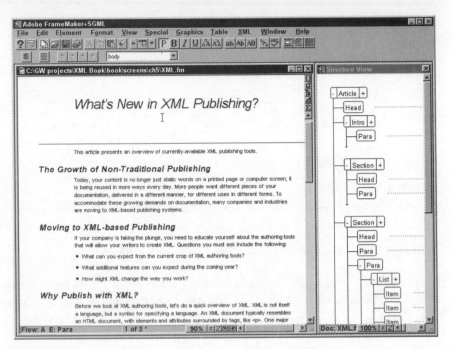

Figure 5-3
Structured document, which can be saved as an XML document, created in Adobe FrameMaker+SGML

Creating XML documents from other XML documents

It was clear from the start that people would want to manipulate XML documents, extract XML content from XML documents, sort XML documents, and customize the display of XML documents. If you don't want to do anything with the content of your XML documents, you can write them with a standard text processor and be done with it.

The XML Transformation Language (XSLT) is a new programming language created exactly for the purposes of selecting, sorting, and manipulating XML documents and creating new XML documents. You learn to work with this language in Session 16.

Creating XML documents from databases

Many similarities exist between XML documents and databases. In both XML documents and databases, content is stored in a structured form, which enables you to query, sort, select, and manipulate the content.

It's only natural that databases would support data entry operations to and from XML documents. A database that understands XML markup could update its tables appropriately. By writing the results of a database query in XML, that query could be further manipulated to format the results for display in a Web browser, personal digital assistant (PDA) screen, hard copy print-out, or other output device.

One advantage of tying databases and XML documents together is manageability. If you only need to update a database and create your output, then you're saving time over the alternative: updating your database and then updating separate non-XML documents. An ideal use for a database is a product catalogue.

The disadvantage of creating XML documents from databases is that without an understanding of database connectivity — ODBC — you may find yourself having to hire consultants to do the connectivity. Automated processes must be put in place properly. With an advanced database or relational database information, construction can be difficult. Plus, any changes in the future would be difficult or limited by your knowledge of the systems.

Automatically creating XML documents

Because XML syntax is relatively simple, albeit strict, it's easy for application developers to write programs that provide information in the form of XML documents. This information can be used in several forms: It might be displayed to human users in a Web browser or on the screen of a PDA; it might be passed between businesses in the form of electronically processed invoices. These documents are likely to serve multiple purposes.

If you are writing a system that creates and distributes billing invoices from your company to its customers, do you want to require that somebody manually create each invoice in an XML editor? Probably not! You're likely to generate the invoices, even as XML documents, automatically from your company's existing accounting infrastructure.

REVIEW

- XML documents may be created with a variety of tools.
- Many XML tools are free.
- More and more computer software manufacturers are adding XML editing utilities and XML creation utilities to their packages.

Done!

- All tools or processes have advantages and disadvantages, which you must consider before selecting a tool.
- Some tools provide XML-related assistance utilities that would be helpful to you as a beginner.

QUIZ YOURSELF

1. Can a text editor create an XML document? (See "Creating XML Documents.")

2. If you use the "save as XML" option in a desktop software package, can you view the resulting XML document in a text editor and in an XML editor? (See "Creating XML documents from other applications.")

3. What is one of the disadvantages of creating XML documents in a text editor? (See "Creating XML documents with a text editor.")

4. Name one XML editor that is available for free download. (See "Creating XML documents with an XML editor.")

5. True or False: In the future, you are likely to code XML invoices and other business documents by hand, instead of using applications for automatically creating XML business documents. (See "Automatically creating XML documents.")

Tour of XML Syntax: Elements and Attributes

Session Checklist

✔ Learning the two major building blocks of XML documents

✔ Understanding how elements and attributes are used to contain and label the content of XML documents

✔ Using nested elements to represent relationships within an XML document

✔ Understanding the trade-offs between using elements or attributes to contain or label content

**30 Min.
To Go**

The previous sessions have focused on what an XML document looks like. The next several sessions get into some details of XML syntax and explain the building blocks of XML documents.

XML provides a platform- and vendor-neutral means of exchanging information. XML documents are self-revealing — information about the content of the document is embedded in the document. This information is available to, and used by, applications that will process the information in the XML document. In this session, you find out how information is encoded in an XML document.

Containers of Information: XML Elements

The term *tag* refers to a string of characters surrounded by a greater-than and less-than sign. A *begin tag* looks like this:

```
<father>
```

An *end tag* begins with a forward slash, like this:

```
</father>
```

The begin tag, end tag, and content between the tags is known as an *XML element*. Figure 6-1 shows a simple XML element and its component parts.

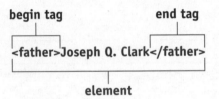

Figure 6-1
XML element with begin and end tags

An XML element is the primary building block of an XML document. Think of elements as containers of information within your XML documents. Each XML element is a container of information. The name of each element is the name string within the begin and end tags. The previous XML fragment, for example, represents an XML element named `father`.

We discuss all the legal content of XML elements in upcoming sessions. For now, an XML element can contain both text content and other XML elements.

Rules for XML tags

The following rules apply to XML tags:

- An XML tag consists of a string delimited by a less-than sign (<) and a greater-than sign (>).
- The start tag and the end tag define the beginning and end of each XML element.
- The name string of an XML tag must conform to the following rules:
  - A tag name must start with a letter (upper- or lower-case) or an underscore (_).

- A tag name may contain letters, numbers, underscores, dashes, or periods.
- Tag names are case sensitive. `<father>` and `<Father>` are two different XML tags.

A tag name may not begin with the letters XML in any case combination. Tags that begin with `Xml`, `xML`, **and** `xMl`, **for example, are forbidden and are reserved for special element names that may be declared by the current or future versions of the XML recommendation.**

Tag names are not limited to alphabetic characters of the Latin alphabet. The XML recommendation permits many non-Latin characters and ideograms from languages including Cyrillic, Hebrew, Arabic, Thai, Chinese, Japanese, and Korean.

Tag names may contain a colon character. But colon characters are used by a special XML construct called a namespace. You should avoid using colon characters in your tag names.

The following are examples of legal XML tags:

```
<inventory>
<_Price.Data>
<Chapter>
```

Empty elements

XML also allows a special kind of element, called an *empty element*. An empty element has no text content — just an element name. Empty elements can serve as markers in your XML documents.

The following are examples of empty elements:

```
<linebreak/>
<img src="xmltable.gif"/>
```

An empty element consists of a less-than sign, followed by a tag name, followed by a forward-slash, followed by a greater-than sign. The rules for naming an empty element are the same as the rules for naming any other XML element.

An XML empty element has the same meaning as an element with no content between the begin and end tags. `<linebreak/>` **and** `<linebreak></linebreak>`, **for example, have the same meaning to an application that processes XML documents. Empty element syntax is provided only for convenience.**

Containers within containers: Using nested elements

You can nest XML elements within other XML elements. By doing so, you can implicitly represent relationships between your XML elements. Your family tree (Session 3), for example, uses the root element `<family>`.

```
<family>
    <father>Joseph Q. Clark</father>
    <mother>Mary J. Clark</mother>
    <child>Jennifer Clark</child>
    <child>Joseph Q. Clark II</child>
</family>
```

In this example, the contents of elements `<father>`, `<mother>`, and `<child>` represent members of the same family. When you design your XML documents in later sessions, you will make explicit use of this sort of relationship when you define the legal content of each element.

Element relationships

When you nest XML elements, the structure of the XML document conveys implicit meaning. Nesting elements enables you to create complex hierarchical relationships in your XML documents. When you begin to create rich, deeply nested documents, it's especially helpful to have a terminology to describe the relationships between elements. XML provides the following terms to describe the relationship between nested elements:

- A *parent element* is the element that contains the current element. In the previous example, `<family>` is the parent element of `<father>`, `<mother>`, and `<child>`.

- A *child element* is an element contained within the current element. In the previous example, `<father>`, `<mother>`, and `<child>` are child elements of `<family>`.

- A *sibling element* is a peer of the current element. Sibling elements share the same parent element. In the previous example, the two `<child>` elements are siblings.

Why are these relationships important? First, they provide clues about the relationships between content of elements in an XML document. Second, they provide the means for you to write programs to select and manipulate specific chunks of content in your XML documents — treating your XML documents like a database. In later sessions, you'll write programs to select parent, child, and sibling elements, and you'll encounter even more terms for describing the relationship between nested elements.

Nesting rules

The XML recommendation is very strict about how elements are nested. Elements must be properly nested in order to conform to the XML version 1.0 recommendation. Elements that meet the following rules are considered properly nested:

- Each start tag must have a corresponding end tag. The name of the start tag and the end tag must be identical.
- The end tag for a child element must precede the end tag of any parent elements. In other words, each element must be closed before its parent element is closed.

Let's look at an example. The following XML fragment is properly nested because the child element <ticker> is closed before the parent element <company>:

```
<company>Apple Computer<ticker>AAPL</ticker></company>
```

The following XML fragment is not properly nested because the parent element <company> is closed before the child element <ticker>:

```
<company>Sun Microsystems<ticker>SUN</company></ticker>
```

Adding More Information: XML Attributes

**20 Min.
To Go**

Now that you know the rules for XML elements, it's time to look at the second major building block. What if you want to label your containers with additional information? Sure, your containers have a name (the XML element name), but you may want to place other labels on your elements. Just as you might want to label a container of chemicals with a "hazardous materials" sticker, you will frequently want to attach additional labels or property information to the content of your XML elements.

XML *attributes* enable you attach additional information to XML elements. If you think of an XML element as a container, then XML attributes are labels on the container. Here are a few simple examples to help you get the idea:

```
<message urgency="low">Be sure to brush your teeth twice each
day.</message>

<message urgency="high">Touching a live wire may cause serious
injury or death.</message>
```

In these examples, we used an XML element to represent a message. But not all messages have the same severity, impact, or importance. Our `message` element includes an attribute called `urgency`, which can be set to denote the urgency of the message.

Why is this useful? Without the `urgency` attribute, we would need to create another XML element for each type of message. That would make our XML documents more complex and make it more difficult to write applications that process those XML documents. Furthermore, we may want to display only certain messages to the end-user, depending on things like message urgency. The user, for example, may only want or need to see messages whose `urgency` attribute value is set to `high`. This allows you to be more flexible when you write applications that process your XML documents.

Rules for XML attributes

XML attributes are an example of the computer science term *name/value pair*. Each XML attribute has a name and a value. Figure 6-2 shows the name and value components of an XML attribute within a start tag.

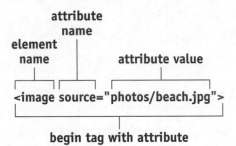

Figure 6-2
Setting name and value components of an XML attribute

An element can have as many attributes as you want. For practical reasons, however, you should limit the number of attributes on each element. Having more than ten attributes in an element is rare.

Attributes are set within the start tag of an element, after the name string but before the closing greater-than sign. Attributes are separated from the tag name by white space — normally a single space, but legally one or more spaces, tabs, or carriage returns. The value of an XML attribute must be enclosed in quotation marks.

Attributes and empty elements

An empty XML element can contain an attribute. The following are typical examples of using attributes with empty elements:

```
<author name="William of Occam"/>
<image source="images/photo.jpg" height="10 cm" width="5 cm"/>
```

**10 Min.
To Go**

Comparison of Elements and Attributes

XML enables you to create your own set of tags to represent your information. XML also allows you to specify the legal attributes on those tags. Sometimes information can be incorporated into either an XML element or an XML attribute. The following two image representations, for example, contain the same information. Given either of these XML fragments, an XML application could find and display the graphic file photos/beach.jpg.

```
<image source="photos/beach.jpg"/>
<image><source>photos/beach.jpg</source></image>
```

Because both representations provide the same information, any assessment of which is better is subjective.

XML users frequently ask, "When should I use elements and when should I use attributes?" There are no absolute rules, but Table 6-1 presents some guidelines.

Table 6-1
Guidelines for Using Elements or Attributes

	Element	Attribute
Can contain text content	Yes	Yes, but anything more than several characters is unwieldy
Can contain child elements	Yes	No

Table 6-1 gives the hard and fast rules. If you need to represent content that may contain child elements, you must use an XML element. If you're attaching labels or properties to XML content, you probably want to use an attribute.

Beyond the fixed rules, however, there's a common-sense component that may govern your choice. If you're authoring or creating XML documents, you should consider how easily other users can understand and process your documents. The following, for example, is a legal XML document:

```
<poem content="Mary had a little lamb, her fleece was white as
snow.  And everywhere that Mary went, her lamb was sure to go.">
</poem>
```

This document uses the <poem> tag to denote a poem. The content of the poem is included as the value of the content attribute.

Although legal, this document is somewhat unwieldy. What if a poem is longer, contains special characters, or contains other XML elements? Although this style works for this particular poem, it won't work in many situations. Instead, you can use the following markup for a poem:

```
<poem>
Mary had a little lamb, her fleece was white as snow.  And
everywhere that Mary went, the lamb was sure to go.
</poem>
```

This session covers the building blocks of learning XML syntax. The next session moves on to other important components of an XML document.

Done!

REVIEW

- XML elements represent containers of information.
- XML elements can contain text and other XML elements.
- XML attributes represent labels on those containers.
- XML attributes have must have a name and a value.
- An empty element is a special XML construct that has no content.

QUIZ YOURSELF

1. How many attributes can an XML element have? (See "Rules for XML attributes.")
2. How many attributes can an empty XML element have? (See "Rules for XML attributes.")
3. Can an XML element name contain a space? (See "Rules for XML tags.")
4. Can an XML attribute value contain a space? (See "Rules for XML attributes.")
5. What specific type of content is legal within an element but illegal within an attribute? (See "Comparison of Elements and Attributes.")

Tour of XML Syntax: Special Constructs

Session Checklist

✔ Learning about XML declarations

✔ Adding information to XML documents with comments

✔ Reviewing special character handling with entity references

✔ Understanding character data and special characters

30 Min. To Go

I n this session, we explore several XML special constructs. These include the XML declaration, comments, processing instructions, CDATA sections, and entities. Depending on your project, you may use all of these, some of these, or none in your XML documents.

Understanding the XML Declaration

All XML documents that you create by using this book begin with an XML declaration. But a declaration is an optional part of your XML document. You use XML declarations to minimize issues with your browsers or other tools that interact with your XML documents. In general, it's a good habit to use a declaration.

If you choose to use an XML declaration, it must be the first line of your XML document with no white space or other characters above it.

The XML declaration you see most often in your examples includes the XML version used to create the XML document.

```
<?xml version="1.0"?>
```

Right now, there's only one version of XML — 1.0. But that may not always be the case. The W3C will most likely issue revisions at some time in the future. It's helpful for the applications and browsers that use your XML document to know the XML version used to create the XML document.

You can also use the character set — the language of the document — within the XML declaration.

```
<?xml version="1.0" encoding="UTF-8" ?>
```

Depending on how you're using XML, you may have additional information in the declaration or other types of encoding. The declaration — again, it's optional — must contain the version number.

Inserting Comments in XML Documents

You may decide to include comments along with your content and markup. XML provides a means for you to type comments in your XML documents. Similar to comment functions in word processors, this capability allows you to include information about your XML document directly in the document itself. You and others can then read your comments as they use or edit your XML document.

Comments are identified in XML with special symbols at the start and end of the comment. Here's an example:

```
<!--Created by Anon E. Mouse-->
```

The exclamation mark and dashes at the start of the line and dashes at the end tell your browser that the information is a comment and should not be displayed. After you place your comments, anyone who reads or edits the XML document may read them. Any machine or application that parses (reads) or validates your XML document ignores commented information.

Comments do not require an end tag.

In Listing 7-1, see if you can tell which lines are comments.

Listing 7-1
An XML document with comments

```xml
<?xml version="1.0"?>
<!--A small piece of a family tree-->
<family>

<father>Joseph Q. Clark</father>
<mother>Mary J. Clark</mother>
<!--This document continues to include children below-->
<offspring>
    <child>Jennifer Clark</child>
    <child>Joseph Q. Clark II</child>
    <child>Margaret M. Clark</child>
    <child>Mark J. Clark</child>
</offspring>
<!--Document created April 2001 in Pittsburgh, Pennsylvania-->
</family>
```

Listing 7-1 is available on your CD-ROM as `family-comments.xml`.

To confirm your suspicions, view this document in Internet Explorer (see Figure 7-1).

Upon viewing the file in the browser, you will see that several lines are shown in lighter text. This confirms your guesses, hopefully. Those are the three comments in this XML document.

```xml
<!--A small piece of a family tree-->
<!--This document continues to include children below-->
<!--Document created April 2001 in Pittsburgh, Pennsylvania-->
```

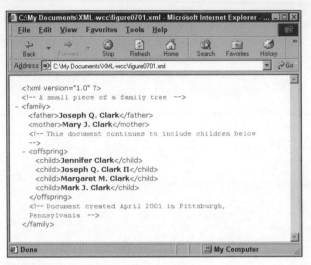

Figure 7-1
Viewing Listing 7-1 in Internet Explorer

Notice that the comments are allowed to wrap to multiple lines. There's no limit on the length of comments you include in your XML document, so feel free to include any information you feel is pertinent or that helps you to remember what each part of your document does.

Using Processing Instructions to Include Application-Specific Information

20 Min. To Go

A processing instruction tells an application how to use your XML documents. You can use a processing instruction for the following purposes:

- To associate a particular style sheet with an XML document.
- To pass formatting information to an application that will render your XML document for printing.
- To include other information in your document that will be recognized by your particular application, but not by an XML parser.

Later, in Session 22 of this book, you will use a processing instruction to associate a cascading style sheet (CSS) with your XML documents.

Using Entity References for Special Characters

Certain characters you might include in your content have special meaning in XML documents. If not typed properly, these characters can cause errors. Entity references enable these characters or symbols to appear without conflicting with their counterparts in the XML markup.

To understand entity references for special characters, you first need to review your syntax. In your XML documents, your tags are included in angle brackets:

```
<Annotation>Family members are listed in birth order whenever
possible.</Annotation>
```

Any time your browser or an application encounters an angle bracket, it assumes a tag is beginning or ending. If you actually have an angle bracket in your content, you can confuse the machine trying to read your XML document. For example:

```
<Annotation>If the number of children is greater than (>) four but
less than (<) ten, this family has been included in the "Honorable
Mention" section of this book but not in the "Record Setters"
section.</Annotation>
```

With the inclusion of (<) and (>), there's the possibility of confusion by a browser or application attempting to parse your XML document, as shown in Figure 7-2.

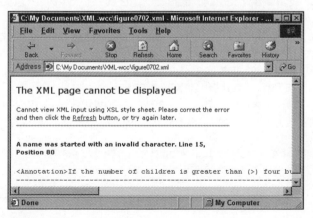

Figure 7-2
Annotation containing angle brackets is misunderstood by the browser

To avoid confusion, you substitute entity references. Instead of angle brackets, you use representations:

- Left angle bracket or less than: <
- Right angle bracket or greater than: >

Any other symbol that has special meaning within your XML document can cause similar problems. In fact, the preceding example uses double quotes. Apostrophes (single quotes), double quotes, and ampersands must also be represented by entity references:

- Apostrophe: '
- Double quote: "
- Ampersand: &

This is similar to HTML. In HTML, for example, when you want to show a registered trademark, you must type ® to display the symbol. With HTML, however, the goal was a special display; with your XML examples, the goal is a legal XML document. You can also use character entities to insert non-ASCII characters, such as symbols or foreign language characters.

Using Entities for Text Snippets

10 Min. To Go

Another type of entity reference allows you to name chunks of XML text so that you can refer to the text with a few short characters. This saves you typing time and enables you to change the text in one spot to update it everywhere. To do so, you create an entity that has a name (the few short characters you will type) and the text chunk you want in place of those characters.

A copyright notice, for example, may appear in many places but only be typed once. When it's needed, it is referenced. In Session 9 of this book, we discuss document type definitions and place entities. For now, we will include it in a `family-cp.xml` document (save your `family.xml` file from Session 3 to this new name).

Under your XML declaration, type the following text to create your copyright:

```
<?xml version="1.0"?>
<!DOCTYPE famtree [
<!ENTITY cp "This book is copyright 2001 Hungry Minds.">
]>
```

Ignore the DOCTYPE famtree stuff for now. What's most important here is

```
<!ENTITY cp "This book is copyright 2001 Hungry Minds.">
```

The first part — the ENTITY — lets the XML know that you're creating an entity. The next part — cp — is the characters you will type. These could have been just about any characters and could have been more than two characters. The part in quotations is the text that will show up in the document.

To check to see if your cp is working, type it after the </offspring> tag between an ampersand and semicolon. Your family-cp.xml XML document should now look like this:

```
<?xml version="1.0"?>
<!DOCTYPE famtree [
<!ENTITY cp "This book is copyright 2001 Hungry Minds.">
]>
<family>
<father>Joseph Q. Clark</father>
<mother>Mary J. Clark</mother>
<offspring>
    <child>Jennifer Clark</child>
    <child>Joseph Q. Clark II</child>
    <child>Margaret M. Clark</child>
    <child>Mark J. Clark</child>
</offspring>
&cp;
</family>
```

Viewed in the browser, you will see This book is copyright 2001 Hungry Minds. (see Figure 7-3) instead of &cp;.

 You may also open this file, family-cp.xml, **from the CD to view.**

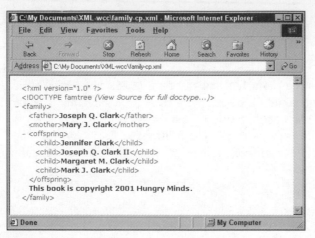

Figure 7-3
The copyright, viewed in the browser

Hiding Content from the Parser with CDATA Sections

Sometimes you may include information in your XML document that you want to display without worrying about substituting special characters in the XML itself. One example is a mathematical equation. You don't want to replace all the greater thans, less thans, and other symbols with special characters — it's time consuming and leaves too much room for error. Another example is scripts, which must contain specific characters. The same drawbacks apply to that scenario.

In these instances, you use XML character data or CDATA sections to get the browser or parser to pass over these characters. You can enter any information you like within a CDATA section. The XML processor sees the special symbols denoting the content as CDATA and sends it through without trying to parse it. As a result, you can have angle brackets and all sorts of other symbols in your document without the fuss of using entity references.

Take a look at the example in Figure 7-4. This document contains a CDATA section. At the start, the section begins with <![CDATA[and ends with]]>. All the information between the beginning and the end are sent directly to the application or browser without being changed.

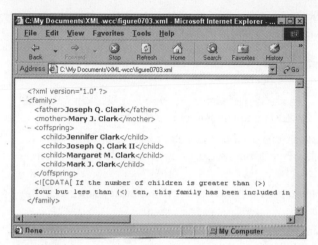

Figure 7-4
Using CDATA the angle brackets display

For the purposes of your example, this enables you to pass through the special characters without retyping them as entity references. But notice that you have also pulled the information out of the Annotation tag. If you want it to be part of the Annotation tag, you may want to stick with entity references.

CDATA is discussed in more detail in Session 14.

Your XML documents are more than just content and markup. They are special entities and data exceptions, and scripts and application information. While you don't need to worry about every type of script and processing instruction — just worry about what you need to get your own job done — it's important to know that you do have options.

Done!

REVIEW

- XML declarations are optional but provide important information to XML processors about the XML document.

- Comments may be placed in an XML document.

- Special characters can cause conflicts within an XML processor. To prevent this, you can use entity references and CDATA in your XML documents.

QUIZ YOURSELF

1. Can an XML declaration be placed at the end of an XML document? (See "Understanding the XML Declaration.")

2. Are you limited in the number of comments you can place in any XML document? (Refer to "Inserting Comments in XML Documents.")

3. Are processing instructions used by an XML processor or are they ignored? (See "Using Processing Instructions to Include Application-Specific Information.")

4. Why must entity references be used? (See "Using Entity References for Special Characters.")

5. What is the purpose of CDATA sections? (Refer to "Hiding Content from the Parser with CDATA Sections.")

Working with Well-Formed XML Documents

Session Checklist

✔ Learning the guidelines for well-formed documents

✔ Understanding the term *vocabulary*

✔ Creating well-formed documents

**30 Min.
To Go**

I n previous sessions, you created short and loosely structured XML documents — also known as *well-formed* XML documents. In this session, we take a closer look at document structure and the rules XML documents need to follow.

Passing the Parser's Syntax Check: A Well-Formed XML Document

XML documents follow certain minimum syntax rules. For most applications, well-formed XML documents are good enough. More complex systems, such as e-commerce systems, require documents to be more rigidly structured (valid) and are dealt with in Session 10.

Documents that are not well-formed do not follow the syntax rules of XML. Well-formed XML documents meet certain basic criteria, which include the following:

- If the XML document includes an XML declaration, the declaration is at the beginning of the document.
- All tags in the document are nested within a root tag.
- Every begin tag has an end tag, and the begin and end tags match.
- Any empty tags must include an ending slash.
- All entities or special characters are used properly.

Understanding Syntax

XML syntax is the rules you follow as you type your XML document. When you're enclosing tags in angle brackets and surrounding content with tags, for example, you are using proper syntax.

Comparing the XML syntax to the vocabulary

You may also read the term *vocabulary* relating to XML documents. In XML, the vocabulary is all the tags available for your documents. In Session 10, you will see a list of tags for a particular type of document: a document type definition (DTD). This is where the vocabulary is defined and modified.

Another term that comes up is grammar, which has to do with setting up languages like XML and SGML.

The next section takes a closer look at syntax and what makes a well-formed document.

Reviewing rules for well-formed XML documents

You must adhere to the following rules when creating well-formed documents:

- The XML document should start with an XML declaration. Although an XML declaration is technically optional for well-formed XML documents, if a document does not start with a declaration, a browser or parser may not recognize the content as XML.

- One root tag must surround the rest of the tags in your XML document. Its begin tag is above your first tag (though after the XML declaration) and the end tag is after your last element.

- Every begin tag must have an end tag, and the begin and end tags must match in name *and* in case. Unlike HTML, XML is case sensitive — `</Family>` and `</FAMILY>` are not end tags for the start tag `<family>`. The only appropriate end tag is `</family>`.

- Tags cannot include spaces, but they can include underscores, letters, and numbers. Note that the tag may start with a letter or underscore but cannot start with a number. Legal tags would be `<family>`, `<_birthdate>`, and `<STATE>`. Unacceptable names would be `<1st_place>` and `<start date>`.

- Any empty tags that have been used — in other words, tags with no end tag — must include an appropriate ending slash, as in `<author name="Jean Yalogi"/>`. To avoid this issue, you may replace the empty tag format with begin and end tags, thus `<author name="Jean Yalogi"></author>`.

- Attribute values, discussed in Session 6, must be enclosed in double quotes or single quotes; there are no exceptions. You may have been sloppy with your HTML quotes, but you cannot be so with your XML quotes! XML will not accept `<meal time=noon>` as a substitute for the proper `<meal time="noon">`.

- All entities or special characters must be used properly with appropriate symbols, specifically beginning with an ampersand and ending with a semi-colon. An example is your angle bracket represented as `gt` instead of `&gt;` (refer to Session 7 for more details).

If you follow these rules, you're likely to create well-formed XML documents. These documents view properly in your browser and can be easily understood and used by related applications

Creating Well-Formed XML Documents

In this section, you experiment with the rules by creating documents with intentional syntax errors.

To begin, open your favorite text editor. For simplicity, all examples in this book use Microsoft Notepad. In your text editor, you will create your sports standings document. Type the document as follows:

**20 Min.
To Go**

```
<?xml version="1.0" ?>
<team_standing>
    <team>Pittsburgh Pirates</team>
    <wins>49</wins>
    <losses>42</losses>
    <standing>3rd</standing>
</team_standing>
```

Use your Enter key to separate the text into logical chunks so that you can edit them more easily. When viewing your XML document, you will not see these dividing spaces; the browser ignores them the same way browsers ignore spaces in HTML.

Now, save this file as standings1.xml. If your operating system version adds the extension .txt to the filename, you may need to enclose the file name in quotes to save it properly.

Now that you have your XML document, view it in your browser. Launch Microsoft Internet Explorer 5 (or higher), if it's not already open. Choose File ⇨ Open, browse to your recently created standings1.xml file in the XML-wcc folder, and double-click to open it. Figure 8-1 shows what it should look like in your browser.

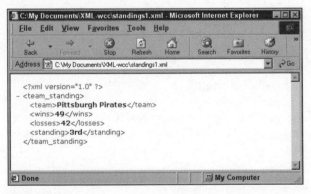

Figure 8-1
An XML document displayed in Internet Explorer

Now place your cursor in front of <team>Pittsburgh Pirates</team>, press the Enter key, type **<record>**, and press the Enter key again. You have added a begin tag. Go ahead and view this in your browser before you type the end tag. That way, you definitely have a syntax error and can see what happens to your XML document.

Here is your document's text:

```
<?xml version="1.0"?>
<team_standing>
    <record>
    <team>Pittsburgh Pirates</team>
    <wins>49</wins>
    <losses>42</losses>
    <standing>3rd</standing>
</team_standing>
```

Figure 8-2 shows the same document in the browser.

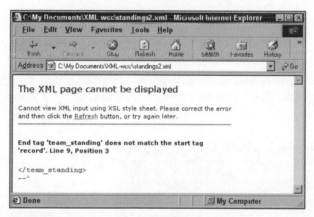

Figure 8-2
An XML Document with a syntax error

**10 Min.
To Go**

The browser becomes confused when it does not see an end tag for <record>. Because of the mathematical way that tags are nested, the browser expects to see an end to <record> before the end to <team_standing>. That is why the error shows a carat pointing to the t in </team_standing>. To fix this error, add the </record> tag before the </team_standing> end tag. Try making a few other intentional errors in your document, such as omitting an angle bracket.

In the next example, you're going to intentionally create an entity as you did in Session 7, but forget to use the ampersand when referencing the entity.

After your XML declaration, type this text:

```
<!DOCTYPE sportbook [
<!ENTITY Brd "Sports Broadcasting Service of America">
]>
```

Now modify your standings1.xml XML document to include a reference to the entity, like this:

```
<?xml version="1.0"?>
<!DOCTYPE sportbook [
<!ENTITY Brd "Sports Broadcasting Service of America">
]>
<team_standing>
    <record>
    <team>Pittsburgh Pirates</team>
    <wins>49</wins>
    <losses>42</losses>
    <standing>3rd</standing>
    <brand>This document created by &Brd;.</brand>
    </record>
</team_standing>
```

Save your document. When viewed in the browser, as shown in Figure 8-3, you will see the replacement text, "Sports Broadcasting Service of America," instead of &Brd;

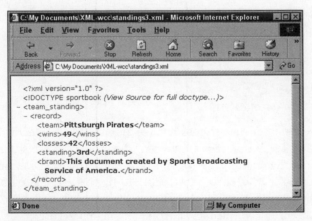

Figure 8-3
The well-formed document with working entity

Now remove the ampersand in front of Brd; where it is referenced in your document.

```
<brand>This document created by Brd;.</brand>
```

Try viewing again. As shown in Figure 8-4, you do not get an error, but your replacement text, Sports Broadcasting Service of America, also does not appear.

Part II—Saturday Morning
Session 8

```
C:\My Documents\XML-wcc\standings3.xml - Microsoft Internet Explorer
File   Edit   View   Favorites   Tools   Help
 ↩         ⇨           ⊗        ↻         ⌂          🔍        📁          🕘
Back    Forward      Stop    Refresh    Home      Search   Favorites   History
Address  C:\My Documents\XML-wcc\standings3.xml                              Go

<?xml version="1.0" ?>
<!DOCTYPE sportbook (View Source for full doctype...)>
- <team_standing>
  - <record>
      <team>Pittsburgh Pirates</team>
      <wins>49</wins>
      <losses>42</losses>
      <standing>3rd</standing>
      <brand>This document created by Brd;.</brand>
    </record>
  </team_standing>

Done                                                      My Computer
```

Figure 8-4
The well-formed document with broken entity, displayed in browser

To ensure that your XML documents are well-formed, make sure when creating them that your syntax is correct. If your syntax is not correct, your document may not view properly in the browser or applications may not be able to process it.

Done!

REVIEW

- Syntax is key in producing well-formed XML documents.
- Syntax errors can keep your documents from parsing or cause errors when applications access your XML.
- The browser doesn't always produce an error message when your syntax is wrong, as shown in Figure 8-4.

QUIZ YOURSELF

1. If you don't follow the syntax rules outlined in this session, will your documents be well-formed? (See "Reviewing rules for well-formed XML documents.")

2. Do empty tags have end tags? (See "Reviewing rules for well-formed XML documents.")

3. Do missing characters in entities keep your document from displaying in a Web browser? (See "Creating Well-Formed XML Documents.")

4. True or False: If your XML documents are not well-formed, the browser will still display them. (See "Creating Well-Formed XML Documents.")

5. True or False: If your XML documents have syntax errors, they may still display in the browser. (See "Creating Well-Formed XML Documents.")

Specifying an XML Vocabulary with a DTD

Session Checklist

✔ Learning about document type definitions (DTDs)

✔ Viewing external DTDs

✔ Creating a DTD

✔ Using a DTD with an XML document

**30 Min.
To Go**

Up to this point, you have created documents that were structured, but did not follow set rules. Now it's time to move from these loosely structured XML documents to rigidly structured, more reusable documents. To produce rigidly structured documents, you need to begin using a document type definition, or DTD.

In this session, you review your loosely structured documents, cover the reasons for using a DTD, walk through a DTD sample, and create a simple DTD.

Defining Elements in Your DTD

A *DTD*, which can be a separate file or included in your XML document, is a listing of elements — your tags — and their properties. Each element is associated with a pattern called a *content model* that defines the element's content. By defining the set of elements and rules for each element, you create an XML vocabulary for your documents. This gives your documents a rigid structure to follow.

Using XML tags without a DTD

In previous sessions, you created an XML document by typing begin tags, content, and end tags. Your document had multiple tags — some were nested, and all were contained inside the root tag. But you essentially made those tags up as you went along. You were making a structured document, and for the most part it worked. You had a loose structure and decided what to call the elements (family, father, child, and so on) and how many of each to have (four child elements, for example). Review the following simple family.xml document:

```
<?xml version="1.0"?>
<family>
<father>Joseph Q. Clark</father>
<mother>Mary J. Clark</mother>
<offspring>
    <child>Jennifer Clark</child>
    <child>Joseph Q. Clark II</child>
    <child>Margaret M. Clark</child>
    <child>Mark J. Clark</child>
</offspring>
</family>
```

At this point, no rules are controlling the document. The document will appear in a browser. You can remove the father element or add three more child elements and the XML document will still appear.

Understanding your DTD's purpose

The purpose of the DTD is to define elements — your tags — for use in your XML documents and to specify the relationship between those elements.

If you want to reuse your XML information, build applications based on your XML documents, and even exchange your XML documents with others, you probably want to make sure that your documents conform to a common structure. Applications that process your XML documents rely on your documents' vocabulary to figure out how to process the contents. You can't effectively reuse and share your XML documents if each document uses a different set of tags.

To maximize the benefits of XML and have many documents consistently work together and perform properly, you need to set up a formal, rigid structure. You can then create XML documents that abide by that structure. After that, you can *validate* your documents, which is a way of ensuring that the XML documents follow the DTD rules. You can do more with valid XML documents than you can with the loosely structured documents discussed in previous sessions.

An XML document that follows a DTD is valid XML. An XML document that does not follow a DTD, but is loosely structured instead, is well-formed XML.

Do you need a DTD? No. Many, but not all, XML documents use DTDs. If you have one, though, you can ensure that your documents are consistently structured. Then you can reuse them. If you are creating the DTD, you name the tags and set the rules for how the tags fit together. If your industry or company already has a DTD, you need to learn its tags and rules.

You may find a DTD that suits your purpose by searching the Web or checking with industry groups. If a DTD already exists for your type of document, you may be able to use it as is or modify it. This can save you weeks — months even — in defining your own DTD from scratch.

In this session, you create your own DTD from scratch. You will set up a small list of elements (tags) and the rules they must follow. You may, for example, create a rule that says that if there is an offspring element, there must also be both father and mother elements. You may add a rule that says that if there is an offspring element, there is at least one child element. Or, you could write a rule that requires both a mother and father element within the family element. (As your document expands, you may replace the family element with two elements — individual and family — and under that scenario such a rule might make more sense.)

In the next section, you will write a DTD with rules that force a file to have mother and father elements, but make the offspring element (and thus the child element) optional.

Walking through a DTD

You can understand a DTD more easily by walking through an example. To build a DTD, you need to know the pieces that you are expected to put together.

*20 Min.
To Go*

The following lines of your DTD define tags that you can use for your XML documents. Each tag that you use in your document is created as an *element* in a DTD. In your `family.xml` document, you had your root tag called `family`. As an element, its definition here is:

```
<!ELEMENT family (father, mother, offspring?)>
```

This creates the root element `family`, and designates the structure that must exist within `family`. In the `family.xml` example from Session 3, you list the `father`, `mother`, and `offspring` in your XML document. Those tags are listed in the `family` element in the order that they are allowed to occur.

The `offspring` element includes a ? denoting that it's optional — a `family` may be a valid element with `father` and `mother`. This is a simplistic example, but is intended just to give you an idea how a DTD and XML document works.

Now if the `family` element is allowed to contain `father`, `mother`, and `offspring`, you must create those elements so that the tags are available for you to use. First, you add the `father` and `mother` elements to the DTD:

```
<!ELEMENT father (#PCDATA)>
<!ELEMENT mother (#PCDATA)>
```

PCDATA is short for parsed character data. The designation PCDATA means that text may be typed within the `father` and `mother` tags.

The third element, `offspring`, does not allow text to be typed in it; instead, it must contain other elements that are called `child`. (We discussed nested elements in Session 6.) We add to the DTD both the `offspring` and `child` elements.

```
<!ELEMENT offspring (child+)>
<!ELEMENT child (#PCDATA)>
```

The `offspring` element contains `child` elements instead of text. The plus (+) means that `offspring` requires one `child` element and the `child` element can repeat. This `child` element can now contain PCDATA, meaning text may be typed in the element. For example purposes, this means that you can type the children's names directly between the begin and end tags. With what you now know about the tags and their creation within a DTD, take a look at the listing that follows.

```
<?xml version="1.0"?>
<family>
<father>Joseph Q. Clark</father>
<mother>Mary J. Clark</mother>
<offspring>
    <child>Jennifer Clark</child>
```

```
   <child>Joseph Q. Clark II</child>
   <child>Margaret M. Clark</child>
   <child>Mark J. Clark</child>
</offspring>
</family>
```

Creating a DTD

In this section, you create a simple DTD for the family tree XML document.

The first step in creating your DTD is to type your XML declaration. This line is an optional beginning for your XML documents and — as an XML document — your DTD has it, too.

Open Notepad and type the following:

```
<!ELEMENT family (father, mother, offspring?)>
```

Now save this file as genealogy1.dtd. If your operating system version adds the extension .txt to the filename, you may need to enclose the file name in quotes to save it properly, as shown in Figure 9-1.

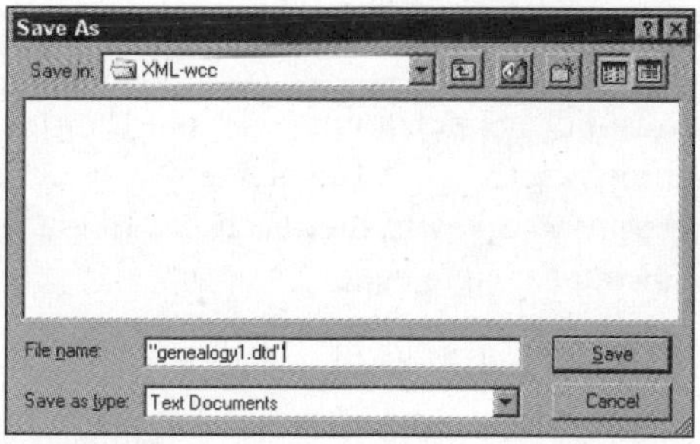

Figure 9-1
Save your DTD as a text file in MS Notepad

Now type the remainder of the text necessary to complete your first DTD. After you type all the text as shown, save the file genealogy1.dtd again.

```
<!ELEMENT family (father, mother, offspring?)>
<!ELEMENT father (#PCDATA)>
<!ELEMENT mother (#PCDATA)>
<!ELEMENT offspring (child+)>
<!ELEMENT child (#PCDATA)>
```

Expanding your DTD

After you set up your DTD and create your main elements, you can expand it. One of your options is to add more tags. You can add tags for the surname (last name) or mother's maiden name. You can add grandmother and grandfather tags, or — to suit that same need — adjust the mother and father elements to contain other mother and father elements for the additional generations!

You could also add attributes to hold information on each person. Attributes are discussed in Session 6.

To keep this example easy to follow, you will expand your DTD by adding a surname (last name) element as well as a maiden element. As we have stated before, because XML is extensible, you can keep adding tags and name them whatever you want.

Before you add these tags, you need to review the rules for your current tags and how your rules need to adjust for new tags.

Reviewing Content Models

The content model may sound mysterious, but it's nothing more than the rule for each element. The content model specifies exactly what the element may contain, the order in which those elements may appear, and whether each child element is optional and/or repeatable. In the following example code

```
<!ELEMENT family (father, mother, offspring?)>
```

the content model for the family element (your tag) is (father , mother , offspring?), which designates the structure that must exist within family. Because commas separate the element names, they must occur in the order shown. If another symbol — a pipe (|), for example — had been used and combined with an asterisk after the end parenthesis, then the elements could occur in any order.

Understanding special symbols in content models

**10 Min.
To Go**

The father, mother, and offspring elements are listed in the family element in the order they are allowed to occur. The offspring element includes a ? denoting that it is optional — family may be a valid element even if it contains only father and mother. Because father and mother do not have a question mark, they are required to occur in family.

In addition to the question mark (?) for tags that are optional and cannot repeat, you can also use an asterisk (*) for tags that are optional and may repeat, and a plus (+) for tags that are required — not optional — and may repeat many times. Table 9-1 contains a complete list of symbols.

Table 9-1
Possible Symbols in the Content Model

Symbols After Element Name		
Content Model Symbol	**Is the Element Required or Optional?**	**Is the Element Able to Repeat?**
Question mark (?)	Optional	No
Asterisk (*)	Optional	Yes
Plus (+)	Required	Yes
No Symbol	Required	No

Symbols Between Element Names	
Content Model Symbol	**Meaning**
Comma (,)	Elements must occur in the order listed.
Pipe (|)	Only one of the elements listed may occur. Sometimes the pipe is combined with parentheses with an asterisk outside; this allows all elements to occur in random order.
Parentheses ( )	Used to combine elements in a mathematical way

Let's take a look at several possible variations for your family element's content model. We review each variation, so the differences depend on the symbols used.

```
<!ELEMENT family (father, mother, offspring?)>
```

This is your original rule. The comma separators means the family element must have father and mother, and father must come first. If there's an offspring element — the question mark that it's optional and might not be there — then it must come after mother.

```
<!ELEMENT family (father | mother)+, offspring?)>
```

Using the pipe and extra parenthesis, this rule is changed so that father and
mother may occur in any order. With the plus, you allow the choice (father or
mother) to occur more than once. The offspring element is still optional with the
question mark.

The content model of the family **element is not ideal, because it
allows multiple** father **or multiple** mother **elements. When you
define a content model, you need to use these symbols in the
best possible combination to produce documents that follow the
rules and make logical sense.**

The next content model example uses multiple question marks, denoting
optional items.

```
<!ELEMENT family (father?, mother?, offspring?)>
```

In this last example, commas again separate the elements so they must occur in
this order. Because they all have question marks, any or all of them may be omit-
ted. We chose this content model for example purposes to familiarize you with the
meaning of the symbols. It is not, for a genealogical DTD, necessarily a sensible
content model.

Expanding your element set and content model

With the addition of the surname, your XML document now becomes larger. In the
following code (from an expanded example in Session 3), the surname tag is added
to the last names of all six people and a maiden tag with new content is added to
the mother. You need to adjust your DTD to recognize and allow these tags.

```
<?xml version="1.0"?>
<family>
<father>Joseph Q. <surname>Clark</surname></father>
<mother>Mary J.
<surname>Clark</surname><maiden>Jones</maiden></mother>
<offspring>
    <child>Jennifer <surname>Clark</surname></child>
    <child>Joseph Q. <surname>Clark</surname> II</child>
    <child>Margaret M. <surname>Clark</surname></child>
    <child>Mark J. <surname>Clark</surname></child>
</offspring>
</family>
```

One rule that you may want to define for this expanded model is that surname is required within all elements (just about everyone has a last name or family name). Another rule (yet to be written in your DTD) is that the maiden element is restricted so that it can only be included in the mother element.

Edit your DTD to include the following text.

```
<!ELEMENT surname (#PCDATA)>
<!ELEMENT maiden (#PCDATA)>
```

Now you have to modify father, mother, and child to allow surname to be nested within them. You must also adjust mother to allow maiden to be a part of it.

```
<!ELEMENT family (father, mother, offspring?)>
<!ELEMENT father (#PCDATA | surname)*>
<!ELEMENT mother (#PCDATA | maiden | surname)*>
<!ELEMENT offspring (child+)>
<!ELEMENT child (#PCDATA | surname)*>
<!ELEMENT surname (#PCDATA)>
<!ELEMENT maiden (#PCDATA)>
```

The next session takes a look at your DTD and XML document combination and how you can ensure that your XML document is following the structure rules within the DTD.

Done!

REVIEW

- Many XML documents use a DTD.
- A DTD defines the tags that may be used in an XML document and the order of occurrence and frequency with which tags may occur.
- DTDs may be expanded to allow nesting of multiple levels of elements.
- The rules created by a DTD give you control over where elements may be used.

QUIZ YOURSELF

1. Is it possible to have an XML document that does not conform to a DTD? (See "Using XML tags without a DTD.")

2. Who decides what information is in a DTD? (See "Understanding your DTD's purpose.")

3. What does the term PCDATA mean in the context of a DTD? (See "Walking through a DTD.")

4. Do you have to adjust your content model if you add tags? (See "Reviewing Content Models.")

5. What are the special symbols used in the content model? Hint: One of the symbols may be found in this question, in front of the word *hint*. (See "Understanding special symbols in content models.")

Validating an XML Document and Expanding Its Structure

Session Checklist

✔ Learning about valid versus well-formed

✔ Validating your XML document against your DTD

✔ Walking through the validation process

✔ Modifying our XML document and DTD

✔ Validating the newly expanded structure

**30 Min.
To Go**

Your XML documents up to this point have been well-formed. The next step is validating your XML document against its DTD. By validating your XML document, you verify that the document conforms to the rules for vocabulary and structure that you've created in the DTD.

While not all XML documents need to be valid, for some usages they must be. Why validate your XML documents? Just as computer programs must follow syntax and language rules, XML documents must also follow similar rules. Applications that process XML documents depend on the consistent use of XML tags to identify specific information. If you design an application to recognize part numbers based on the `<part_number>` tag, that application won't work if your part numbers are labeled `<partNum>`. By validating your XML documents, you verify that the documents contain the XML tags that you've specified in your DTD.

Validation does not verify that the content of each XML tag is valid, just that the tags themselves conform to the structure specified in the DTD. XML documents are just as prone to the "garbage in, garbage out" complex as any computer program.

Determining How to Validate

Several tools enable you to validate an XML document against a DTD. When you validate your XML document, you basically compare your XML document against the DTD structure rules to ensure your document is following those rules. When you validate, your validation tool may return errors relating to missing pieces or improperly nested elements. It may even return errors relating to well formedness (missing quotes on attributes, for example).

On this book's CD-ROM, there is a link to a set of Microsoft browser utilities called "Internet Explorer Tools for Validating XML and Viewing XSLT Output." The installer file that you can download, `iexmltls.exe`, adds an XML validation tool to your browser. Once installed, two new choices are available: View XSL Output and Validate XML. These choices are shown in Figure 10-1.

Back
Forward
Save Background As...
Set as Wallpaper
Copy Background
Set as Desktop Item...
Select All
Paste
Create Shortcut
Add to Favorites...
View Source
Encoding ▶
Print
Refresh
View XSL Output
Validate XML
Properties

Figure 10-1
Right-click to see new validation options (Internet Explorer 5.5)

Install the `iexmltls.exe` component and follow the `readme` instructions. Then open one of your XML documents in Internet Explorer 5 or higher. Right-click and Validate XML appears in the menu. Select this item and you will get either a list of errors or a confirmation of validity (see Figure 10-2).

```
Microsoft Internet Explorer                    ☒
    ⚠   Validation Successful.
        file:///C:/My Documents/XML-wcc/familyatt1.xml

            ┌──────────────┐
            │     OK       │
            └──────────────┘
```

Figure 10-2
The XML validation plug-in declares an XML document valid

Temporarily modify your family.xml document to create an error. Within your DTD, the content model states that child elements must be contained within offspring elements.

```
<!ELEMENT offspring (child*)>
```

Remove the <offspring> and </offspring> tags from your XML document. Save the file as family10.xml. Now, specify the DTD that your document should be validated against. This is done within your XML document, family10.xml. We add a line after our XML declaration that names the DTD and shows its path. Thus,

```
<?xml version="1.0"?>
<!DOCTYPE family SYSTEM "genealogy.dtd">
<family>
<father>Joseph Q. Clark</father>
<mother>Mary J. Clark</mother>
    <child>Jennifer Clark</child>
    <child>Joseph Q. Clark II</child>
    <child>Margaret M. Clark</child>
    <child>Mark J. Clark</child>
</family>
```

Do not modify your DTD. Just make sure the genealogy.dtd you created in the last session is located in the same directory as the family10.xml document just created.

Both the family10.xml XML document and the genealogy.dtd DTD are located in the session10 folder of your book's CD.

Now open your family10.xml document in the browser. After it displays, right-click and select Validate XML. You should get the error shown in Figure 10-3, because the child tags are not properly contained within an offspring tag.

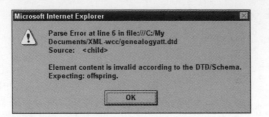

Figure 10-3
An error due to invalid document structure

**20 Min.
To Go**

Expanding Your DTD with New Elements

You can add elements, such as birthday, gender, or birthplace, to expand your
XML documents. Right now, our genealogy.dtd document looks like this:

```
<!ELEMENT family (father, mother, offspring?)>
<!ELEMENT father (#PCDATA | surname)*>
<!ELEMENT mother (#PCDATA | maiden | surname)*>
<!ELEMENT offspring (child+)>
<!ELEMENT child (#PCDATA | surname)*>
<!ELEMENT surname (#PCDATA)>
<!ELEMENT maiden (#PCDATA)>
```

To add birthplace, you create its element information in your DTD by adding
something like the following:

```
<!ELEMENT birthplace (#PCDATA)>
```

**Remember, PCDATA (parsed character data) means that text can
be typed inside the tag.**

If a new tag is available, you must also specify where the tag may be placed.
Suppose that you want to modify the child element to allow birthplace.
Instead of

```
<!ELEMENT child (#PCDATA | surname)*>
```

you modify the element to include `birthplace`

```
<!ELEMENT child (#PCDATA | surname | birthplace)*>
```

and you can use the `birthplace` tag in XML documents.

If PCDATA is not stated (such as in the `offspring` **element), then text cannot be typed inside the tag, but other tags may be nested (such as the nesting of** `child` **inside** `offspring`**). Because PCDATA and elements may be in** `child`**, this element is considered to have *mixed* content.**

Save your DTD as `genealogy10.dtd`. Make sure you adjust the DTD filename in your DOCTYPE reference. Now you can use the `birthplace` tag in your XML document, as in the following code.

This listing is available on your CD-ROM under the session10 folder. It is called `family10a.xml`.

```
<?xml version="1.0"?>
<!DOCTYPE family SYSTEM "genealogy10.dtd">
<family>
<father>Joseph Q. <surname>Clark</surname></father>
<mother>Mary J.
<surname>Clark</surname><maiden>Jones</maiden></mother>
<offspring>
    <child>Jennifer <surname>Clark</surname>
    <birthplace>Pittsburgh PA</birthplace></child>
    <child>Joseph Q. <surname>Clark</surname> II
    <birthplace>Kenmore NY</birthplace></child>
    <child>Margaret M. <surname>Clark</surname>
    <birthplace>Pittsburgh PA</birthplace></child>
    <child>Mark J. <surname>Clark</surname>
    <birthplace>Washington PA</birthplace></child>
</offspring>
</family>
```

Save this file as `family.xml` and display it in your browser. Figure 10-4 shows how the last few `child` elements should appear.

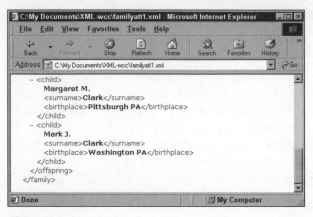

Figure 10-4
The child element with nested birthplace

The next section looks at a new way to expand your DTD.

Expanding Your XML Document

**10 Min.
To Go**

Before moving into attributes and adding them to your DTD and XML document, you need to take a few moments and adjust how your information is structured, which will make your data more flexible. For now, you're going to modify the content of the `child` element in your XML document. Then you'll adjust the content model of the `child` element in your DTD, and validate your example document.

Adjust your `family10a.xml` document as shown in the following code. You are making your document into a higher quality document with more searchable and sortable parts. Concentrate on the `child` element content for now, and only modify those sections of your XML document. For real-world use, you would probably make similar adjustments to the `mother` and `father` elements, but you want to focus on the `child` element right now.

```
<?xml version="1.0"?>
<!DOCTYPE family SYSTEM "genealogy10.dtd">
<family>
<father>Joseph Q. <surname>Clark</surname></father>
<mother>Mary J.
<surname>Clark</surname><maiden>Jones</maiden></mother>
<offspring>
    <child>
```

```
      <firstname>Jennifer</firstname>
      <surname>Clark</surname>
      <birthplace>Pittsburgh PA</birthplace></child>
  <child>
      <firstname>Joseph</firstname>
      <midname>Q.</midname>
      <surname>Clark</surname><ext>II</ext>
      <birthplace>Kenmore NY</birthplace></child>
  <child>
      <firstname>Margaret</firstname>
      <midname>M.</midname>
      <surname>Clark</surname>
      <birthplace>Pittsburgh PA</birthplace></child>
  <child>
      <firstname>Mark</firstname>
      <midname>J.</midname>
      <surname>Clark</surname>
      <birthplace>Washington PA</birthplace></child>
</offspring>
</family>
```

Viewed in the browser, the document appears as shown in Figure 10-5.

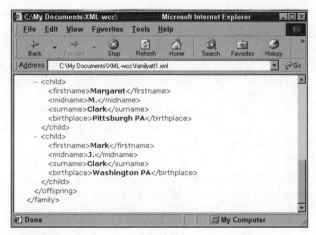

Figure 10-5
The child element with name expanded

To take advantage of all these new parts within `child`, you need to modify your DTD to allow these elements. Modify your `genealogy10.dtd` as shown in the following code:

```
<!ELEMENT family (father, mother, offspring?)>
<!ELEMENT father (#PCDATA | surname)*>
<!ELEMENT mother (#PCDATA | maiden | surname)*>
<!ELEMENT offspring (child*)>
<!ELEMENT child (firstname, midname*, surname, ext?, birthplace)>
<!ELEMENT firstname (#PCDATA)>
<!ELEMENT midname (#PCDATA)>
<!ELEMENT surname (#PCDATA)>
<!ELEMENT ext (#PCDATA)>
<!ELEMENT maiden (#PCDATA)>
<!ELEMENT birthplace (#PCDATA)>
```

Save your DTD.

Validating Your Expanded Document

To validate `family10a.xml` against `genealogy10.dtd`, start Internet Explorer and open `family10a.xml`. You don't need to open your DTD, because it is already specified within your XML document by the line:

```
<!DOCTYPE family SYSTEM "genealogy10.dtd">
```

Notice the minus to the left of the `<child>` element in Figure 10-5. Click this minus and it will change to a plus. If you watch carefully, you will see several lines disappear from your XML document.

You have just collapsed your structure. Because XML documents are structured, you can manipulate what you see in the browser. You could actually collapse all the child elements, as shown in Figure 10-6.

Now click inside your browser to activate the window, and then right-click. After right-clicking, select Validate XML from the pop-up menu (see Figure 10-1). In a few moments, you should get either a list of errors in your Window (similar to Figure 10-3) or a notification that your XML document is valid (as shown in Figure 10-2).

You will work with this expanded document more in the next session.

```
C:\My Documents\XML-wcc\          Microsoft Internet Explorer    _ □ ×
 File  Edit  View  Favorites  Tools  Help
   ←      →      ⊗      ↻      ⌂      ◎      ▣      ⬥
  Back   Forward   Stop   Refresh  Home   Search  Favorites  History
 Address  C:\My Documents\XML-wcc\familyatt1.xml              ▼  ⬿ Go
      <surname>Clark</surname>                               ▲
    </father>
  - <mother>
      Mary J.
      <surname>Clark</surname>
      <maiden>Jones</maiden>
    </mother>
  - <offspring>
    + <child>
    + <child>
    + <child>
    + <child>
    </offspring>
  </family>                                                  ▼
 ②                                    ▣ My Computer
```

Figure 10-6
All the child elements collapsed in the browser

Done!

REVIEW

- Validating a document means ensuring that the structure within the XML document matches the structure rules of the DTD.

- Valid documents are more than just well-formed; they are well-formed and are compared against a DTD.

- Many tools for validating exist, including a free tool within Internet Explorer 5 or higher.

- Validating helps you locate mistakes and fix them in your documents.

QUIZ YOURSELF

1. Do all your XML documents need to be valid? (See "Determining How to Validate.")

2. Name one tool that allows you to validate your XML documents. (See "Validating Your Expanded Document.")

3. What happens if your document has errors and does not validate? (See "Validating Your Expanded Document.")

4. When you adjust or rename your DTD, what change do you need to make to your XML document? (See "Validating Your Expanded Document.")

5. True or False: If you add a DOCTYPE line to your XML document, you must do an update of your DTD. (See "Determining How to Validate.")

PART

II

Saturday Morning

1. What does the term *syntax* refer to?
2. Is the syntax for XML the same as HTML?
3. Name three ways to create an XML document.
4. Which of the following snippets shows proper form for a begin and end tag combination?

   ```
   <father>Joseph Q. Clark</father>
   <Father>Joseph Q. Clark<Father>
   <father/>Joseph Q. Clark</father>
   ```

5. Which of these may start the name of an XML tag: a space, an underscore, the number 5, the letter q?
6. True or False: An XML attribute value must be enclosed in quotes.
7. What is the version number of the first XML Recommendation?
8. Is it possible to insert comments in XML, or only in HTML?
9. True or False: Angle brackets require special handling to avoid parser errors.
10. Name three characters that must be represented with entity references.
11. What capability of XML allows you to define chunks of XML for reuse?
12. True or False: A CDATA section can be used to pass scripts to a browser without adjustment.
13. Name three criteria of well-formed XML documents.
14. Do XML documents have to have a root tag to be well-formed?

15. Is a DTD required to work with XML?

16. What term is used in the DTD when you define your tags `<!ELEMENT` or `<!TAG` ?

17. Do all elements have a content model?

18. Which content model symbol means that a tag is optional but may repeat?

19. Do all XML documents need to be validated?

20. True or False: Microsoft Notepad can be used to validate an XML document against a DTD.

PART

III

Saturday Afternoon

Exploring XML DTDs: Specifying Attributes

Session Checklist

✔ Discovering attributes and their proper form in the DTD

✔ Understanding the available attribute types

✔ Expanding your DTD to add attributes to elements

✔ Using attributes to change your display

**30 Min.
To Go**

Thus far, you've used XML elements to embed metadata — data about your data — within your documents. In this session, you're introduced to XML attributes. Attributes provide a way to attach even more metadata to your XML elements. You'll later learn to manipulate your XML documents based on both elements and attributes.

Understanding Attributes

In the sections that follow, you find out how to expand your elements to include extra information. These bits of extra information — meta-information — are called attributes. Any element in your DTD can have an attribute or multiple attributes. Attributes are not required, but are an option for including extra details in a document whether the details are for display or are for hidden metadata about the document.

Attributes are associated with a specific element. They are usually created for pieces of information that you want to have readily available with related data. In the next section, for example, you will create a `gender` attribute for the `child` element so that as children are added to the genealogical data, male or female may be specified.

The rules for attribute naming are the same as for element naming. Element names may include underscores, letters, numbers, dashes, but no spaces.

You can even place attributes in an empty element. These attributes can hold data in the document that does not display but can be accessed by machine or read by a human reader. Let's first take a look at an attribute from an HTML perspective; one of the assumptions this book makes is that you have some understanding of HTML.

In HTML, you have tags with attributes. Here are a few examples:

```
<table width="100%">
<td width="30%" valign="top" bgcolor="red">
<p align="center">
<li class="parts">
```

In each of these examples, the word just inside the left angle bracket is the tag. It is separated from the attribute(s) that follow by a space. Each of the attributes has a name: `width`, `valign`, `align`, `bgcolor`, `class`. Each attribute also has a specific value, which is after the equal sign and enclosed in quotes.

Just as XML allows you to define your own elements to represent your XML content, you can also define your own attributes. Examples of XML attributes are the following:

```
<child gender="male">
<child gender="female">
```

Understanding Attribute Values

Here's what you know about attributes so far:

- Attributes have a name
- Attributes have a value
- The value must be enclosed in quotes

Table 11-1 shows different types of values your attributes may have.

Table 11-1
Attribute Values

Attribute Value Type	Explanation
CDATA	May contain text (string)
ENTITY	The name of an external entity
ENTITIES	A list of external entities (separate using spaces)
Enumeration/Enumerated	A list of single words that serve as choices
ID: a unique identifier	See Session 12 for usage examples
IDREF	A reference to a unique identifier (see Session 12)
IDREFS	A list of references to unique identifiers (separated by spaces)
NMTOKEN	A single word
NMTOKENS	A list of NMTOKEN separated by spaces
NOTATION	Allows you to declare in a DTD; then access in your XML

Adding Attributes to Elements

Instead of adding elements for all the data in your documents (and then having to type begin and end tags around their content), you can add information by using attributes. These attributes would be added to your existing elements.

Take a look at your DTD as it now stands.

```
<!ELEMENT family (father, mother, offspring?)>
<!ELEMENT father (#PCDATA | surname)*>
<!ELEMENT mother (#PCDATA | maiden | surname)*>
<!ELEMENT offspring (child*)>
<!ELEMENT child (firstname, midname*, surname, ext?, birthplace)>
<!ELEMENT firstname (#PCDATA)>
<!ELEMENT midname (#PCDATA)>
```

```
<!ELEMENT surname (#PCDATA)>
<!ELEMENT ext (#PCDATA)>
<!ELEMENT maiden (#PCDATA)>
<!ELEMENT birthplace (#PCDATA)>
```

Continue using `genealogy10.dtd`, which you created in the preceding session. If you did not complete the prior session, you may want to take a moment and create this document in Microsoft Notepad or another text editor. Or, you can open the file from the session11 folder on your CD-ROM.

Consider the type of XML document this DTD defines. A genealogical document or database may contain hundreds of facts about each person represented. For example, Margaret M. Clark, female, born in Pittsburgh PA, birth date September 14, birth year 2000, birth weight 9 lbs 11 oz, marital status single, current residence Raleigh NC, ethnicity not recorded, father Joseph Q. Clark, mother Mary J., siblings number three, occupation not recorded, and so forth.

 A DTD created for genealogical data, called GedML, is available via a link on this book's CD. GedML contains hundreds of elements containing bits of genealogical information. You can also start with that DTD instead of creating your own, should you desire to create a family tree in XML.

In some instances, you can choose to place these hundreds of facts into elements that already exist, rather than creating new elements for them. These attributes may relate directly to the elements in which they reside.

Earlier in this book, we made reference to the fact that XML can be read by a human and understood fairly easily because of the tags. In your XML document, `family10.xml`, it's easy to see that Mark is the child of Joseph and Mary. Mark has two sisters, Jennifer and Margaret, and a brother, Joseph.

Well, what if one of the children was named Chris or Riley? These names may be boys' or girls' names. To clarify your data, you might decide to put `gender` into the `child` element. But instead of including it as a nested element — as done for `birthplace` — you add it to `child` as an attribute of `child`! With nonspecific names, the `gender` specification (`male | female`) is especially helpful. The adjustment to make to your DTD is shown. This allows you to add an attribute of gender with two options — female and male.

```
Author: So what is this code? JZHope is clarified with addition
above.Kay.<!ELEMENT child (#PCDATA | surname | birthplace)*>
<!ATTLIST child  gender  (female | male )  #IMPLIED >
```

Taking the attribute information apart, you have ATTLIST, which starts the list of attributes for any element. Then comes child, which is the name of the element that has the attributes, followed by the name of an attribute, gender in this case. After that are possible values. The pipe in female | male means the same thing that it meant for element definitions: that either of the values may occur.

At the end of the line is #IMPLIED, which is where you might put the default value for an attribute. If nothing is selected, the XML processor assumes that the attribute is set to the default value. You might use a default if, for example, you wanted female to be the default gender value if none is present in the XML document. That way, if nothing is specified a value comes in automatically.

```
<!ATTLIST child  gender  (female | male ) 'female' >
```

Save your genealogy.dtd DTD. It should now look like the following:

```
<!ELEMENT family (father, mother, offspring?)>
<!ELEMENT father (#PCDATA | surname)*>
<!ELEMENT mother (#PCDATA | maiden | surname)*>
<!ELEMENT offspring (child*)>
<!ELEMENT child (firstname, midname*, surname, ext?, birthplace)>
<!ATTLIST child  gender  (female | male ) 'female' >
<!ELEMENT firstname (#PCDATA)>
<!ELEMENT midname (#PCDATA)>
<!ELEMENT surname (#PCDATA)>
<!ELEMENT ext (#PCDATA)>
<!ELEMENT maiden (#PCDATA)>
<!ELEMENT birthplace (#PCDATA)>
```

Once gender is a part of the child element, you can then use it within your XML document to identify the children as male or female. Save your family10.xml file as familyatt1.xml. View your familyatt1.xml XML document. Make it include the gender information like this:

```
<?xml version="1.0"?>
<!DOCTYPE family SYSTEM "genealogy.dtd">
<family>
<father>Joseph Q. <surname>Clark</surname></father>
<mother>Mary J.
<surname>Clark</surname><maiden>Jones</maiden></mother>
<offspring>
    <child gender="female">
        <firstname>Jennifer</firstname>
```

```
        <surname>Clark</surname>
        <birthplace>Pittsburgh PA</birthplace></child>
    <child gender="male">
        <firstname>Joseph</firstname>
        <midname>Q.</midname>
        <surname>Clark</surname><ext>II</ext>
        <birthplace>Kenmore NY</birthplace></child>
    <child gender="female">
        <firstname>Margaret</firstname>
        <midname>M.</midname>
        <surname>Clark</surname>
        <birthplace>Pittsburgh PA</birthplace></child>
    <child gender="male">
        <firstname>Mark</firstname>
        <midname>J.</midname>
        <surname>Clark</surname>
        <birthplace>Washington PA</birthplace></child>
</offspring>
</family>
```

Session 8 covers the rules an XML document must follow to be well-formed. Part of those rules include rules for attribute syntax, which say that attributes must have a name and a value and the value must be enclosed in quotes.

After making these adjustments, save your `familyatt1.xml` document again and view it in the browser.

To save you time, the DTD and XML document above are available in the session11 folder on your book's CD-ROM.

Utilizing Attributes: What Can They Do?

10 Min. To Go

Using something called a style sheet (discussed later), you can now do neat things like make the document display *females* in *italic* and *males* in **bold.** In Session 16, we discuss XSLT, and you will have an opportunity to modify your documents based on element attributes. An example of a document utilizing attributes is shown in Figure 11-1.

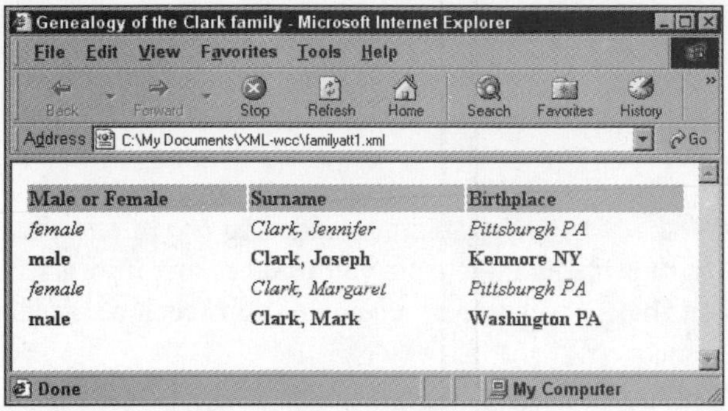

Figure 11-1
Our data with the attribute affecting the display

If the data were to change, the formatting adjusts automatically based on that attribute without you worrying about adjusting the formatting. You just tweak your data — or database. If you create a style sheet, then tell the XML document to reference it, the formatting is now taken care of as you adjust and display your XML document.

Checking Our Attribute Handling

To further test the attribute handling, in familyatt1.xml remove the child Mark's attribute gender. Save the XML document and redisplay in the browser. Notice Mark's data are shown with a female attribute. This is because female is set as the default in your DTD.

Before continuing, set Mark's gender attribute to male within your XML document and save. Redisplay if you like to ensure the gender shows up properly.

Adding More Attributes

Now let's add more attributes to your elements. This allows you to expand the information associated with the child element and with some of its nested elements.

Add one more attribute to child, entering it in front of the right angle bracket after the default value specification, ('female').

```
<!ELEMENT family (father, mother, offspring?)>
<!ELEMENT child (firstname, midname*, surname, ext?, birthplace)>
<!ATTLIST child  gender      (female | male )  'female'
                 birthyear   CDATA             #IMPLIED >
```

Now add an attribute for birthplace, which contains text (PCDATA), to specifically name the country.

```
<!ELEMENT birthplace (#PCDATA)>
<!ATTLIST birthplace  country CDATA              #IMPLIED >
```

These extra attributes — the `birthyear` attribute added to `child` and the `country` attribute added to `birthplace` — enable you to later sort information, or select information based on these attributes or a combination (such as a specific `gender` within a `birthyear`).

Deciding When to Use Attributes Instead of Creating New Elements

Why use an element when an attribute seems easier to use? With attributes, there are no messy end tags to remember and the data are similar. Each has its place and it's up to the document designer to decide which fits best. There are no hard and fast rules because there are so many possibilities with XML. XML is extensible, so any variety of attributes and elements may be defined.

If you are creating your DTD, you get to choose what will be elements and what will be attributes of those elements. Think about how your information will be displayed and how it will be sorted. Information within your elements is metadata — information about your document. Information within your attributes is meta-information — information about the data in your document.

When in doubt, try creating your document with an item as an attribute of an existing element. If you cannot access that information as you like, or you want to have attributes attached to that information, you may have to move it out into an element of its own.

Done!

REVIEW

- A DTD can define elements and element attributes.
- Attributes provide information about an element.
- An element may have no attributes, or it may have many.
- An attribute can be placed in an empty element, which serves as an information holder.
- Some information might fit as either an element or an attribute, and it's up to the DTD designer to determine the best fit.

QUIZ YOURSELF

1. How many attributes can an element have? (See "Understanding Attributes.")

2. When you add an attribute to a tag in an XML document, do you have to make any adjustments to the DTD? (See "Adding Attributes to Elements.")

3. How can you make an attribute value come in automatically? (See "Adding Attributes to Elements.")

4. Are there any hard and fast rules for selecting an attribute versus a new element? (See "Deciding When to Use Attributes Instead of Creating New Elements.")

5. True or False. You must use attributes in your XML documents. (See "Understanding Attributes.")

Exploring XML DTDs: Creating Cross-References and Links

Session Checklist

✔ Learning about XML document cross-references

✔ Declaring ID attributes for unique element identifiers in your DTD

✔ Using ID and IDREF attributes to create cross-references in XML documents

**30 Min.
To Go**

A typical cross-reference in a book is text that refers you to other text or to an object. In an online HTML document, these references are hypertext links to anchors within the same or other HTML documents. With XML, you use a new technique for linking that involves identification numbers (IDs).

Cross-Reference Links Using ID and IDREF

An ID is a special type of attribute. IDs provide a target that can be used to link to an element. Within a document, the XML processor checks ID attributes for uniqueness. If the processor discovers that two ID attributes have the same value, the processor reports an error and stops.

In your sample family tree, for example, you may wish to provide IDs for mothers and fathers so that children can be cross-referenced with their parents. This way, the parents may be kept in the database as individuals alongside the children. In the long term, this format would allow entire family trees to be maintained or built around the selection of a specific set of offspring.

How IDREF links work

IDREF links work by linking to a unique element identifier: an attribute. If you're using a software tool to create your XML, the unique identifiers may be created for you. When FrameMaker+SGML 6.0 creates the cross-reference in Figure 12-1, for example, the program automatically assigns the same identifier to the paragraph that is being referenced to and the location where the cross-reference text appears.

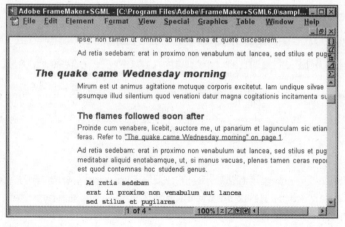

Figure 12-1
A structured document with a cross-reference to a nearby item

Notice in Figure 12-2 the unique ID given to the item being referenced. The software, FrameMaker+SGML, provides the BABJEICC identifier and tracks it. The IDREF in the cross-reference matches the ID, which enables the program to produce the initial cross-reference text and also ensure the cross-reference updates if the text (at the ID) changes.

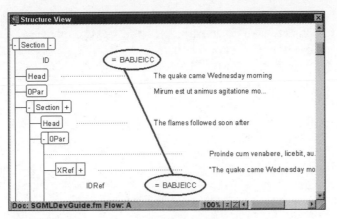

Figure 12-2
A unique identifier automatically provided to a cross-referenced item by FrameMaker+SGML.

If you're coding by hand, you need to track your IDs and ensure that your IDREFs are pointing precisely to that identifier.

Defining ID attributes in your DTD

**20 Min.
To Go**

You can name the ID attribute, or the unique identifier you apply to some element, whatever you like. Names may contain spaces, numbers, or letters. The only limitation is that names must not start with a space.

> **Your element names (tags) and attributes cannot contain spaces. The ID can contain spaces. To avoid confusion, you should avoid using spaces in your ID names.**

An ID is just an attribute, so you need to decide which elements should have this attribute. You can then add this attribute to each ATTLIST within the DTD. Suppose that you want to assign unique ID numbers to each person in your family tree XML documents. To do so, you need to add an id attribute to mother, father, and child elements within your DTD, as shown in the following code. To follow along, modify your genealogy.dtd.

```
<!ELEMENT family (father , mother , offspring?)>
<!ELEMENT father (#PCDATA | surname)*>
<!ATTLIST father  id ID  #IMPLIED >
<!ELEMENT mother (#PCDATA | maiden | surname)*>
<!ATTLIST mother  id ID  #IMPLIED >
```

```
<!ELEMENT offspring (child*)>
<!ELEMENT child (firstname, midname*, surname, ext?, birthplace)>
<!ATTLIST child  gender    (female | male )  'female'
                 birthyear CDATA  #IMPLIED
                 id        ID     #IMPLIED >
<!ELEMENT firstname (#PCDATA)>
<!ELEMENT midname (#PCDATA)>
<!ELEMENT surname (#PCDATA)>
<!ELEMENT ext (#PCDATA)>
<!ELEMENT maiden (#PCDATA)>
<!ELEMENT birthplace (#PCDATA)>
<!ATTLIST birthplace  country CDATA  #IMPLIED >
```

Your ID type attribute in this example is id, **but the attribute name could be anything you like. You could just as easily have called it** PersonID **or** ident.

Now you have an attribute in your XML document that you can use. Note that some tools, like Adobe FrameMaker+SGML, assign these attributes as you go (as discussed in the preceding section).

Now open your familyatt1.xml document and save it as familyatt2.xml. Add the following attribute values to your father and mother start tags:

```
<father id="CL02">
<mother id="J001">
```

Now add the following identifiers to the children in order. Be sure to place these in the child start tags:

```
<child gender="female" id="CL03">
<child gender="male" id="CL04">
<child gender="female" id="CL05">
<child gender="male" id="CL06">
```

Viewed in the browser, you see the id numbers, as shown in Figure 12-3.

Right-click your mouse and choose Validate XML to verify that your document is valid (following your DTD's structure rules). Now modify your familyatt2.xml document so that father reads as the following:

```
<father ident="CL02">Joseph Q. <surname>Clark</surname></father>
```

```
C:\My Documents\XML-wcc\familyatt2.xml - Microsoft Internet Explorer

File   Edit   View   Favorites   Tools   Help

Back   Forward   Stop   Refresh   Home   Search   Favorites   History

Address  C:\My Documents\XML-wcc\familyatt2.xml                    Go

<?xml version="1.0" ?>
<!DOCTYPE family (View Source for full doctype...)>
- <family>
  - <father id="CL02">
      Joseph Q.
      <surname>Clark</surname>
    </father>
  - <mother id="JO01">
      Mary J.
      <surname>Clark</surname>
      <maiden>Jones</maiden>
    </mother>
  - <offspring>
    - <child gender="female" id="CL03">
        <firstname>Jennifer</firstname>
        <surname>Clark</surname>
        <birthplace>Pittsburgh PA</birthplace>
      </child>

                                                 My Computer
```

Figure 12-3
Your document, complete with id attributes, viewed in the browser

Save your document and view it in the browser. Be sure to reload the page so that the browser can reread the document. You still see the attribute (now with a new name) and the file displays properly. If you run the Validate XML command again, however, you get an error, as shown in Figure 12-4.

```
Microsoft Internet Explorer                            X

  ⚠    Parse Error at line 4 in file:///C:/My
        Documents/XML-wcc/genealogyatt.dtd
        Source:   <father ident="CL02">Joseph Q.
        <surname>Clark</surname></father>

        The attribute 'ident' on this element is not defined in the
        DTD/Schema.

                       OK
```

Figure 12-4
Validation error caused by incorrectly named ID attribute

To correct the error, change your father tag so that the attribute is id again, instead of the error-producing ident attribute name not supported by your DTD.

You will also get an error (see Figure 12-5) if you begin your unique identifier with an integer (number) or if you make two of the child tags use the same unique identifier (making it non-unique). Change both Margaret and Mark to CL05; then save and reload in the browser.

Figure 12-5
Validation error caused by a duplicated ID

Creating an IDREF link

**10 Min.
To Go**

After you add ID attributes to some of your elements, you can create IDREF links to reference (in other words, cross-reference) those elements. If you create an ID for a table element, for example, you can then put IDREF items within other elements that reference the table element.

Using your example, you have ID attributes for your father, mother, and child items within your familyatt2.xml XML document. You need to make IDREF attributes available in your DTD to refer to these IDs. To your attribute list or ATTLIST for an element, you add an attribute called mother and another called father. For each of these, you set the type as IDREF. This allows you to reference the parents' identification numbers in the XML. If no element contains the ID attribute value of the IDREF (i.e., if the IDREF does not point to another element), the XML parser will report an error. This guarantees that your IDREF specifies a legal link.

 Once the attribute is set up, multiple children — in our genealogical document — may point to their mothers and fathers. It is all right to have multiple IDREF to an ID.

```
<!ATTLIST child  gender    (female | male )  'female'
                 birthyear CDATA #IMPLIED
                 id        ID    #IMPLIED
                 mother    IDREF #IMPLIED
                 father    IDREF #IMPLIED >
```

You can then reference from the children to their parents, which you can later use to create complex family tree outputs. For now, you're just referencing to mother, as shown in the following code:

```
<?xml version="1.0"?>
<!DOCTYPE family SYSTEM "genealogy.dtd">
<family>
<father id="CL02">Joseph Q. <surname>Clark</surname></father>
<mother id="J001">Mary J.
<surname>Clark</surname><maiden>Jones</maiden></mother>
<offspring>
    <child gender="female" id="CL03" mother="J001">
        <firstname>Jennifer</firstname>
        <surname>Clark</surname>
        <birthplace>Pittsburgh PA</birthplace></child>
    <child gender="male" id="CL04" mother="J001">
        <firstname>Joseph</firstname>
        <midname>Q.</midname>
        <surname>Clark</surname><ext>II</ext>
        <birthplace>Kenmore NY</birthplace></child>
    <child gender="female" id="CL05" mother="J001">
        <firstname>Margaret</firstname>
        <midname>M.</midname>
        <surname>Clark</surname>
        <birthplace>Pittsburgh PA</birthplace></child>
    <child gender="male" id="CL06" mother="J001">
        <firstname>Mark</firstname>
        <midname>J.</midname>
        <surname>Clark</surname>
        <birthplace>Washington PA</birthplace></child>
</offspring>
</family>
```

Depending on how your XML document is being authored, you may be able to assign the values in advance, such as in a database of individuals.

Done!

REVIEW

- You can add ID and IDREF attributes to link between document elements.
- No two items within an XML document can have the same ID.
- Using software tools designed to handle structure can assist you in assigning and referencing your identifiers.
- Validating a document can help you troubleshoot your IDs (though in your examples, it's the user's responsibility to assign the correct parents).

QUIZ YOURSELF

1. If your end result must be a valid document, can you add ID attributes to an XML document without adding that attribute to a DTD? (See "Cross-Reference Links Using ID and IDREF.")

2. How many ID attributes of the same name can a begin tag contain? (See "Defining ID attributes in your DTD.")

3. True or False: You may use HTML links without defining them in your DTD (See "Cross-Reference Links Using ID and IDREF.")

4. True or False: You may have multiple references to an ID (See "Creating an IDREF link.")

5. True or False: The value of an IDREF attribute must correspond to the value of an ID attribute elsewhere in the XML document. (See "Creating an IDREF link.")

Exploring XML DTDs: External Files

Session Checklist

✔ Learning about options for combining multiple XML documents

✔ Including external entities in your DTD

✔ Exploring syntax for external entities in your XML documents

**30 Min.
To Go**

I n Session 7, we discussed using entities for special characters and for text snippets. In this session, we discuss external entities and the potential for reusing large blocks of XML. Because external entities have potential for content reusability, we look at these entities in depth in this session.

Using External Entities to Create Reusable XML Content

Now that you have created XML documents, stop for a moment and think about your XML. What are your options for working with your documents? How will you manage your information? Depending on your plans for XML, you may want to work with your XML as a series of small files. You can then work with these small files as separate entities.

Here are just a few advantages of authoring — or mechanically producing — small XML files:

- You can simultaneously edit several parts of a whole document. If a larger document is broken into numerous small XML documents, one person can work with one file, while another person works with a different file in the group. This can speed up the editing process. Conversely, if you had all the XML in one file, only one person at a time could edit it.

- You can reuse parts of a document more easily. If, for example, you have a corporate overview blurb that appears in all your documents, you can create it as a separate file and reference it in many other XML documents. Otherwise, each document must include its own copy of the corporate overview blurb.

- If part of a document that you're going to reuse is located in one place, then you can reference it, which would decrease editing time. You can edit that part, thereby updating all the files to which it's referenced. Conversely, if the document part were included in each file, you would have to search for that content within every file and update each by hand.

- Managing your XML in small chunks facilitates a database-like set up. With add-on software or scripting, you may be able to revision track and perform other actions on these small components.

- Along with same lines as the previous item, you may be able to produce an on-demand XML assembly system with the small components. This may promote implementation of e-commerce or catalog-type systems (depending on your needs).

XML provides a lot of potential — in creation, in management, and in use. For now, let's take a look at the potential for creating many separate documents that work together. You can decide later if this is the best approach for you.

Creating the XML documents

20 Min. To Go

You're now going to create several small XML documents of similar, simple structure. You will make several, and then deal with the DTD. Please be sure to save all documents into the same directory (preferably the XML-wcc directory created early in this book).

You may save yourself some typing time by pulling the examples off the CD-ROM. You'll find them in folder session13.

Create a small XML document containing the XML as shown in the following code. When you finish typing, save it as intro.ent.

```
<module>
<heading>Introduction</heading>
<para>This document is transmitted as our response to your request
for proposal. We believe that we at XYZ Corporation can perform
all tasks outlined in the proposal project and with due
speed.</para>
<para>This document is subject to revision and final approval and
is for bidding purposes only. (etc., etc.) </para>
</module>
```

After you have your intro.ent, create the following document, and save it as scope.ent:

```
<module>
<heading>Scope of Work</heading>
<para>The project outline includes the following phases:
evaluation, recommendation, implementation, and follow-up
support.</para>
<para>All phases are included in this scope (etc., etc.)</para>
</module>
```

Then create the following document and save it as summary.ent:

```
<module>
<heading>Summary</heading>
<para>(etc., etc.) We believe that we at XYZ Corporation can
perform all tasks outlined in the proposal project and with due
speed. We also believe we can come in within the budget range
specified.</para>
<para>Please contact us at (919)555-5555 to discuss this project
and award timeframe. </para>
</module>
```

You now have three separate XML documents. The next step is to create an XML document that references these three smaller documents, creating a composite document.

 Please notice that these three small XML documents do not need to have an XML declaration (`<?xml version="1.0"?>`). Also notice that you named them with the file extension `ent` instead of `xml`. This is because you're going to use them as external entities. The file extension you use is not important; you could give these documents any extension you want.

Type the following and save it as a separate file called `proposal.xml`.

```
<?xml version="1.0"?>
<proposal>
<title>XYZ Corporation Technical Project Proposal</title>
</proposal>
```

Adding entities to the DTD

Now you're going to create your DTD. You need to create a DTD with elements for the composite document and for the small documents.

```
<!ELEMENT proposal (title? , module*)>
<!ELEMENT title (#PCDATA)>
<!ELEMENT module (heading , para+)>
<!ELEMENT heading (#PCDATA)>
<!ELEMENT para (#PCDATA)>
```

 These element names were chosen for simplicity's sake. We are *not* advocating meaningless names like `heading` for XML data. Part of XML's strength is the ability to provide strong, meaningful names for your XML elements.

Save your DTD as `proposal_guide.dtd` and keep it open. You now have your DTD and a batch of XML documents ready for use. In the next section, you put them all together.

Combining XML Documents

In your DTD, you need to create an entity reference for each small XML document so that you can refer to them in your XML document, `proposal.xml`. The proper form for these external general entities is as shown, with the `<!ENTITY` beginning, a name for use in your XML document (you pick the name), `SYSTEM` designating it as local, and finally the filename (using the files named in this section: intro.ent, scope.ent, and summary.ent).

```
<!ENTITY intro SYSTEM "intro.ent">
<!ENTITY scope SYSTEM "scope.ent">
<!ENTITY summary SYSTEM "summary.ent">
```

Save your `proposal_guide.dtd` again and go to your `proposal.xml` document.

You need to include the DOCTYPE in your proposal. Notice the special instruction added to the XML declaration. You must add this specification so that the parser recognizes that the main document does not stand alone but requires other XML documents in order to be valid.

```
<?xml version="1.0" standalone="no" ?>
<!DOCTYPE proposal SYSTEM "proposal_guide.dtd">
<proposal>
<title>XYZ Corporation Technical Project Proposal</title>
</proposal>
```

Now you can pull all the units together. Reference the entities by using the entity syntax (`&somename;`).

In `proposal.xml`, add the following external entity references:

```
&intro;
&scope;
&summary;
```

Place these in your XML document just in front of the `proposal` end tag.

```
<?xml version="1.0" standalone="no"? >
<!DOCTYPE proposal SYSTEM "proposal_guide.dtd">
<proposal>
<title>XYZ Corporation Technical Project Proposal</title>
&intro;
&scope;
&summary;
</proposal>
```

Viewing Your Composite Document

After you make the changes to your `proposal.xml` document, you're ready to view it. You can view your document in any browser or XML editor that supports external entities.

When you open `proposal.xml` in Internet Explorer Version 5, you should see the result shown in Figure 13-1.

A bug in certain configurations of Internet Explorer render entities incorrectly. It may list them at the top of the document or show them in reverse order. If your results do not match those in Figure 13-1, your configuration has this bug.

There does not seem to be a complete fix for this bug. In testing, some installations of Internet Explorer 5 and higher displayed these entities properly; most displayed in the wrong order. As of this writing, Internet Explorer 6.0 is still in beta and not available for complete testing.

Consistency in display can be achieved by putting the files on a Web server, and opening them via their "http..." address. If you do not have proper access to a Web server, you could try viewing the files in an XML parser or another browser, such as Amaya (`http://www.w3c.org`).

Feel free to experiment with the addition of other files to ensure that you understand what's going on. There's no limit to the number of external entities you can reference. For now, remove one of the entities from your `proposal.xml` to see what happens. Remove the `&summary;` line from the document so that the resulting file looks like this:

```
<?xml version="1.0" standalone="no"? >
<!DOCTYPE proposal SYSTEM "proposal_guide.dtd">
<proposal>
<title>XYZ Corporation Technical Project Proposal</title>
&intro;
&scope;
</proposal>
```

In Figure 13-2, the display for the `summary.ent` document is gone.

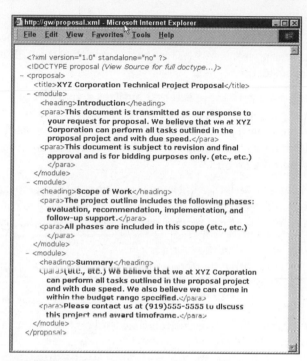

Figure 13-1
The content of all files appears in proposal.xml.

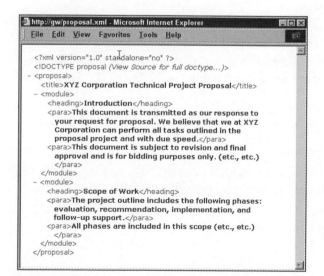

Figure 13-2
The modified proposal.xml with two entities instead of three

The summary.ent document still exists, the information is still in the DTD describing it, but it's not in use in the document. Keep this in mind as you move forward with XML. You can design many entities, set them up within the DTD, but not use them in all your documents.

Experiment more with these external entities more, perhaps adding another section after scope for a timeline. Make sure that you create your entity as an XML file (no declaration needed); then add the appropriate data to the DTD so that you can reference it within the proposal.

After you finish experimenting with these files, you can close all the proposal-related XML documents and proposal_guide.dtd. In the next session, you will get into other types of entities and special references, and revert to your family tree examples.

Done!

REVIEW

- XML documents may contain all the information that you want, or you can split the content among multiple XML documents.

- If you author XML documents specifically for use within other XML documents, you don't need to include the XML declaration.

- To let the parser know other files are needed, you add standalone="no" to your XML declaration.

- You must declare your external entities within your DTD before using them.

- To reference an external entity in your XML document, you must use the form &somename; where name is defined in the DTD's ENTITY declaration.

QUIZ YOURSELF

1. True or False: You can combine XML documents to form a larger XML document. (See "Using External Entities to Create Reusable XML Content.")

2. Is it possible to use an external entity without identifying it in a DTD? (See "Combining XML Documents.")

3. What is the maximum number of external entities you may include in a combined document, such as your `proposal.xml`? (See "Viewing Your Composite Document.")

4. What happens if you create entities and reference them in the DTD, but do not use them in your compilation document? (See "Viewing Your Composite Document.")

5. Is it possible to create new entities in the future, or only at the time the others are created? (See "Viewing Your Composite Document.")

Exploring XML DTDs: Special Characters

Session Checklist

✔ Reviewing special characters and parser errors

✔ Defining general entities for frequently-used text strings

✔ Using general entities to insert content from external files

✔ Using CDATA sections to hide text from the parser

I n this session, we take a look at including special characters in our XML documents, creating entities for reusable text, and code for passing content through a parser. Samples are included for each section within this session.

**30 Min.
To Go**

Reviewing Special Character Entities

Certain characters have special meaning in XML documents. If the parser encounters these characters in the content of your XML documents, the document will not parse and the XML processor will display an error message. XML provides a special construct called an entity reference that you can use to include these characters in your XML documents without confusing the XML parser.

In Session 7, we discussed entity references for special characters. We looked at several entities that are standard for XML documents:

- Left angle bracket or less than: <
- Right angle bracket or greater than: >
- Apostrophe: '
- Double quote: "
- Ampersand: &

We also noted in Session 7 that it is possible to add entity references by defining them in your DTD. Representing your registration symbol is an important step in XML. With HTML, the ® is built-in and ready to use; with XML, you must define it first.

In your DTD, you first add the entity declaration to make the character available. If you skip this step and do not declare the entity in your DTD, your parser will display an error message when you attempt to view your XML document.

If you are viewing your XML document in Internet Explorer, because it is designed to handle HTML special characters, it may display the registration symbol, copyright symbol, and other HTML-defined symbols. This is generally not the case with XML parsers.

After you make the character entity available, and your XML document properly references the DTD, you can then use this entity freely in your XML document.

Defining and Using General Entities

General entities are another type of entity that you can represent in your DTD — or in a DTD declaration within your XML document. General entities allow you to define abbreviations, strings of repeating text (such as copyright notices), and boilerplate text (chunks or entire XML documents that you reuse).

Using general entities to represent text strings

You can represent a text string by using a general entity. Think about your information that you plan to put online. Do you have any text, such as a copyright notice, that appears in many documents? Do you have any smaller strings — perhaps a product name or department name — that appear throughout your information? If so, you can set them in your DTD as general entities.

Let's use your family tree example. You have identified `birthplace` as an available tag (it is an element within your DTD). In your example, several Clark children were born in Pittsburgh, Pennsylvania. To save yourself some typing time, you can assign a much smaller abbreviation for this city and state. Use the airport code of `PIT`.

In your favorite text editor, open your `genealogy.dtd` file and save it as `genealogy14.dtd`. Then open your `familyatt2.xml` document used in the last few sessions and save it as `family14.xml`. Be sure to change your DOCTYPE reference to your new DTD name.

To make your general entity text string available, you must add an entity declaration in your DTD as shown in the following code:

```
<!ENTITY PIT "Pittsburgh PA">
```

Save your DTD and open your `family14.xml` XML document. View it in a browser for a moment to see how the cities now appear. After you view it, change the `birthplace` content for every child born in your key city (Pittsburgh PA) to the entity, `&PIT;`. (See Listing 14-1.) In this document, it affects the content for both Margaret and Jennifer. Don't forget the ampersand and semicolon.

Listing 14-1
Replacing birthplace content with an entity

```
<?xml version="1.0"?>
<!DOCTYPE family SYSTEM "genealogy14.dtd">
<family>
<father id="CL02">Joseph Q. <surname>Clark</surname></father>
<mother id="JO01">Mary J.
<surname>Clark</surname><maiden>Jones</maiden></mother>
<offspring>
    <child gender="female" id="CL03" mother="JO01">
        <firstname>Jennifer</firstname>
        <surname>Clark</surname>
        <birthplace>&PIT;</birthplace></child>
    <child gender="male" id="CL04" mother="JO01">
        <firstname>Joseph</firstname>
        <midname>Q.</midname>
        <surname>Clark</surname><ext>II</ext>
        <birthplace>Kenmore NY</birthplace></child>
```

Continued

Listing 14-1   *Continued*

```
<child gender="female" id="CL05" mother="J001">
    <firstname>Margaret</firstname>
    <midname>M.</midname>
    <surname>Clark</surname>
    <birthplace>&PIT;</birthplace></child>
<child gender="male" id="CL06" mother="J001">
    <firstname>Mark</firstname>
    <midname>J.</midname>
    <surname>Clark</surname>
    <birthplace>Washington PA</birthplace></child>
</offspring>
</family>
```

**20 Min.
To Go**

Don't forget that XML is case sensitive, and &PIT; is not the same as &pit; or &Pit;. If you really want to have the choice of PIT and Pit, you could define two entities with those case sensitive names. You may only have one entity with a specified name within your DTD. If you have more than one, you will not get an error in your parser, but the parser will only use the first value.

> **Note**
>
> **While this may seem more work than it's worth now, keep in mind all the potential additions to your family and other family XML documents, and the amount of time you'll save typing. You're basically turning 13 keystrokes for Pittsburgh PA into 5 keystrokes for** &PIT;.

Save your family14.xml document and view it in the browser (see Figure 14-1). Notice that your text, Pittsburgh PA, still shows up in your XML. This is because your XML document is parsed and the entity reference replaced with your text string.

Not only can you have this text string "typed" for you over and over, you can also modify it in one spot to fix all occurrences of that text! To check this out, temporarily modify the DTD entity reference as shown in the following code:

```
<!ENTITY PIT "Pittsburgh, Pennsylvania USA">
```

View your family14.xml document in the browser and notice that all references to your city show the modified Pittsburgh, Pennsylvania USA text instead of the former Pittsburgh PA text. Be sure to change your DTD back to Pittsburgh PA before continuing.

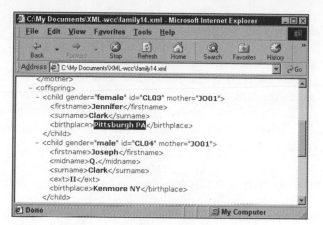

Figure 14-1
Our text string showing in the browser

Using general entities to draw an external file

You can pull an entire XML document in the same way that you create a general entity to pull a text string. Suppose that you have a copyright notice that must appear in every document. For simplicity, you'll place one within your family tree example, though it certainly can translate to other types of XML documents.

Open your `genealogy14.dtd` document, if not already open. Add an entity referencing a file with your copyright content. You will make that XML document in a moment.

```
<!ENTITY cp SYSTEM "copyright.xml">
```

You can name this entity anything that you want. Be sure to use logical names so that you and others working with these documents can easily understand and remember your entities.

Now create a document called `copyright.xml` and, for simplicity's sake, save it in the same directory as your DTD and XML document. Its content should appear like the following:

```
<annotation>This book is copyright 2001 Hungry Minds. All rights reserved.</annotation>
```

You want this general entity to be well-formed so that it does not cause any errors; be careful using special characters.

Defining and Using CDATA Content

You may want to display information without substituting special characters. Perhaps you have text that contains many characters that need replacing. In these instances, you use XML character data, or CDATA sections, to get the browser or parser to pass over these characters — to essentially skip entire portions of your XML documents. This was introduced briefly in Session 7. In this session, we walk through examples and create a CDATA section in an XML document.

Keeping the parser out of entire sections

**10 Min.
To Go**

One example of information that you may want the parser to skip is a mathematical equation. You don't want to replace all the greater thans, less thans, and other symbols with special character entities. It's time consuming and leaves too much room for error. Therefore, you place the equation inside a CDATA section so that the parser sends it through as is and doesn't choke on the special symbols.

You can enter any information you like within a CDATA section. The XML processor sees the special symbols denoting the content as CDATA and sends that content through without trying to parse it.

Another example is scripts, which have to contain specific characters for the script to run properly. Scripts may be included in CDATA sections so that the parser passes them through as-is.

CDATA for an annotation

In this section, we place a CDATA section in our family tree XML document. At the start, the section begins with <![CDATA[and ends with]]>. All the information between the beginning and the end are sent directly to the application or browser without being changed or causing errors.

You will use an annotation tag for this and future examples, so you may want to take a moment and make this an official element within your family14.dtd document.

```
<!ELEMENT annotation (#PCDATA)>
```

Modify your family element to include one or more annotation elements as an option.

```
<!ELEMENT family (father , mother , offspring?, annotation*)>
```

Add the following within your `family14.xml` document between the `offspring` and `family` end tags:

```
<annotation>
<![CDATA[If the number of children is greater than (>) four but
less than (<) ten, this family has been included in the "Honorable
Mention" section of this book but not in the "Record Setters"
section.]]>
</annotation>
```

This example enables you to pass through the special characters without retyping them as entity references. The result is shown in Figure 14-2.

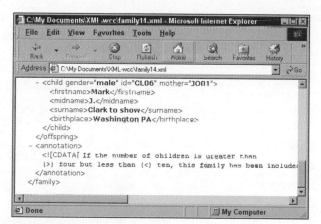

Figure 14-2
Using CDATA, the angle brackets display properly.

CDATA for a mathematical equation

Let's move away from your family tree example and look at a new XML document. This particular document is a snippet from a technical report and contains mathematical data. You use a simple mathematical statement to demonstrate the usefulness of a CDATA section.

Here's a simple mathematical equation:

```
Z = <X - 4>2
```

Now place this equation within a simple XML document.

```
<?xml version="1.0"?>
<report>
<heading>Introduction</heading>
<para>Our analysis produced the answer to the Z = <X - 4>^2
equation.</para>
</report>
```

This equation won't display in the browser because of the angle brackets included in the equation. Type the listing above in your text editor and save it as Treport.xml. Displayed in the browser, you see the error shown in Figure 14-3.

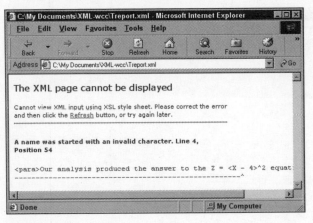

Figure 14-3
Equation angle brackets cause an error in your browser.

Now modify your document to enclose the equation in a CDATA section.

```
<?xml version="1.0"?>
<report>
<heading>Introduction</heading>
<para>Our analysis produced the answer to
the <![CDATA[ Z = <X - 4>^2 ]]>equation.</para>
</report>
```

Your XML document parses without any errors, as shown in Figure 14-4.

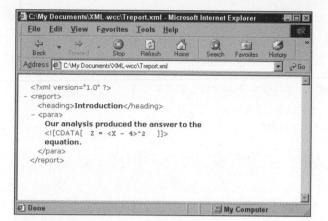

Figure 14-4
Your equation brackets within a CDATA section

Any time you have information in your XML document that contains special characters or scripts, you may choose to enclose them in a CDATA section.

Done!

REVIEW

- Special characters cannot just be typed within your text; some characters must be represented by entities.

- Symbols and other special characters must be made available via DTD entity declarations before being used in XML documents.

- CDATA sections may help you to avoid parser errors by allowing their content to pass to the browser or application without parsing.

QUIZ YOURSELF

1. What are the five entity references predefined in XML? (See "Reviewing Special Character Entities.")

2. How must new entity references be added? (See "Defining and Using General Entities.")

3. What would you place in your XML document to take advantage of the following entity:

```
<!ENTITY RDU  "Research Triangle Park, North Carolina USA">
```

(See "Using general entities to represent text strings.")

4. What happens if you add a character entity in your XML document but do not place it in the corresponding DTD? (See "Reviewing Special Character Entities.")

5. What is the purpose of the CDATA section? (See "Keeping the parser out of entire sections.")

Exploring XML DTDs: Graphics

Session Checklist

You have now created several XML documents and worked with DTDs. Before moving forward into adjusting the look and feel of your text, you're going to find out about another important aspect of working with DTDs: adding graphics to your XML document.

Including Graphics and Other Binary Files in Your XML Document

XML is a character-based format, but much of your data is binary. You may, for example, want to include graphics, sound, video, or multimedia files in your documents. XML would be severely limited if you couldn't include these file types in your XML documents. This session discusses how to do so.

You may have heard the term *external data type*. This means that you are referencing a non-XML file in your XML document. If you refer to a GIF in your XML document, for example, you're referencing an external data type.

In the next section, we will first review the way graphics are referenced within HTML. Then, we take a look at how graphics may be referenced within XML documents.

The HTML approach

You can add graphic images to an HTML document by using the HTML tag, img. A common format uses src="graphicname.xxx", where the src attribute refers to the source of the image and the attribute value (in quotes) is the graphic's location and name. The file extension, represented here as xxx, is usually GIF or JPG. You can, therefore, refer to a basic graphic in HTML in one of the following ways:

```
<img src="baby.jpg">
<img src="images/baby.jpg">
<img src="images/baby.jpg width="100">
```

In the third example, we threw in the width attribute to show that you can use additional attributes. If you've worked with HTML, then you're most likely familiar with width, as well as height, border, align, and alt.

HTML enables you to include different graphic types. But most browsers only support display of GIF and JPEG, with some added support for other formats.

The XML approach

The code for placing graphics in XML is more complex than for HTML. With XML, you modify your DTD to accept certain types of graphics, create applicable elements, and reference the images within your XML documents.

These steps are necessary because XML documents are encoded in ASCII or Unicode. You cannot, therefore, include binary formats directly in your XML document. As a result, XML provides a procedure for including binary formats. You may include these by adding the following to your DTD.

- In your DTD, you declare an entity for your binary file by typing **NDATA** and providing an NDATA type (such as GIF).

- Also in the DTD, you use a NOTATION declaration to define the NDATA type (to identify what a GIF is) and provide a system pathname for resolving entity references of that type (to identify the pathname for finding GIF files).

Keep in mind that no browsers currently support the display of graphics in XML documents. To see graphics now, you need to use XSLT (discussed in Session 21) to convert documents to HTML. Later, you will have the option of using XLink (discussed in Session 30) to show your graphics.

Adding a graphic element to a DTD

To work with graphics, you need to create an element that you can use in your XML documents. With HTML, the browser is designed to understand img. With XML, the browser doesn't understand your tag, so you can call it whatever you want. In this example, you're going to use img just to keep it familiar; you could just as easily use image, graphic, pic, picture, or photograph — just about anything.

To define your img element within the DTD, start by typing **<!ELEMENT**; then add a name such as img for your element (the tag you will use in your XML documents), followed by EMPTY> (see the following code):

```
<!ELEMENT img EMPTY>
```

Your element also needs attributes. You must be able to use source (again, a name you select) to include a filename or other reference within your img tag.

```
<!ATTLIST img source ENTITY #REQUIRED>
```

You may recall from the discussion of attributes that #REQUIRED means that a value must be given. This means that any time you use the img tag, you are required to provide a source attribute that specifies a graphic location.

Providing the NOTATION

Placing the entity references within your DTD only gets you halfway. Now you need to set up the notations for GIF, JPG, and any other types used. Once both pieces are created — the entity references and the notations — you may reference the entity within your XML documents

Because the files (entities) are not parsed, the notation allows you to specify the tool to use. In your DTD, you place a notation referring to the file type (such as GIF), a URL (such as http://www.somebody.com/GIF/), or a Windows application reference (such as image/gif).

You must also include the entity syntax in your DTD. After the initial <!ENTITY, you provide a name such as logo for the entity. Then type **SYSTEM**, followed by the location. After the location is the NDATA notation and the name designated within the notation. The following are some examples of graphic ENTITY definitions within a DTD:

```
<!ENTITY logo SYSTEM "http://www.logoworks.com/hmi.gif" NDATA GIF>
<!ENTITY baby SYSTEM "images/baby.jpg" NDATA JPG>
```

The notation is typed in the DTD below the ENTITY that uses its type. Notations list the location of information for a specific file type. "image/gif", for example, may be the location for GIF management information on your local system. Here are some sample notations:

```
<!NOTATION GIF SYSTEM "image/gif">
<!NOTATION jpg SYSTEM "image/jpeg">
<!NOTATION pdf SYSTEM "application/pdf">
```

For your two example ENTITYs, the applicable NOTATIONs may look like the following:

```
<!ENTITY logo SYSTEM "http://www.logoworks.com/hmi.gif" NDATA GIF>
<!NOTATION GIF SYSTEM "image/gif">
<!ENTITY baby SYSTEM "images/baby.jpg" NDATA JPG>
<!NOTATION JPG SYSTEM "image/jpeg">
```

After you set the NOTATIONs within the DTD, you can use them within your XML documents.

SYSTEM, **which has come up several times in this book, means the location of the entity, file, or other resource on the local file system.**

Including a graphic in your XML document

After you prepare the element and notation in the DTD, you can add the appropriate code within any XML document. The following are several independent examples:

**20 Min.
To Go**

```
<img source="baby.jpg"/>
<img source="graphics/baby.jpg"/>
```

XML requires /> at the end of any empty tag. This is unlike your HTML img tag. Do not forget the slash, or your document will not be well-formed and your browser will report an error that your document is missing an end tag.

Creating a simple example

The next step is to create a small XML document that includes a graphic. You're going to use your family tree example. Listing 15-1 is the DTD for family tree. To follow along, open your `genealogy14.dtd` document and save it as `genealogy15.dtd`, or retype and save it as `genealogy15.dtd`.

If you do not wish to type this DTD, you may open `genealogy.dtd` **from your session15 folder on your CD. To follow the examples below, save it as** `genealogy15.dtd`.

Listing 15-1
Our Genealogy DTD

```
<!ELEMENT family (father, mother, offspring?, annotation*)>
<!ELEMENT father (#PCDATA | surname)*>
<!ATTLIST father  id ID  #IMPLIED >
<!ELEMENT mother (#PCDATA | maiden | surname)*>
<!ATTLIST mother  id ID  #IMPLIED >
<!ELEMENT offspring (child*)>
<!ELEMENT child (firstname, midname*, surname, ext?, birthplace)>
<!ATTLIST child  gender    (female | male )  'female'
                 birthyear  CDATA  #IMPLIED
                 id         ID     #IMPLIED
                 mother     IDREF  #IMPLIED
                 father     IDREF  #IMPLIED >
<!ELEMENT firstname (#PCDATA)>
<!ELEMENT midname (#PCDATA)>
<!ELEMENT surname (#PCDATA)>
<!ELEMENT ext (#PCDATA)>
<!ELEMENT maiden (#PCDATA)>
<!ELEMENT birthplace (#PCDATA)>
<!ELEMENT annotation (#PCDATA)>
<!ATTLIST birthplace  country CDATA #IMPLIED >
```

Listing 15-2 is the XML document for family tree. To follow along, open your `family14.xml` document and save it as `family15.xml`, or retype and save it as `family15.xml`. (You must also adjust the DOCTYPE to reflect the change in Sessions 14 and 15.)

If you do not wish to type this XML document, you may open `family14.xml` **from your session15 folder on your CD. To follow the examples below, save it as** `family15.dtd` **in the same folder as the** `genealogy15.dtd` **document you just created.**

Listing 15-2
Our Family XML Document

```
<?xml version="1.0"?>
<!DOCTYPE family SYSTEM "genealogy15.dtd">
<family>
<father id="CL02">Joseph Q. <surname>Clark</surname></father>
<mother id="J001">Mary J.
<surname>Clark</surname><maiden>Jones</maiden></mother>
<offspring>
    <child gender="female" id="CL03" mother="J001">
        <firstname>Jennifer</firstname>
        <surname>Clark</surname>
        <birthplace>Pittsburgh PA</birthplace></child>
    <child gender="male" id="CL04" mother="J001">
        <firstname>Joseph</firstname>
        <midname>Q.</midname>
        <surname>Clark</surname><ext>II</ext>
        <birthplace>Kenmore NY</birthplace></child>
    <child gender="female" id="CL05" mother="J001">
        <firstname>Margaret</firstname>
        <midname>M.</midname>
        <surname>Clark</surname>
        <birthplace>Pittsburgh PA</birthplace></child>
    <child gender="male" id="CL06" mother="J001">
        <firstname>Mark</firstname>
        <midname>J.</midname>
        <surname>Clark</surname>
        <birthplace>Washington PA</birthplace></child>
</offspring>
<annotation>
<![CDATA[If the number of children is greater than (>) four but
less than (<) ten, this family has been included in the "Honorable
Mention" section of this book but not in the "Record Setters"
section.]]>
</annotation>
</family>
```

Modifying the DTD

You're now going to add a photograph element to your DTD so that you can include pictures of the family members. You include the new element in your DTD with a source attribute.

```
<!ELEMENT photograph EMPTY>
<!ATTLIST photograph source ENTITY #REQUIRED>
```

You also need to allow photograph to be nested in some other element. In this case, you're going to make it available within the child element, and it's going to be optional (denoted with a question mark) so that you don't have to provide an image with every person.

```
<!ELEMENT child (firstname, midname*, surname, ext?, birthplace,
photograph?)>
```

In order to use different types of files (non-XML files), you must include a notation as to what specific types of document (GIF, BMP, JPG) you plan to use. The notation within your DTD sample is

```
<!FNTITY baby SYSTEM "baby.jpg" NDATA jpg>
```

If you attempt to view an XML file in the browser with just this notation, you get an error. You also need to define a GIF. The other part of your notation, placed below ENTITY, is

```
<!NOTATION jpg SYSTEM "image/jpeg">
```

After preparation, your DTD should look like the following:

```
<!ELEMENT family (father, mother, offspring?, annotation*)>
<!ELEMENT father (#PCDATA | surname)*>
<!ATTLIST father  id ID  #IMPLIED >
<!ELEMENT mother (#PCDATA | maiden | surname)*>
<!ATTLIST mother  id ID  #IMPLIED >
<!ELEMENT offspring (child*)>
<!ELEMENT child (firstname, midname*, surname, ext?, birthplace,
photograph?)>
<!ATTLIST child  gender     (female | male )  'female'
                 birthyear  CDATA    #IMPLIED
                 id         ID       #IMPLIED
                 mother     IDREF    #IMPLIED
                 father     IDREF    #IMPLIED >
```

```
<!ELEMENT firstname (#PCDATA)>
<!ELEMENT midname (#PCDATA)>
<!ELEMENT surname (#PCDATA)>
<!ELEMENT ext (#PCDATA)>
<!ELEMENT maiden (#PCDATA)>
<!ELEMENT birthplace (#PCDATA)>
<!ELEMENT annotation (#PCDATA)>
<!ATTLIST birthplace  country CDATA #IMPLIED >
<!ELEMENT photograph EMPTY>
<!ATTLIST photograph source ENTITY #REQUIRED>
<!ENTITY baby SYSTEM "baby.jpg" NDATA jpg>
<!NOTATION jpg SYSTEM "image/jpeg">
Save your DTD and go to your XML document.
```

**10 Min.
To Go**

Modifying the XML document

You can now use the photograph tag within your XML document to display a graphic. Well, you can't actually display it because the browser doesn't support it, but it will be part of your valid XML document!

A JPEG photograph is available in the folder XML-wcc with your XML document (see Figure 15-1).

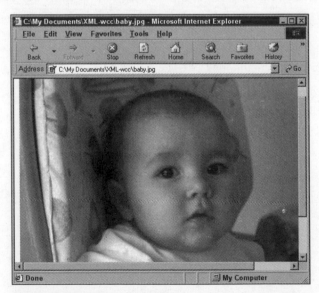

Figure 15-1
The available JPG file in the same directory as your XML document

Within the information for the child named Margaret, use the photograph tag to place the baby.jpg file.

```
<child gender="female" id="CL05" mother="J001">
     <firstname>Margaret</firstname>
     <midname>M.</midname>
     <surname>Clark</surname>
     <birthplace>Pittsburgh PA</birthplace>
     <photograph source="baby"/></child>
```

Be sure to insert photograph *after* the birthplace end tag and *before* the child end tag to keep your structure valid.

Viewing the result

Figure 15-2 shows the result of viewing this XML document in Internet Explorer. The code is highlighted so that you can more easily see it; the highlight is not something the browser does.

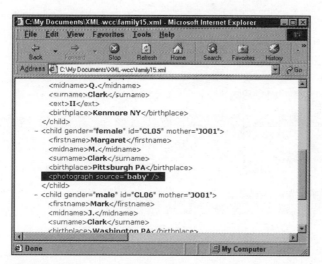

Figure 15-2
XML document includes a photograph but does not display.

Although the JPG file is available, it's not displayed by the browser or linked to it in any way. You can make the picture display by using XML with XSLT. That topic is covered later in this book.

Peeking at SVG

SVG is an XML vocabulary for creating graphics using XML. SVG graphics are graphically represented XML. Because SVG is made of XML, the graphics integrate well with XML documents. You can view SVG graphics by using a viewer tool, such as Adobe's SVG viewer. To create SVG graphics, you can use any of several available creation tools, such as Adobe's Illustrator 9.0 SVG export plug-in, or just hand code (if you're so inclined).

Because SVG graphics are XML, it becomes easy to cross-reference information in an XML document with information in an SVG graphic. This can then allow you to modify the graphic's display in a browser by activating an XML area.

If the mouse is moved over the XML document or the SVG graphic, information "lights up" both in the table and in the graphic (see Figure 15-3).

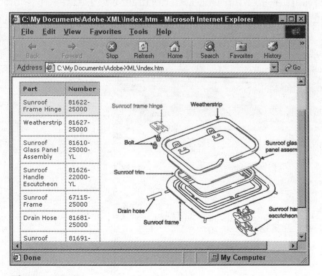

Figure 15-3
An XML document with an SVG graphic

For more information on SVG, visit the W3C Web site (http://www.w3.org) and check out the latest news.

The SVG specifications from the W3C are included on this book's CD, along with sample SVG graphics files. Also included is an Adobe SVG viewer plug-in, designed for installation within Internet Explorer 5 or higher.

Done!

REVIEW

- You can place graphics and binary files in XML documents.
- You can include any file type in your XML document, but the file type must be recognized by the application that processes your XML documents.
- The future of graphics will be determined by the path that browsers and other applications take.
- SVG is an XML-based graphics language.

QUIZ YOURSELF

1. What is the appropriate tag to include an image within an HTML document? (See "The HTML approach.")

2. Why do you have to create an element instead of just using the HTML img tag? (See "The XML approach.")

3. True or False: You may refer to URLs instead of local files with both notations and images. (See "Providing the NOTATION.")

4. True or False: Support for images is limited because of shortcomings in XML. (See "Modifying the XML document.")

5. True or False: SVG images are XML documents. (See "Peeking at SVG.")

16

Publishing XML Documents: Introduction to XML Transformations

Session Checklist

✔ Learning why you need to transform XML documents to other XML vocabularies

✔ Introducing the XML style sheet language, XSLT

✔ Creating and testing our first XSLT style sheet

30 Min. To Go

XML allows you to separate the content of a document from the format of a document. Why would you want to do this? Separating content from format provides several capabilities:

- You can extract the content from your documents
- You can transform that content to other forms
- You can publish that content to a variety of output devices

If our XML documents include only content information, where does the formatting information come from? How do we specify the format of an XML document? This is a major topic that we will address over the next nine sessions.

Challenges of Information Repurposing

Reuse and repurposing of information presents some interesting challenges. Different output devices don't provide the same display capabilities. Display screens vary widely in size and amount of content they can present. Different output devices don't even understand the same file formats! Web browsers, printers, and cell phone displays each require a significantly different set of instructions for rendering information. Take a look at the following typical XML document, and the instructions you need to render the content of that XML document on a Web browser, cell phone display, and hardcopy printer:

- XML fragment:

```
<headline>MegaCorp Merger Announced</headline>
```

- HTML version:

```
<h1>MegaCorp Merger Announced</h1>
```

- WML version (for cell phone screens):

```
<wml><card>MegaCorp Merger Announced</card></wml>
```

- Printed version:

```
<fo:block>MegaCorp Merger Announced</fo:block>
```

You must render your documents differently on various output devices. You may also want to customize the content of your documents for each output device. You may, for example, publish news articles to subscribers on a number of different display devices. Users of cell phones probably only want to read the headlines — it's just not practical to display or read the entire text of a news article on the screen of a typical cell phone.

But subscribers on personal computers with full-size monitors will want the full content of your news feed. How can you publish two versions of your news feed from a single XML source file? You create two style sheets — one for transforming your content for display in Web browsers, another for transforming your content for display on cell phone screens.

Figure 16-1 is a block diagram of an XML document. It shows an XML source transformed to three different markup languages for three different types of renderings.

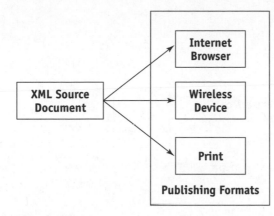

Figure 16-1
Transforming an XML document for publishing to the Web, to a wireless device, and to print

Introduction to XML Style Sheets

Because transforming XML is such an important part of any XML-based application, a language was created specifically for the task of transforming XML documents. This language, called the XML style sheet language, or XSLT, has the following capabilities:

- Transforms XML documents from one XML vocabulary to another
- Selects specific content from an XML document
- Sorts content from an XML document
- Combines content from multiple XML documents

An XML style sheet is applied to an XML source document by an application called an XSLT processor. The XSLT processor applies the style sheet rules to the XML source document and writes the results of the transformation to a *result document*. This process is shown in Figure 16-2.

Because a style sheet does not modify the source document, multiple style sheets can be applied to perform multiple transformations. You may have as many style sheets as you have output devices.

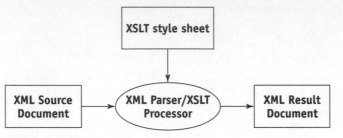

Figure 16-2
Flow diagram of XML source document, XSLT style sheet, and result document

XSLT Design Principles

You should understand some important things about XSLT if you plan to use it to its fullest potential.

An XSLT style sheet is an XML document

The XSLT language is expressed as an XML vocabulary — simply a set of tags. An XSLT style sheet must be a well-formed XML document. This has several effects:

- You can use the same editors that you use for creating XML documents to create your XSLT style sheets.
- You can check that your XSLT style sheets are well-formed by using the same tools that you use to verify that your XML documents are well-formed.
- You can write applications to create XSLT style sheets.

An XSLT style sheet can only be well-formed. It's not possible to validate an XSLT style sheet because there is no DTD for XSLT. Because it is possible to include any literal result elements in an XSLT style sheet, an XSLT DTD would have to define an infinite number of content models for XSLT elements.

XSLT is a declarative language

XSLT is a full-featured programming language with a rich set of capabilities. But XSLT differs from many conventional programming languages in a significant way.

Many programmers are only familiar with *procedural* languages — languages whose statements are executed a single line at a time, starting at the beginning of the program and ending at the last statement that is executed. (This may or may not be the last line of the program. The program may terminate based on some condition that is met midway through the program.)

XSLT is a *declarative* language. An XSLT program is comprised of a set of *templates*. The templates match patterns — XML element and attributes — in the source tree and define the contents of the result tree when those patterns are encountered. Here's an example:

- XML fragment

  ```
  <message>This is a very important message!</message>
  ```

- XSLT fragment

  ```
  <xsl:template match="message">
      <H1><xsl:value-of select="."/></H1>
  </xsl:template>
  ```

- Result document

  ```
  <H1>This is a very important message!</H1>
  ```

An XSLT template consists of both XSLT elements, which are the commands and functions of the XSLT language, and literal result elements, which are copied to the result document without modification. In this example, the HTML tags `<H1>` and `</H1>` are literal result elements — these elements are written as-is to the result document. The XSLT statement `<xsl:value-of select="."/>` matches the string content of the current element — in this case the `<message>` element. The XSLT statement gets replaced with the value of the current element.

Because XSLT is declarative, and not procedural, no template can affect the results of another template. Most significantly, this means that an XSLT style sheet cannot update variables or maintain counters during execution. In theory, the template rules of an XSLT style sheet could be distributed across a multiprocessor machine, with each template executed by a different processor, and the results of each processor combined in the end.

Your First XSLT Style Sheet

You're now going to create and apply a simple XSLT style sheet. In this exercise, you will extract information from a simple XML document for publishing on a Web page.

Specifying your XSLT style sheet vocabulary

An XSLT style sheet must have a root element `<xsl:stylesheet>`. This root element informs the XSLT processor that the file is an XSLT style sheet, tells the processor that all elements that begin with `xsl:` are XSLT instructions, and tells the processor that the instructions conform to version 1.0 of the XSLT Recommendation. Here is the literal begin tag for the root element of your XSLT style sheet:

```
<xsl:stylesheet
    xmlns:xsl="http://www.w3.org/1999/XSL/Transform"
version="1.0">
```

The following begin tag is also legal:

```
<xsl:transform
    xmlns:xsl="http://www.w3.org/1999/XSL/Transform"
version="1.0">
```

You may occasionally see style sheets that start with this line:

```
<xsl:stylesheet xmlns:xsl="http://www.w3.org/TR/WD-xsl">
```

The `xmlns:xsl` attribute value of `http://www.w3.org/TR/WD-xsl` means that the style sheet uses an older draft version of the XSLT language and may not work with many current XSLT processors.

The XSLT language was published as a W3C Recommendation in November 1999. Microsoft's Internet Explorer Version 5.5 was released before this date and supports an older draft version of the language. This session discusses the final Recommendation version of XSLT.

To run this book's examples in Internet Explorer Version 5.5, you must install the Microsoft XML Processor Upgrade, MSXML3 and Microsoft's xmlinst configuration tool. Links to MSXML3 and xmlinst are provided on the CD that accompanies this book.

Your XML source file

Suppose that you maintain the baseball standings for your favorite team in an XML file that looks like this:

```
<?xml version="1.0"?>
<team_standing>
  <team>Pittsburgh Pirates</team>
  <wins>49</wins>
  <losses>42</losses>
  <standing>1st</standing>
</team_standing>
```

You can create these files on your system and try them yourself. Save your XML document as `standings.xml`.

You can view the XML file as-is in a Web browser. Without any formatting information, the browser displays your baseball standings, as shown in Figure 16-3. Although you can read the file in the browser, you probably don't want to publish the information this way. To make your results look more like a real Web page, you're going to create an XSLT style sheet.

Figure 16-3
Baseball standings XML source file

Creating an XSLT style sheet

You're going to create a simple XSLT style sheet that will process your XML source file and create an HTML result file that allows you to do the following:

- Create a parent <html> element for the Web page.
- Create a title for the Web page that includes the name of the team.
- Create a heading for the information that also includes the name of the team.
- Print the name of the team and the team standing.

We go into more detail about the XSLT language in the next section. For now, the following style sheet should do the trick. The style sheet consists of a root <xsl:stylesheet> element and a single <xsl:template> element. Remember that style sheet elements that begin with xsl: are XSLT instructions. All other elements in the style sheet are literal result elements and are copied as-is to the result tree. You use these literal result elements in this style sheet to create the skeleton of your HTML result file. You then select strings — team name and standings — from the XML file to fill in the HTML skeleton.

You may notice that you use the element <xsl:value-of select="team"/> three times in this XSLT template — once to populate the HTML <title>, once to populate the header, and once to build the sentence that provides the standings. You can use this information multiple times, even though it occurs only once in the source XML file.

```
<xsl:stylesheet version="1.0"
                xmlns:xsl="http://www.w3.org/1999/XSL/Transform">
<xsl:template match="team_standing">
<html>
  <head>
    <title>Standing for <xsl:value-of select="team"/></title>
  </head>
  <body>
    <h1>Standing for <xsl:value-of select="team"/></h1>
    <p>
       The <xsl:value-of select="team"/> are in
       <xsl:value-of select="standing"/> place.
    </p>
  </body>
</html>
</xsl:template>
</xsl:stylesheet>
```

After typing the preceding information, save your style sheet as `standings.xsl` and you can complete the style sheet. As a last step, verify that the style sheet is well-formed. You can do so by opening the style sheet in Internet Explorer version 5.5. If the style sheet is well-formed, Internet Explorer will display the style sheet in the color-coded tree pattern that it uses to display other XML documents (see Figure 16-4).

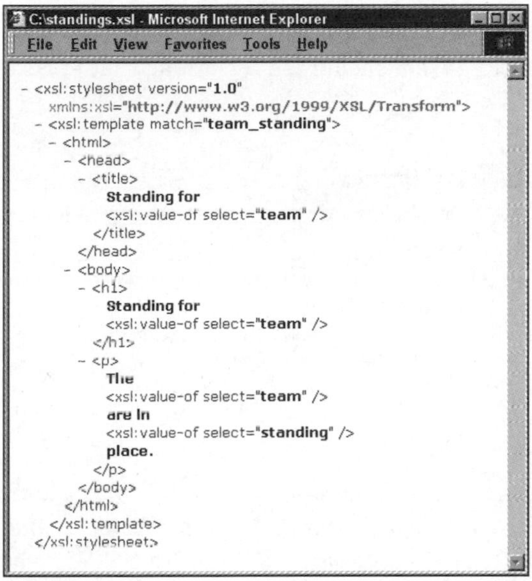

Figure 16-4
Well-formed XSLT style sheet displayed in Internet Explorer 5.5

If Internet Explorer returns an error when you try to view your style sheet, check the style sheet for well-formedness. Make sure that all begin tags have a corresponding end tag, and make sure that all tags are properly nested.

Attaching a style sheet to an XML document

Thus far, you have created a simple XML document and an XSLT style sheet to transform that document into a publishable HTML file. Now you need to apply the style sheet to the document.

You can do this easily, especially if you're letting your browser apply the XSLT transformation. In your XML document, you can specify the name of the default style sheet that you want to apply. Just add the following processing instruction to your XML file, immediately following the XML declaration:

```
<?xml-stylesheet type="text/xsl" href="standings.xsl"?>
```

This processing instruction is recognized by Microsoft Internet Explorer version 5.5, but not by all XML processors. Check the documentation that comes with your XML processor if you're unsure.

Testing your style sheet

Now try testing your XSLT style sheet in Internet Explorer. All you need to do is open the XML file in Internet Explorer. You should see something that looks like Figure 16-5.

Figure 16-5
Result of XSLT transformation in browser

If your result does not match Figure 16-5, verify that you have installed the Microsoft XML Processor Upgrade, MSXML3 and run Microsoft's xmlinst configuration tool. Links to MSXML3 and xmlinst are provided on the CD that accompanies this book.

Done!

REVIEW

- XML enables you to separate your content from your format. You can specify the format of an XML document by applying a style sheet.
- To publish your XML documents to a variety of output devices, you typically must transform the XML document to the vocabulary of the target device.
- The XML style sheet language, XSLT, enables you to write style sheets that transform your XML documents to other XML vocabularies.

QUIZ YOURSELF

1. True or False: An XSLT style sheet must be a well-formed XML document. (See "An XSLT style sheet is an XML document.")

2. What is the required root element of an XSLT style sheet? (See "Specifying your XSLT style sheet vocabulary.")

3. What is the term for an element in an XSLT style sheet that is not defined by the XSLT vocabulary? (See "XSLT is a declarative language.")

4. What happens to these elements when the style sheet is processed? (See "XSLT is a declarative language.")

5. How can you associate an XML document with an XSLT style sheet so that the style sheet is invoked automatically? (See "Attaching a style sheet to an XML document.")

PART

III

Saturday Afternoon

1. Must all attributes have a name and value?
2. Can attributes be used to drive text formatting?
3. True or False: Attributes can sometimes be used instead of elements.
4. Is it necessary to have an ID when using IDREF?
5. What is the purpose of an ID attribute?
6. Can attributes cause parser errors?
7. True or False: XLink supports bidirectional linking.
8. Is it possible to reference an external file in XML?
9. True or False: < and > are predefined entity references in XML.
10. True or False: If you want to use special symbols, you must define them as character entities in your DTD prior to using them in an XML document.
11. Can a general entity be used to substitute repeating text?
12. Are CDATA sections allowed in XML documents?
13. True or False: XML does not support binary graphics files.
14. True or False: XML only supports GIF and JPG graphic formats.
15. True or False: Different devices render XML differently.
16. Can XML documents be printed or only displayed online?
17. Are XSLT style sheets XML documents?

18. Does XSLT change XML documents to HTML?

19. True or False: An XSLT style sheet can generate an HTML table.

20. Do XSLT documents require a root tag?

PART

IV

Saturday Evening

Simple Transformations with XSLT and XPath

Session Checklist

✔ Understanding XSLT template rules

✔ Learning common XSLT instructions

✔ Learning common XSLT mistakes

**30 Min.
To Go**

I n the previous session, we introduced the concept of XML transformations and discussed why you probably need to transform your XML documents to other formats. We introduced XSLT, the language for transforming XML documents, and looked at a simple example of using an XSLT style sheet to transform XML into an HTML page suitable for display in a Web browser.

In this session, we're going to take a more detailed look at the XSLT language. Although there's not enough space in this book to cover all of XSLT, this chapter will give you a good start.

To explore XSLT more fully, see the XSLT Recommendation at
`http://www.w3.org/TR/xslt`.

Reviewing a Typical Style Sheet Processing Model

The following code shows how a typical style sheet is applied to an XML source document. Most style sheets have a template rule that looks something like this:

```
<xsl:template match="/">
[literal result elements]
<xsl:apply-templates/>
[literal result elements]
</xsl:template>
```

This template rule does the following:

- Matches the document's top-level element, including all of its content, with `<xsl:template match="/">`. (The / symbol is XSLT short-hand for the top-level element.) By matching the document's top-level element, the style sheet grabs all of the document's content for processing — including text, child elements, and attributes.

- Writes some literal result elements to the result file. These aren't shown here but are likely to be HTML tags used to "wrap" the content of your XML document. Literal result elements are copied as-is to the result document. We will see examples of literal result elements later in this session.

- Applies the remaining templates in the style sheet to the children of the top-level element with `<xsl:apply-templates/>`.

- Writes more literal result elements to the file (if any are provided), and stops processing the source document.

The third template rule result in the preceding list is critical. The style sheet invokes the remaining style sheet template rules on the children of the top-level element. These templates may write literal result elements to the result file. They may also invoke template rules on their child elements.

Writing XSLT Instructions

An XSLT style sheet is comprised of a set of statements that match patterns in the XML source document and create corresponding patterns in the result document. The following sections look at the most common ways to match patterns in the source document.

Using *<xsl:template/>*

The most common way to match patterns in an XML source document is with the `<xsl:template/>` statement. An `<xsl:template/>` element looks like this:

```
<xsl:template match="[pattern]">
  [literal result elements and XSLT elements]
</xsl:template>
```

The `pattern` can be an element name or an expression to identify specific fragments of our XML document. For the purposes of this book, assume that `pattern` is an element name.

Using *<xsl:apply-templates/>*

You can use the XSLT element `<xsl:apply-templates/>` in one of two ways:

- With no attributes, `<xsl:apply-templates/>` means "apply any templates in this style sheet that match patterns in the source document."
- With a *match* attribute, `<xsl:apply-templates match="[expression]"/>` means "apply any templates in this style sheet that match the specified XPath expression."

XPath expressions are statements for selecting an element or elements from an XML document. An XPath expression can be as simple as an element name. We will discuss XPath expressions in more detail in Session 18.

Using *<xsl:for-each select="[expression]"/>*

`<xsl:for-each select="[expression]"/>` enables your style sheet to iterate over a series of content in the source document. `<xsl:for-each select="[expression]"/>` is particularly useful for populating HTML tables with the content of XML elements.

Using *<xsl:value-of select="[expression]"/>*

`<xsl:value-of select="[expression]"/>` enables you to write the string value of a particular element to a location in the result document. `<xsl:value-of select="[expression]"/>` does have one danger: If the element you're writing has child elements, the text of the child elements is also included. This may not be the result you intended.

Iterating over XML element content

You're now going to work with a more complete version of the sample XML source document that you used in the previous session. This time, you'll work with standings from several teams.

```
<?xml version="1.0" ?>
<?xml-stylesheet type='text/xsl' href='division_standings.xsl'?>
<division_standing>
  <name>National League Central</name>

    <name>Pittsburgh Pirates</name>
    <record>
      <wins>49</wins>
      <losses>42</losses>
    </record>
    <standing>1st</standing>
  </team>
  <team>
    <name>Chicago Cubs</name>
    <record>
      <wins>41</wins>
      <losses>50</losses>
    </record>
    <standing>3rd</standing>
  </team>
  <team>
  <team>
    <name>St. Louis Cardinals</name>
    <record>
      <wins>46</wins>
      <losses>45</losses>
    </record>
    <standing>2nd</standing>
  </team>
</division_standing>
```

The next step is to build a style sheet to generate an HTML document that contains a table row for each `<team>` element. This XSLT style sheet does the following:

- Matches the top-level element with `<xsl:template match="/">`
- Sets up an HTML page
- Uses `<xsl:value-of />` elements to populate the title and header of the HTML page
- Uses `<xsl:for-each select="team"/>` to populate an HTML table with the team data from the XML source file
- Closes the HTML page

Remember that the style sheet is an XML document. All this work is happening within the `<xsl:template match="/"/>` element.

```
<xsl:stylesheet version="1.0"
                xmlns:xsl="http://www.w3.org/1999/XSL/Transform">

<xsl:template match="/">
  <html>
    <head>
      <title>Standings for <xsl:value-of
select="division_standing/name"/></title>
    </head>
    <body>
    <h1>Standings for <xsl:value-of
select="division_standing/name"/></h1>
    <table>
      <tbody>
        <th>
        <hr />
          <tr>
            <td>Team</td>
            <td>Wins</td>
            <td>Losses</td>
            <td>Standing</td>
          </tr>
        </th>
        <xsl:for-each select="//team">
          <tr>
```

```
            <td><xsl:apply-templates select="name"/></td>
            <td><xsl:apply-templates select="./record/wins"/></td>
            <td><xsl:apply-templates
   select="./record/losses"/></td>
            <td><xsl:apply-templates select="./standing"/></td>
         </tr>
       </xsl:for-each>
     </tbody>
   </table>
   </body>
  </html>
</xsl:template>


</xsl:stylesheet>
```

When you provide your source document and your style sheet to an XSLT processor, the following HTML result document is created:

```
<html>
<head>
<META http-equiv="Content-Type" content="text/html; charset=UTF-
16">
<title>Standings for National League Central</title>
</head>
<body>
<h1>National League Central</h1>
<table>
<tbody>
<th>
<tr>
<td>Team</td>
<td>Wins</td>
<td>Losses</td>
<td>Standing</td>
</tr>
</th>
<hr />
<tr>
<td>Pittsburgh Pirates</td>
<td>49</td>
```

```
<td>42</td>
<td>1st</td>
</tr>
<tr>
<td>Chicago Cubs</td>
<td>41</td>
<td>50</td>
<td>3rd</td>
</tr>
<tr>
<td>St. Louis Cardinals</td>
<td>46</td>
<td>45</td>
<td>2nd</td>
</tr>
</tbody>
</table>
</body>
</html>
```

Notice that HTML tags have replaced your original XML tags. Only the content of the original XML source document — not the tags — has been copied to the HTML result document. The XML tags are gone from the result document, although you did use the XML tags in the style sheet to identify exactly which content to copy to the result document. You've wrapped that content in the appropriate HTML tags instead of your original XML tags. Figure 17-1 shows how this looks in a Web browser:

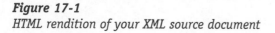

Figure 17-1
HTML rendition of your XML source document

You can see the results of Figure 17-1 yourself by opening the file `standings.xml` **from the session17 folder on your book's CD-ROM. Open** `standings.xml` **in Microsoft Internet Explorer, Version 5.5 or higher, with the MSXML3 and xmlinst packages installed.**

To run this book's examples in Internet Explorer Version 5.5, you must install the Microsoft XML Processor Upgrade, MSXML3 and Microsoft's xmlinst configuration tool. Links to MSXML3 and xmlinst are provided on the CD that accompanies this book.

Sorting XML content

Your HTML document does have one problem — the teams aren't displayed in order of team standing. You can fix this in your style sheet by using an `<xsl:sort/>` statement.

   `<xsl:sort/>` appears as an immediate child to an `<xsl:apply-templates/>` or `<xsl:for-each/>` element. `<xsl:sort/>` accepts an attribute named `select`, which can specify an element to be used as the sort key. In this case, we will sort the order of the elements processed by the `<xsl:for-each/>` loop by team standing:

```
<xsl:for-each select="//team">
  <xsl:sort select="./standing"/>
[rest of xsl:for-each element]
</xsl:for-each>
```

You can see the results of Figure 17-2 yourself by opening the file `standings_sorted.xml` **from the session17 folder on your book's CD-ROM. Open** `standings_sorted.xml` **in Microsoft Internet Explorer, Version 5.5 or higher, with the MSXML3 and xmlinst packages installed.**

To run this book's examples in Internet Explorer Version 5.5, you must install the Microsoft XML Processor Upgrade, MSXML3 and Microsoft's xmlinst configuration tool. Links to MSXML3 and xmlinst are provided on the CD that accompanies this book.

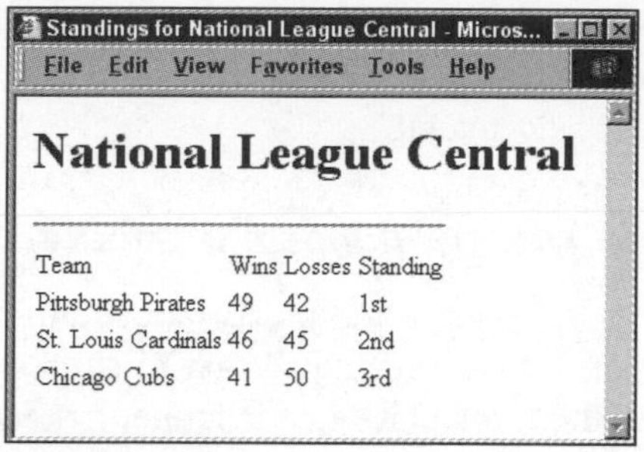

Figure 17-2
HTML rendition of your XML source document, sorted by team standing

XSLT default templates

You don't need to explicitly match each element in your source document that you want to pass through to the result document. XSLT provides default — or built-in — templates, which process elements in your source document in the absence of an explicit template rule.

These default templates are invoked when a template on a parent or ancestor element invokes `<xsl:apply-template/>` on its children, but there is no explicit template rule for the child elements. In this case, the default template will copy the text of any child elements to the result document.

Suppressing content

How do you suppress content from being copied from your source document to your result document? Because XSLT's built-in template rule copies text from elements that aren't matched by a template to the result tree, you may think that all text in your source document is copied to your result document. This is not so. There are two ways, discussed in the following sections, that you can exclude the content of specific elements from being copied from your source document to your result document.

Define a template rule that does nothing

You can suppress the content of specific elements in your source document by defining an "empty" template rule for these elements — that is, a template rule that does nothing. The following template rule, for example, would suppress the contents of the element `<standings>` from being copied to the result document:

```
<xsl:template match="standings"/>
```

Note that this template is an empty element with no body. Because the template body contains neither literal result elements nor XSLT instructions, the matched element has no effect on the result document.

Avoid using *<xsl:apply-templates/>* without a match attribute.

Without a match attribute, `<xsl:apply-templates/>` will process all children of the current node and apply the default template — copying all text of child elements to the result document — if no matching template rule is found. Instead, explicitly select the elements you want to process with `<xsl:for-each select="`*[expression]*`"/>` or `<xsl:apply-templates match="`*[expression]*`"/>`.

Common XSLT mistakes

The following sections cover some common XSLT mistakes that you should know about. Anyone who writes XSLT style sheets runs into these at some time, especially when first learning how to write them.

The XSLT style sheet is not well-formed

Your XSLT style sheet must be a well-formed XML document. This means that all tags are properly nested, that all begin tags have a corresponding end tag, and that all empty elements use the empty element syntax.

Because XSLT style sheets usually consist of a mix of XSLT elements (whose tag names begin with `xsl:`) and literal result elements, it's easy to create a style sheet that's not well-formed. Be especially careful when embedding HTML elements in your style sheet. You must express empty HTML elements by using XML empty element syntax, or your XSLT style sheet will not be well-formed. To include an HTML line break in your style sheet, for example, use `<br />`, not `<br>`.

The XSLT style sheet does not match the root template element

An XSLT style sheet should have an `<xsl:template match="`*[expression]*`">` that matches either of the following:

- The entire XML document, `<xsl:template match="/">`
- The highest-level element in the XML document

If you create and apply a style sheet that creates an empty result document, you must verify that either of these two template elements is present. If not, the style sheet will miss the contents of your XML document.

XSLT statements within `<xsl:template/>` *are relative to the current node*

Within the body of your `<xsl:template match="[expression]">` statements, you're likely to reference other elements within your XML document. Be aware that any element references are with respect to the current element — in other words, with respect to the particular element to which the `<xsl:template match="[expression]">` statement applies.

In this session, you were introduced to the XML transformation language in some detail. In the next session, you will learn about XPath, which is a language for selecting components of XML documents. After you learn XSLT and XPath, you will be able to create powerful style sheets for selecting, sorting, and publishing your XML documents.

Done!

REVIEW

- An `<xsl:template/>` element can include both literal result elements and XSLT statements.
- `<xsl:apply-templates/>` and `<xsl:for-each/>` are two XSLT statements that select content in your source XML document for style sheet processing.
- `<xsl:sort/>` will cause the current template to match elements in sorted order.

QUIZ YOURSELF

1. True or False: You can define an empty template to suppress element content from being copied from the source XML document to the result XML document. (See "Reviewing a Typical Style Sheet Processing Model.")
2. True or False: An XSLT style sheet must be a well-formed XML document. (See "The XSLT style sheet is not well-formed.")
3. What is the XSLT term for text that is copied as-is from the style sheet to the result document? (See "Reviewing a Typical Style Sheet Processing Model.")
4. Why might you typically want to include such text in your style sheets? (See "Reviewing a Typical Style Sheet Processing Model.")
5. Which XSLT element will iterate over elements in the source document? (See "Writing XSLT Instructions.")

Introducing the XML Path Language (XPath)

Session Checklist

✔ Learning how XPath expressions can select specific pieces of XML documents

✔ Understanding the building blocks of XPath expressions

✔ Performing Boolean tests with XPath predicates

**30 Min.
To Go**

S ession 18 continues your tour of the XML transformation language. Thus far, you've been introduced to XML transformations, looked at the basic elements that comprise an XSLT style sheet, and worked with a few practical examples.

In this session, you're going to explore XPath, which is a companion language to XSLT. XSLT enables you to create and apply templates to an XML source document. You used XSLT location paths to select which nodes to process in your XML source document. XPath allows you to create specific rules for addressing parts of an XML source document — enabling you to build precise expressions to select the elements from your source document.

Microsoft Internet Explorer supports an older version of XSLT. To run this book's examples in Internet Explorer Version 5.5, you must install the Microsoft XML Processor Upgrade, MSXML3 and Microsoft's xmlinst configuration tool. Links to MSXML3 and xmlinst are provided on the CD that accompanies this book.

Why do you want to select specific elements from an XML document? We mentioned the power and capabilities of XSLT and XPath. Together, they enable you to create specific transformations. You can select pieces of an XML document to copy to your result tree. You can sort, select, and manipulate elements of your XML source documents based on the following characteristics:

- Element name
- Attribute name
- Attribute value
- Presence of a particular parent element
- Presence of a particular child element

This list is far from complete, and XPath is too comprehensive to cover in this book. But this session introduces you to the basics of using XPath expressions to select specific content from your XML source documents.

To explore XPath more fully, see the XPath Recommendation at http://www.w3.org/TR/xpath.

Performing Selections Based on Document Structure

XPath allows you to select elements and attributes not only by name, but also by their relationship to other elements in the XML source document. Here are some examples, in plain English, of the types of selections you can specify with XPath:

- Select all nodes of the source document that are children of the element `<team>`.
- Select the first child element of `<team>`.
- Select the parent element of `<name>`.

Viewing XML documents as a collection of nodes

Before you jump into exploring XPath syntax and writing XPath statements, you need to take a slightly different view of your XML documents. Thus far, you have looked at XML documents as plain text files that include tags that specify information about the content of the document. But you can nest these tags within other tags in a way that frequently yields even more information.

When you run your XML document through an XML processor, the XML processor does the following:

- Verifies that the XML document is well-formed
- (Optionally) Verifies that the XML document conforms to a specified DTD
- Creates an internal representation of the XML document — a node tree.

The node tree represents both the content and the structure of the XML document. Besides the elements and element content of the source document being available, an XSLT style sheet can also access attributes and attribute values, text, and even comments and processing instructions from the source document.

The sample XML document in Figure 18-1 shows the node tree that is created when the XML document is processed. The sample document is a slightly more complex version of the document that you've worked with in the previous two sessions.

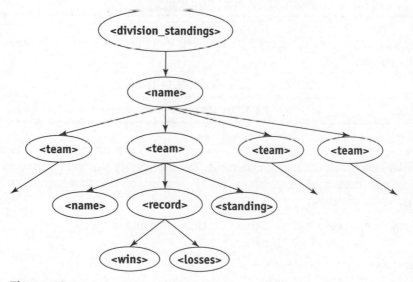

Figure 18-1
An XML document as a tree of elements

XPath statements for specifying element relationships

**20 Min.
To Go**

In the preceding session, you used the match attribute on `<xsl:template/>` and `<xsl:apply-templates/>` to select specific nodes in the source tree to be processed by the style sheet. You can set the value of the match attribute to the name of a child node of the current element. But match allows you to perform much more powerful selections — you can specify a child of the current node as well as almost any other node or collection of nodes in the XML source document. You do this through a powerful set of expressions called location paths.

If you're familiar with Unix and Windows directory structures, then you'll recognize the syntax for location paths. Many similarities exist between addressing an XML document as a tree of nodes and addressing the location of a file in a directory structure. The following are the basic location path expressions that XPath provides:

Symbol	Use in Location Path
/	child of the current node
../	parent of the current node
//	descendant of the current node

XPath provides a few other symbols that you should be aware of for building location paths:

*	matches all child elements of the current node
@league	matches the attribute of the current node named league

You can combine these location path expressions to identify elements within a particular context in the source document. You can specify particular elements by name, or you can use an asterisk to select all elements in the current context. Here are some examples:

- /division_standing/* — Selects all child elements of the <division_standing> element
- /division_standing/name — Selects the <name> child of the <division_standing> element
- //wins — Selects all descendant <wins> elements
- /record/../name — Selects the <name> element that is the child of the parent of the <record> element. <name> and <record> have the same parent element.

You can further refine these location paths by using predicates. *Predicates* enable you to refine the results of a location path with the following types of constraints:

- You can specify elements that have particular values. To extract only the record of the Pittsburgh Pirates from your XML source document, for example, you could construct the following location path expression: "Process all child elements of the `<team>` that has a child element `<name>` with a value of "Pittsburgh Pirates". The resulting expression would look something like this: `//team[name="Pittsburgh Pirates"]/*`.

- You can specify elements that have particular attributes.

- You can specify elements with particular attributes that are set to particular values.

- You can specify a particular element, based on document order, for a location path that matches more than one element. "Give me the first team element listed in the source document.", for example, would look something like `//team[1]`.

Going further with location paths: XPath axes

XPath provides a specific set of location path keywords, called *axes*, to specify an element's relationship with other elements. Table 18-1 shows several of the XPath axes specifiers, and Figure 18-2 provides a graphical representation of the XPath axes.

Table 18-1
XPath Axes Specifiers

Specifier	Explanation
child	Specifies all direct children of the current node. A child node is nested directly within the current node.
descendant	Specifies descendants of the current node. Includes child nodes, all children of child nodes, their children, and so on.
parent	Specifies the direct parent of the current node.
ancestor	Specifies all ancestors of the current node, including the parent node, parents of parents, and so on.

Continued

Table 18-1   *Continued*

following-sibling	All nodes that follow the current node and have the same parent element.
preceding-sibling	All nodes that precede the current node and have the same parent element.
following	All nodes that follow the current node, regardless of nesting level.
preceding	All nodes that precede the current node, regardless of nesting level.
self	Specifies the current node.

Several other XPath axes are available. For a complete list, see the XPath Recommendation at http://www.w3.org/TR/XPath.

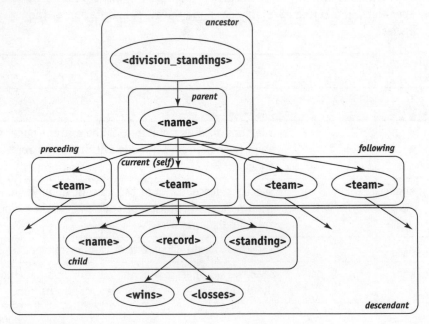

Figure 18-2
Illustration of XPath axes

**10 Min.
To Go**

Using Axes in Location Paths

With XPath axes statements, you can build complex location paths to select specific nodes in your source document. The following are some example location paths using XPath axes:

- `ancestor::name` — Selects all elements named "name" that are ancestors of the current node
- `descendant::team` — Selects all elements named "team" that are descendants of the current node
- `parent::*` — Selects the parent element of the current node

Your location path consists of an axis keyword on the left-hand side, a :: separator, and a node test on the right side. The node test constrains the set of nodes identified by the axis keyword. You may, for example, only want to select ancestor elements with a particular name. You can further constrain the set of nodes with predicates, which we discuss in the next section.

Constraining Location Paths with Predicates

Your location path strings can match a single node or a group of nodes. Sometimes the location path alone isn't enough for selecting the node or group of nodes that you want. You may want a member of a group of nodes that contains a particular text string. Perhaps you want the first or last member of a group of nodes. Maybe you want a node that contains a particular attribute with a particular value. You can accomplish these selections by adding predicates to your location paths.

A predicate is a Boolean expression that further constrains the results of a location path. Take a look at the following examples of location paths with predicates:

- `paragraph[@role="example"]` — Matches a paragraph element, which includes a role attribute whose value is set to example.
- `child::*[position()=first()]` — Matches the first child node of the current element.
- `ancestor::[5]` — Matches the fifth ancestor element, counting from the current node towards the beginning of the document. If the current element does not have 5 ancestor elements, the location path matches nothing.

This session contains a lot of theory and syntax for you to digest. In the next two sessions, you will put this theory to work and build more real-world examples.

Done!

REVIEW

- XPath is a language for addressing components of an XML document.
- XPath axes statements select nodes based on their relationship to the current node.
- XPath predicates enable you to attach Boolean tests to your XPath expressions.

QUIZ YOURSELF

1. True or False: An XPath statement cannot access a processing instruction or comment in the source document. (See "Viewing XML documents as a collection of nodes.")

2. True or False: The child axis includes all descendants of the current node. (See "Going further with location paths: XPath axes.")

3. What is the XPath path expression that selects all descendants of the current node? (See "Going further with location paths: XPath axes.")

4. What is the XPath symbol used to select an attribute node? (See "XPath statements for specifying element relationships.")

5. True or False: XPath statements can address elements by their numerical order within an XML document. (See "Constraining Location Paths with Predicates.")

Using XSLT and XPath to Select XML Content

Session Checklist

✔ Extracting content from an XML file by using XSLT and XPath

✔ Learning to extract the value of an XML element with
  `<xsl:value-of>`

✔ Looping over XML elements with `<xsl:for-each>`

✔ Using XSLT conditional statements

The past few sessions covered XSLT, the language for transforming XML documents. Session 18 introduced XPath, the language for specifying portions of an XML document. XPath provides a syntax for identifying elements, attributes, text, comments, and processing instructions in an XML document based on metadata (tag and attribute names) and location in the XML element hierarchy.

In this session, you're going to find out more about using XPath expressions within your XSLT style sheets. You're going to use the XPath expressions that you've already learned to address real XML content. You will work through several examples at the end of the session.

Understanding the Context Node

As a style sheet processes an XML document, the elements of the XML document are compared to the XSLT element in the style sheet. As the style sheet iterates through the nodes in the document, each element in the style sheet operates on a particular node. At any time during style sheet processing, the particular node being operated on in the source document is the context node. Figure 19-1 shows how the context node shifts as an XML document is processed through an XSLT style sheet.

Even though a node in an XML document can be an element, attribute, text, comment, or processing instruction, for the purpose of this book we assume that a node is an element.

Why is the context node important? Just as a set of directions depends on your starting point, an XPath expression depends on its context node. Think of an XPath expression as the directions for finding another node in the XML source document from the context node.

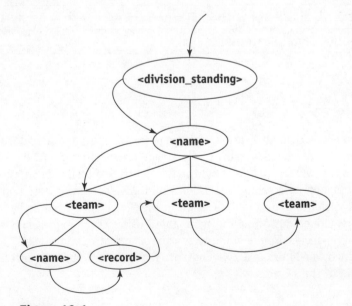

Figure 19-1
Progression of context node during the processing of an XML document

Using <xsl:value-of> to Select Specific XML Content

The `<xsl:value-of>` statement returns the value of an XML element or attribute, as shown in the following syntax:

```
<xsl:value-of select="[expression]"/>
```

The `<xsl:value-of>` statement is useful for extracting the content of specific elements in your XML data file — similar to treating your XML data file as a database. Take a look at a few example expressions:

- `<xsl:value-of select="."/>` writes the value of the context node to the result tree.

- `<xsl:value-of select=".."/>` writes the value of the parent node to the result tree.

- `<xsl:value-of select="../following-sibling::team/name"/>` is more complex. Try reading it from right-to-left, instead of from left-to-right. This expression writes the value of the name element child of the team element that follows the context node's parent.

`<xsl:value-of>` has one gotcha. The value of an XML element is defined as the text content of the element and all of its children. If you select the value of an element that has child elements, the result of `<xsl:value-of>` is the text content of all child elements concatenated together. This may not be what you expect, so you need to be careful if you use `<xsl:value-of>` to access the value of elements that may have children.

Getting attribute values

The `<xsl:value-of>` statement is not limited to extracting element values from an XML data file. You can use `<xsl:value-of>` to get the value of attributes as well. To do so, use the following syntax:

```
<xsl:value-of select="@attribute_name">
```

XSLT uses an @ symbol to specify the name of an attribute. You can use an attribute identifier anywhere in a location path, just as you would an element name. The location path in the following `<xsl:value-of>` statement, for example, selects the value of the city attribute of the name element that is a child of the context element's parent.

```
<xsl:value-of select="../name/@city"/>
```

Using <xsl:for-each> to Iterate over Multiple XML Elements

Your XML documents frequently resemble database records. To process information in your XML documents, you often need to iterate over elements of the same name. You've looked at `<xsl:for-each>` in examples in the previous two sessions, but let's take a closer look:

```
<xsl:for-each select="expression">
```

`<xsl:for-each>` enables you to explicitly choose elements in the source document. The expression attribute value can be specific or general. The following statement, for example, will iterate over each element in an XML document, in the order in which they appear in the document. The `<xsl:value-of>` statement in the body of `<xsl:for-each>` invokes the XSLT `name()` function to return the name of each visited element.

```
<xsl:for-each select="//*">
<xsl:value-of select="name()"/>
</xsl:for-each>
```

**20 Min.
To Go**

Conditional XSLT Processing

If you've done any programming, then you've probably worked with conditional statements. Programmers must frequently test a condition and choose an action based on the result of that test. XSLT programming is no different in its need for conditional testing.

XSLT provides two statements — `<xsl:if>` and `<xsl:when>` — for working with conditional tests.

Testing a condition with <xsl:if>

The `<xsl:if>` statement enables you to test a condition. If the condition is true, the XSLT processor invokes the body of the `<xsl:if>` statement. If the condition is false, the body of the `<xsl:if>` statement is skipped.

Testing for the existence of an attribute

The following `<xsl:if>` statement tests for the presence of an attribute named gender on the current element. The value of gender is not tested. If the gender attribute exists, the statement will evaluate to true and the statements within the `<xsl:if>` element are processed. Otherwise, the statements within the `<xsl:if>` element are ignored.

The following example writes a table cell containing the text Gender to the result document if the current element has an attribute named gender. Note that only the presence of the attribute is tested, not the value:

```
<xsl:if test="@gender">
<td>Gender</td>
</xsl:if>
```

You can get even more creative here. Suppose that you want to test for the presence of the gender attribute, and if the gender attribute exists, use `<xsl:value-of>` to write the value of the gender attribute. See the following code:

```
<xsl:if test="@gender">
<td><xsl:value-of select="@gender"/></td>
</xsl:if>
```

Testing the value of an attribute

The following XSLT statement tests for the presence and value of a gender attribute on the current element. If the gender attribute exists and has a value of 'male', the statement will evaluate to true and the statements within the `<xsl:if>` element are processed. Otherwise, the statements within the `<xsl:if>` element are ignored.

```
<xsl:if test="@gender='male'">
<td>Male</td>
</xsl:if>
```

Note that the attribute value 'male' is in single quotes.

Testing the identity of an element's parent

You may want to process an element differently based on its context. A `<name>` element, for example, may have a different meaning based on the identity of its parent element. The following style sheet fragment uses XPath axes to check that the current element is name and the parent of the current element is team. If so, the style sheet writes the value of the current name element.

```
<xsl:if test="self::name and parent::team">
<h2>Team name is <xsl:value-of select="."/></h2>
</xsl:if>
```

Selecting among multiple conditions with <xsl:choose>

You may need to test multiple conditions and take action on only one. In this case, you can use the `<xsl:choose>` statement.

`<xsl:choose>` presents a series of conditional tests. When a test occurs that evaluates to true, the statements within the `<xsl:when>` element are processed and the `<xsl:choose>` statement terminates. If no test evaluates to true, then the contents of the required `<xsl:otherwise>` element are processed. An `<xsl:choose>` statement looks like this:

```
<xsl:choose>
<xsl:when test="@gender='Male'">
<td>Male</td>
</xsl:when>
<xsl:when test="@gender='Female'">
<td>Female</td>
</xsl:when>
<xsl:otherwise>
<td>Eunuch</td>
</xsl:otherwise>
</xsl:choose>
```

**10 Min.
To Go**

Trying It Yourself: Examples

The next step is to put together everything you've learned thus far about XSLT and XPath. You have the following XML data file, which is your familiar set of baseball team standings. You're going to construct location path expressions and apply `<xsl:value-of>` statements to this document to extract specific information from your standings data. You can find this document on the book's CD-ROM, in folder session19, file standings.xml.

```
<?xml version="1.0" ?>
<?xml-stylesheet type='text/xsl' href='xpath.xsl'?>
<division_standing>
```

```
<name>National League Central</name>
<team>
<name>St. Louis Cardinals</name>
<record>
<wins>46</wins>
<losses>45</losses>
</record>
<standing>2nd</standing>
</team>
<team>
<name>Chicago Cubs</name>
<record>
<wins>41</wins>
<losses>50</losses>
</record>
<standing>3rd</standing>
</team>
<team>
<name>Pittsburgh Pirates</name>
<record>
<wins>49</wins>
<losses>42</losses>
</record>
<standing>1st</standing>
</team>
</division_standing>
```

Here is the style sheet that you will use. For the purposes of this exercise, you're going to assume that the context node is the second <team> element (Chicago Cubs information).

```
<xsl:stylesheet version="1.0"
                xmlns:xsl="http://www.w3.org/1999/XSL/Transform">
<!-- Force context node to be second team element -->
<xsl:template match="/division_standing/team[2]">
  <html>
    <body>
<!-- Select name child -->
<h1><xsl:value-of select="name"/></h1>
    </body>
  </html>
```

```
</xsl:template>
<!-- Supress all other text content from the result file -->
<xsl:template match="text()"/>
</xsl:stylesheet>
```

The CD-ROM contains five different style sheets. Each is exactly the same, except for the expression in the `<xsl:value-of>` statement. To see the results of each expression, we will edit the style sheet processing instruction in the file session19/`division.xml`. For each example, we will et the value of the `href` attribute to the name of the style sheet, provided with each example in parentheses. The following style sheet processing instruction, for example, will invoke style sheet `xpath1.xsl`:

```
<?xml-stylesheet type='text/xsl' href='xpath1.xsl'?>
```

In the following steps, you will view the results of five different stylesheets, with five different expressions.

To run this book's examples in Internet Explorer Version 5.5, you must install the Microsoft XML Processor Upgrade, MSXML3 and Microsoft's xmlinst configuration tool. Links to MSXML3 and xmlinst are provided on the CD that accompanies this book.

1. Copy session19/`division.xml` from the CD-ROM to your hard drive. Open `division.xml` in Internet Explorer Version 5.5 or above. Figure 19-2 shows the result that you should see.

   `division.xml` invokes the style sheet `xpath1.xsl`, which in turn invokes the XSLT statement `<xsl:value-of select="name"/>`. This statement selects the value of the `<name>` child of the current element, which is `Chicago Cubs`.

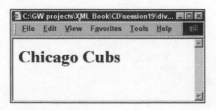

Figure 19-2
Result of applying <xsl:value-of select="name"/> on sample XML data file

2. Edit `division.xml` in a text editor. Change `xpath1.xsl` to `xpath2.xsl`, save `division.xml`, then open `division.xml` in Internet Explorer. The stylesheet `xpath2.xsl` invokes the XSLT statement `<xsl:value-of select="//division_standing/name"/>`. This statement selects the value of the `<name>` child of the `<division_standing>` element, wherever it occurs in the document (`//` is XSLT shorthand for "any descendant of the root element"). This style sheet returns "National League Central".

3. Edit `division.xml` in a text editor. Change `xpath2.xsl` to `xpath3.xsl`, save `division.xml`, then open `division.xml` in Internet Explorer. The style sheet `xpath3.xsl` invokes the XSLT statement `<xsl:value-of select="//team[3]/name"/>`. This statement selects the value of the `<name>` child of the third `<team>` element in the document. This style sheet returns "Pittsburgh Pirates".

4. Edit `division.xml` in a text editor. Change `xpath3.xsl` to `xpath4.xsl`, save `division.xml`, then open `division.xml` in Internet Explorer. The stylesheet `xpath4.xsl` invokes the XSLT statement `<xsl:value-of select="following-sibling::team/record/wins"/>`. This statement selects the value of the `<wins>` child of the `<record>` element child of `<team>` element that follows the context node. This style sheet returns 49.

5. Edit `division.xml` in a text editor. Change `xpath4.xsl` to `xpath5.xsl`, save `division.xml`, then open `division.xml` in Internet Explorer. The stylesheet `xpath5.xsl` invokes the XSLT statement `<xsl:value-of select="preceding-sibling::team/record/wins"/>` (`xpath5.xsl`). This statement selects the value of the `<wins>` child of the `<record>` element child of `<team>` element that precedes the context node. This style sheet returns returns 46. Figure 19-3 shows the result.

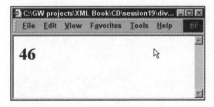

Figure 19-3
Result of applying <xsl:value-of select="preceding-sibling::/record/wins"/>
to sample XML data file

Done!

REVIEW

- You can use style sheets to select specific content from an XML document.
- All location path statements are relative the current context node.
- You can test for the presence or absence of elements and attributes in conditional statements.

QUIZ YOURSELF

1. Name the XSLT statement used to select specific content from an XML source document. (See "Using `<xsl:value-of>` to Select Specific XML Content.")

2. How is the name of an attribute specified in an XSLT expression? (See "Getting attribute values.")

3. Name the XSLT statement used to explicitly choose multiple elements in the source document. (See "Using `<xsl:for-each>` to Iterate over Multiple XML Elements.")

4. Name the two conditional statements provided by XSLT. (See "Conditional XSLT Processing.")

5. What is the XSLT term for the current element that is being processed by the style sheet? (See "Understanding the Context Node.")

Using XSLT and XPath to Fill an HTML Template

Session Checklist

✔ Using XML to fill HTML templates

✔ Embedding HTML templates within XSLT style sheets

✔ Selecting specific content from an XML data file

In this session, we learn how to fill in HTML pages from XML data files. This allows you to maintain a consistent look across multiple HTML pages, and easily update a Web site from XML source files.

30 Min. To Go

Adding XML Content to HTML Pages

You may have noticed that most Web sites have a consistent page design. Navigation and graphic elements are often similar, if not identical, from page to page. These elements tend to appear around each page's body content.

This is no accident. Just as readers expect consistency from page to page in a book or magazine (*Wired* magazine notwithstanding), readers tend to expect the same consistency across pages in a Web site. A Web site with consistent pages and navigation menus is usually easier to navigate, and presents a more pleasing experience overall, than a Web site whose navigation scheme and page layout changes from page to page.

If you have implemented a Web site, you may have already worked with HTML templates. An HTML *template* consists of HTML code that is common for every page. The body content of each page is inserted into the HTML template for publishing to a Web site. A template gives your site a consistent look and makes it easier to maintain.

Working with HTML Templates and XML

You're going to use a slightly different syntax for your style sheets in this session than you have thus far. The W3C XSLT Recommendation enables you to write a style sheet in the form of a *literal result element*. (You included literal result elements in your previous style sheet, but the entire style sheet was not a literal result element.) A literal result element allows you to create an HTML page template and populate content areas in that template with XSLT/XPath statements.

Figure 20-1 shows a simple HTML page for presenting sports standings. Graphic elements that would give this page a more polished appearance are left out; for now, you're concerned about the content of the page.

Figure 20-1
Simple sports standings page

Although the content of this page is fine, you must update the entire page when standings change. In addition, this page isn't flexible — you need to change the page title and header to display standings from another division.

To make your page more adaptable, you're going to maintain your sports standings in an XML file that's updated whenever standings change. You will use an XSLT style sheet to "pull" standings results from the XML file, into an HTML template. You will create the HTML template directly in the XSLT style sheet.

Creating an HTML template and an XML data file

You're going to modify the HTML page that you first saw in Figure 20-1 to serve as a style sheet template. First, you need to figure out which fields in the HTML page to populate from your XML data file. (See Listing 20-1.)

Listing 20-1
HTML Template with Team Standings Information

```
<html>
<head>
<title>Standings for National League Central</title>
</head>
<body>
<h1>National League Central</h1>
<table>
<tbody>
<th>
<tr>
<td>Team</td>
<td>Wins</td>
<td>Losses</td>
<td>Standing</td>
</tr>
</th>
<hr>
<tr>
<td>Pittsburgh Pirates</td>
<td>49</td>
<td>42</td>
<td>1st</td>
</tr>
<tr>
<td>St. Louis Cardinals</td>
<td>46</td>
<td>45</td>
<td>2nd</td>
</tr>
<tr>
```

Continued

Listing 20-1 *Continued*

```
<td>Chicago Cubs</td>
<td>41</td>
<td>50</td>
<td>3rd</td>
</tr>
</tbody>
</table>
</body>
</html>
```

**20 Min.
To Go**

You must examine your XML data file to create the XPath expressions that will extract the XML data from the appropriate fields. Where this data file comes from is inconsequential — you can create it manually, or it can be created automatically from a database. Right now, you're only concerned about the structure of your data file, so that you can write the appropriate XSLT code to extract its content.

Listing 20-2 shows what your well-formed XML data file looks like. You're intentionally not counting on the data file to present your teams in order, sorted by name or standing. You're going to make the style sheet do that for you.

We provide the following XML source file in session20/ `division_standings.xml` **on your book's CD-ROM.**

Listing 20-2
The division_standings.xml XML Document

```
<?xml version="1.0" ?>
<division_standing>
<name>National League Central</name>
<team>
<name>St. Louis Cardinals</name>
<record>
<wins>46</wins>
<losses>45</losses>
</record>
<standing>2nd</standing>
</team>
<team>
```

```
<name>Chicago Cubs</name>
<record>
<wins>41</wins>
<losses>50</losses>
</record>
<standing>3rd</standing>
</team>
<team>
<name>Pittsburgh Pirates</name>
<record>
<wins>49</wins>
<losses>42</losses>
</record>
<standing>1st</standing>
</team>
</division_standing>
```

You're going to extract information from your XML data file based on the structure of your XML document. Take a look at the following fragments from your XML data file to figure out exactly what elements you need to extract:

- The root element, <division_standing>, has a child element called <name>, which contains the name of the division.

- <division_standing> has multiple instances of the child element <team>.

- Each element <team> has a child element <name>. In this context, <name> holds the name of the team.

- Each element team has a child element <record>.

- Each <record> element has child elements <wins> and <losses>. These elements contain — you guessed it! — the number of wins and losses for the team.

- Each element <team> has a child element <standing>, which holds the team's standing within the division.

Creating XPath expressions to extract the appropriate XML information

Your next step is to create the XPath expressions to select the appropriate content from your XML data file. Because you know the order of the XML data, you're going to use `<xsl:value-of/>` statements to select specific content from the XML file to populate the HTML template. To select this specific content, you need to write the proper *location path* statement to serve as the value of your `select` attribute.

To pull the name of the division, you extract the text content of the `<name>` element child of `<division_standing>`:

```
<xsl:value-of select="division_standing/name"/>
```

Team information lives in several `<team>` elements. To iterate over each `<team>` element, you use an `<xsl:for-each>` statement:

```
<xsl:for-each select="division_standing/team">
```

Within the `<xsl:for-each>` statement, the current `<team>` element becomes the context node. Therefore, your XPath expressions within the `<xsl:for-each>` statement are relative to the current `<team>` element.

Because the team name is in the `<name>` element that is a child of `<team>`, you can select it directly:

```
<xsl:value-of select="name"/>
```

Wins and losses are in elements that are a child of `<record>`, which is a child of `<team>`:

```
<xsl:value-of select="record/wins"/>
<xsl:value-of select="record/losses"/>
```

The team standing is in an element called `<standing>`, also a child of `<team>`:

```
<xsl:value-of select="standing"/>
```

Creating the XSLT style sheet

You're going to include these XSLT/XPath statements in your style sheet. This style sheet (in Listing 20-3) is in the form of an HTML page, which you're populating with information from your XML data file via XSLT/XPath statements.

We provide the style sheet in session20/`literal_template.xml` **on your book's CD-ROM.**

Listing 20-3
The XSLT Style Sheet to Populate the HTML Template

```
<html xsl:version="1.0"
      xmlns:xsl="http://www.w3.org/1999/XSL/Transform"
      xmlns="http://www.w3.org/TR/xhtml1/strict">
<head>
<title>Standings for <xsl:value-of
select="division_standing/name"/></title>
</head>
<body>
<h1><xsl:value-of select="division_standing/name"/></h1>
<table>
<tbody>
<th>
<tr>
<td>Team</td>
<td>Wins</td>
<td>Losses</td>
<td>Standing</td>
</tr>
</th>
<hr />
<xsl:for-each select="division_standing/team">
<tr>
<td><xsl:value-of select="name"/></td>
<td><xsl:value-of select="record/wins"/></td>
<td><xsl:value-of select="record/losses"/></td>
<td><xsl:value-of select="standing"/></td>
</tr>
</xsl:for-each>
</tbody>
</table>
</body>
</html>
```

Viewing your results

**10 Min.
To Go**

First, open division_standings.xml in a text editor. Associate the XML data file with the style sheet by adding the following line after your XML declaration (<?xml version="1.0" ?>):

```
<?xml-stylesheet type='text/xsl' href='literal_template.xsl'?>
```

Then open the date file `division_standings.xml` in Internet Explorer 5.5. Figure 20-2 shows what you should see.

> **To run this book's examples in Internet Explorer Version 5.5, you must install the Microsoft XML Processor Upgrade, MSXML3, and Microsoft's xmlinst configuration tool. Links to MSXML3 and xmlinst are provided on the CD that accompanies this book.**

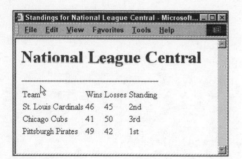

Figure 20-2
Displaying results from an XML data file in an HTML template

Finishing touches: Sorting the results in the template

Something is still wrong with your list — the teams display in the order that they appear in the XML data file. But you really want to order them by standing. You're going to update your XSLT style sheet to extract team information from the XML data file in sorted order.

Within an <xsl:for-each> statement, you can use the <xsl:sort> statement to control the order in which the elements visited by the <xsl:for-each> iteration appear in the result document. The <xsl:sort> command takes a select attribute, which provides the element or attribute upon which the sorting will be based. To modify the `<xsl:for-each>` statement in your previous style sheet, `literal_template.xsl`, add the statement `<xsl:sort select="name"/>` to your `<xsl:for-each>` statement. Your `<xsl:for-each>` statement will then look like the following code:

```
<xsl:for-each select="division_standing/team">
<xsl:sort select="name"/>
<tr>
<td><xsl:value-of select="name"/></td>
<td><xsl:value-of select="record/wins"/></td>
<td><xsl:value-of select="record/losses"/></td>
<td><xsl:value-of select="standing"/></td>
</tr>
</xsl:for-each>
```

Figure 20-3 shows the result of applying this style sheet to the XML data file.

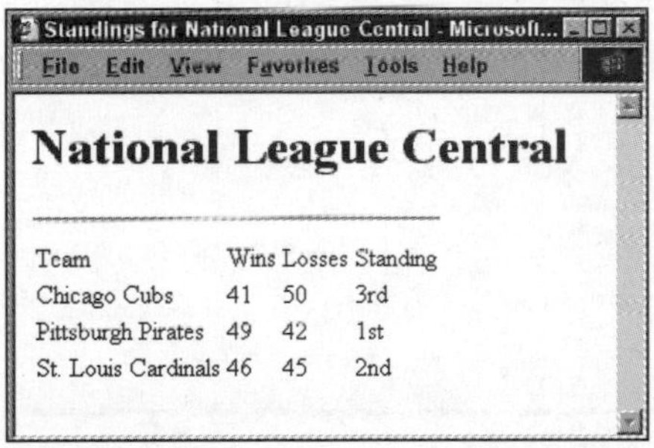

National League Central

Team	Wins	Losses	Standing
Chicago Cubs	41	50	3rd
Pittsburgh Pirates	49	42	1st
St. Louis Cardinals	46	45	2nd

Figure 20-3
Sports standing results sorted by team name with `<xsl:sort>`

You've sorted the results based on the team name. Although this may be useful in some cases, it's not quite what you want here. Change the `<xsl:sort/>` line in `literal_template.xsl` to

```
<xsl:sort select="standing"/>
```

When you reload the page, you should see something like Figure 20-4.

Standings for National League Central - Microsoft...

File   Edit   View   Favorites   Tools   Help

National League Central

Team	Wins	Losses	Standing
Pittsburgh Pirates	49	42	1st
St. Louis Cardinals	46	45	2nd
Chicago Cubs	41	50	3rd

Figure 20-4
Results sorted by standing with <xsl:sort>

That's it! Your XSLT template is complete.

Done!

REVIEW

- You can use XSLT style sheets to create and populate HTML templates.
- You can use the <xsl:for-each> statement to iterate over elements in an XML data file.
- The <xsl:value-of> statement allows you to extract text content from your XML data file.
- <xsl:sort> lets you sort the results.

QUIZ YOURSELF

1. True or False: Using XML style sheets to populate HTML templates maintains consistency across multiple Web pages. (See "Adding XML Content to HTML Pages.")

2. True or False: What is the name of the XSLT style sheet form that allows you to create HTML templates? (See "Working with HTML Templates and XML.")

3. What is the name of the XSLT statement that selects the content of a specific element from an XML data file? (See "Creating XPath expressions to extract the appropriate XML information.")

4. True or False: The `<xsl:sort>` statement sorts results based on the the current element's content. (See "Finishing touches: Sorting the results in the template.")

5. True or False: XSLT templates allow you to easily update your HTML pages when your XML data files change. (See "Working with HTML Templates and XML.")

1. True or False: XSLT style sheets are the same as CSS.

2. Name one way you can match patterns with XSLT.

3. Can an XSLT style sheet be set up to create an HTML page?

4. Does XSLT transformation nest XML tags inside HTML or replace XML tags with HTML tags?

5. Can text from your XML document be excluded by XSLT?

6. True or False: XSLT style sheets are easy to make and not prone to error.

7. True or False: XPath works with XSLT.

8. Can XPath be used to select elements within an XML document?

9. Does XPath allow reference to elements according to their position in the document hierarchy?

10. Is it possible to constrain location path results?

11. What is the context node?

12. Is it necessary to identify a context node?

13. True or False: `<xsl:value-of>` may be used to get attribute values.

14. Does XML allow you to design documents using HTML templates?

15. How do you combine the HTML of a template with your XML document data?

16. Is it possible to sort XML information as it is moved into HTML?

17. True or False: Your HTML document title may be determined by information in your XML document.

18. What XPath expression would you use to extract text from an element?

19. How would the expression of Question 18 be modified to extract text from a child element?

20. Which is the proper form: `<xsl:sort>` or `<xsl-sort>`?

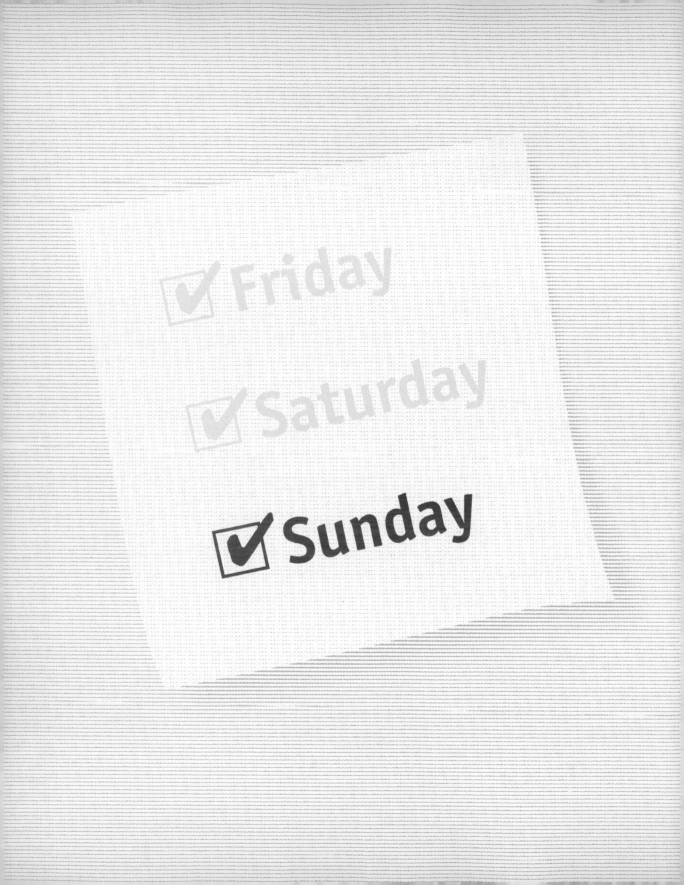
☑ Friday

☑ Saturday

☑ Sunday

Part V — Sunday Morning

Part VI — Sunday Afternoon

PART

V

Sunday Morning

Introduction to Displaying XML Documents

Session Checklist

✔ Applying formats to your XML documents

✔ Reviewing XSLT and XPath for Web publishing

✔ Introducing cascading style sheets (CSS)

✔ Distinguishing between XSLT/XPath and CSS

✔ Using CSS and XSLT together

**30 Min.
To Go**

Because XML is so flexible, you can use it for a variety of information-management applications. Companies and organizations can use XML as a platform-independent format for exchanging business information. XML can provide a simple syntax for software configuration files. Internally, XML can provide a way for different business units to exchange information.

At the end of the day, however, much of the information that exists in XML files exists to be published. You can publish XML files on the Web, in print, to portable wireless devices, or to nonconventional publishing systems, such as a spoken-language interface. Perhaps you have chosen XML as your data format specifically because you plan to publish to several different output devices. XML enables you to maximize the flexibility and value of your publishable data. Using XML, you can publish the right content to the right device.

Reuniting Content and Format

The primary reason that your XML data is so flexible and easy to repurpose is that you've removed *formatting* information from your XML, leaving behind your *content* information. The metadata, or content information, in your XML documents exists in the form of XML elements and attributes within those documents. When you process your XML documents, you use those elements and attributes to understand and manipulate your XML content.

Now you must reunite format with content. You've already spent several sessions looking at XSLT style sheets, which you use to select and sort your XML content, and to transform that content to HTML for Web publishing.

In this session, you're introduced to another formatting mechanism: cascading style sheets (CSS). CSS was originally created as a way to specify the format of HTML elements. But it turned out to be a great way to specify how the contents of XML elements should be rendered in a Web browser.

Alas, both XSLT and CSS are very different beasts — they couldn't be further apart in their operating model, capabilities, and complexity. In this session, we compare and contrast XSLT and CSS and provide enough information so that you will know whether to use XSLT or CSS. We even talk about getting the best of both worlds by combining the two, using each for the things that it does best.

Introduction to CSS

In the beginning, HTML was simple. For headers, you used tags like <h1> and <h2>; for paragraphs, you used <p>. Bold font was <b> and italic was <i>. Your Web browsers figured out how to treat text that was wrapped in each of these tags. One reason that HTML was easy to learn and easy to use was because you let browsers take care of the formatting. HTML was simple, and people across the planet learned how to create HTML documents. The World Wide Web caught on very quickly.

As the Web became more popular, many people wanted to control how their information was rendered in a Web browser. They weren't content knowing that a browser would render an <h1> tag in its largest type size, <h2> a bit smaller, and so on. These people wanted precise control over font face, font size, and font color, even though the simplicity of HTML was based on leaving these aspects up to the browser manufacturers.

Originally, these parameters were set as attributes on HTML tags. If you've looked at much HTML code, you have surely seen code that looks like this:

```
<FONT SIZE="18" FACE="ARIAL, VERDANA, HELVETICA" COLOR="RED">
```

Not only is this code complex to create, but it's complex to read and very difficult to maintain! If you want to change all headers on your site from 18 pt font to 15 pt font, you need to find every single header instance and change the size parameter. Remember that users can provide their own browser settings for rendering fonts. If you specify how a font should be rendered, you're explicitly overriding the wishes of your users, many of whom choose different font settings because of personal preference or visual impairment.

Origin of CSS

CSS provided a way of separating HTML formatting information. By segregating formatting information, CSS brought the following improvements to HTML code:

- HTML again became easier to read, because the inline font information was no longer necessary.
- HTML became easier to maintain. To change format information, you only needed to update a CSS file.

Basic CSS syntax

A CSS style sheet consists of a series of *rules*. Each rule consists of a *selector* and a *declaration*. The declaration is made up of a set of property/value pairs. A single CSS rule has the following syntax:

```
selector {property1: value1; property2: value2;}
```

20 Min. To Go

A simple CSS rule to set the formatting properties for an HTML <h1> element might look like this:

```
h1 {font-size: 18; font-weight: bold; font-color: red;}
```

CSS and XML

If you can use CSS to make an <h1> element big, red, and bold, why can't you use it to make a <parent> element big red and bold? Browsers that support both CSS and XML (including Microsoft Internet Explorer version 5.5) enable you to do just that. The following is what a CSS rule for an XML element might look like:

```
parent {font-size: 18; font-weight: bold; font-color: red;}
```

Comparison of CSS and XSLT/XPath

Before you get too excited about the capabilities of CSS and XML, compare and contrast CSS with XSLT, the style sheet language already discussed. XSLT and CSS have significant differences. These differences will guide you when you figure out which style sheet language to use to display your XML data files.

XSLT/XPath capabilities and limitations

XSLT with XPath allows you to do the following with your XML data:

- Select specific content from XML documents. You often don't want to publish all of a document's content, just as you usually don't want to publish all of a database's content!
- Manipulate or sort content from an XML document
- Combine content from more than one XML document
- Convert an XML document from one vocabulary to another (XML to HTML or XML to Wireless Markup Language)

XSLT also has several limitations:

- XSLT doesn't actually provide a syntax for specifying formatting. XSLT specifies formatting characteristics by converting XML to a markup language, such as HTML, which does specify formatting. No XSLT statement, for example, says make this text 18 point Helvetica bold. XSLT depends on HTML syntax to do this.
- XSLT and its companion language, XPath, are rich languages that present a relatively steep learning curve.
- XSLT requires an XSLT processor, typically run on the server. Few client browsers have XSLT support built-in.

CSS capabilities and limitations

CSS has a single major strength:

- CSS can directly and simply specify the formatting characteristics of HTML or XML elements.

CSS also has its limitations:

- CSS cannot manipulate an XML document in any way (except possibly for suppressing content). CSS cannot select, sort, or manipulate XML content. The XML document is either displayed in its entirety, or not at all.

- CSS depends on browser support, and support for CSS varies widely among browsers.
- CSS cannot specify formatting based on attribute values.

**10 Min.
To Go**

Combining CSS and XSLT

XSLT is a feature-rich programming language that's useful for translating XML documents to other vocabularies, such as HTML, for display. Cascading style sheets (CSS) offer a relatively simple syntax for attaching formatting attributes to particular HTML or XML elements. Why not use the best of both worlds? You can use XSLT to select and manipulate your XML content; then use CSS to specify how the result document should be formatted. You're going to resurrect your genealogy example to see how it's done.

First, you're going to create a simple CSS . You will create two CSS classes: one labeled `male`, the other labeled `female`. You will assign a bold font-weight to the `male` class and an italic font-weight to the `female` class. Your CSS, called `genealogy.css`, looks like this:

```
.male       {font-weight:bold; }
.female     {font-style:italic;  }
```

Now create an XSLT style sheet to extract the appropriate information from your `genealogy.xml` data file. Here's the twist: When you extract `<child>` elements, you're going to place the contents of the `<child>` element in a table row of class `male` or `female`, based on the value of the `<child>`'s gender attribute. You use the `<xsl:choose>` statement to test the gender attribute and create the appropriate element in the result document.

```
<xsl:stylesheet version="1.0"
                xmlns:xsl="http://www.w3.org/1999/XSL/Transform">
<xsl:template match="/">
<html>
<head>
<title>Genealogy of the <xsl:value-of select="//father/surname" />
family</title>
<link rel="stylesheet" href="genealogy.css" type="text/css"/>
</head>
<body>
<table width="100%">
<tbody><tr bgcolor="silver">
```

```
        <td width="33%"><B>Male or Female</B></td>
        <td width="33%"><B>Surname</B></td>
        <td width="33%"><B>Birthplace</B></td></tr>
          <xsl:for-each select="//child">
    <xsl:choose>
    <xsl:when test="@gender='male'">
          <tr class="male">
          <td><xsl:apply-templates select="@gender"/></td>
          <td><xsl:apply-templates select="./surname"/></td>
          <td><xsl:apply-templates select="./birthplace"/></td>
          </tr>
    </xsl:when>
    <xsl:otherwise>
          <tr class="female">
          <td><xsl:apply-templates select="@gender"/></td>
          <td><xsl:apply-templates select="./surname"/></td>
          <td><xsl:apply-templates select="./birthplace"/></td>
          </tr>
    </xsl:otherwise>
    </xsl:choose>
          </xsl:for-each>
    </tbody>
    </table>
    </body>
    </html>
    </xsl:template>
    </xsl:stylesheet>
```

Figure 21-1 shows the results. Note that male children are rendered in bold, and female children are rendered in italics.

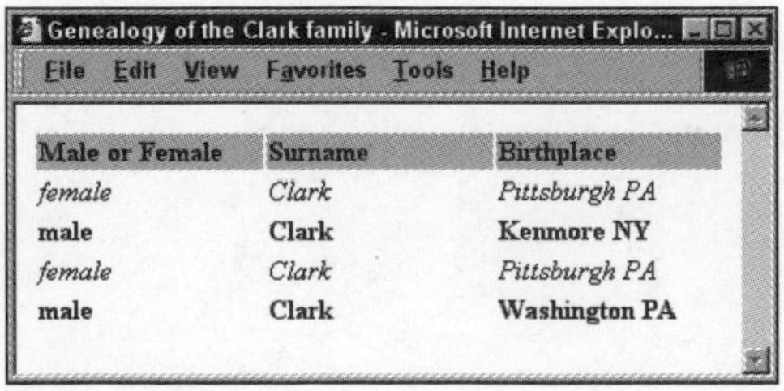

Figure 21-1
Result of combining CSS and XSLT style sheets for displaying XML data

Combining CSS and XSLT has several advantages: You keep your complex XSLT style sheets as simple as possible. Formatting information remains embedded in the simple cascading style sheet. It simplifies maintenance — you're probably more likely to adjust formatting than to adjust style sheet logic. To adjust formatting, you only to need modify the simpler CSS file, not the more complex XSLT file.

In this session, we introduced cascading style sheets, which provide a relatively simple mechanism for formatting XML documents, albeit without the transformation capabilities of XSLT. In upcoming sessions, we take a closer look at CSS syntax, and further investigate how you can use both style sheet languages when you publish your XML documents.

Done!

REVIEW

- CSS was originally conceived as a language for simplifying HTML format overrides.
- CSS provides a syntax for specifying the format of HTML and XML elements.
- CSS is much simpler than XSLT, but it doesn't provide the same capabilities.
- You can use CSS and XSLT together.

QUIZ YOURSELF

1. Name a disadvantage of hard-coded HTML format information (See "Introduction to CSS.")
2. What's the name of the first field in a CSS rule? (See "Basic CSS syntax.")
3. What are the two components of a CSS declaration? (See "Basic CSS syntax.")
4. True or False: CSS is supported equally across all major browsers (See "CSS capabilities and limitations.")
5. True or False: CSS can be used to select and manipulate XML content? (See "Comparison of CSS and XSLT/XPath.")

22

Formatting XML Documents with Cascading Style Sheets

Session Checklist

✔ Learning the syntax and common properties of cascading style sheet (CSS) rules

✔ Understanding CSS conflict resolution

✔ Associating a CSS file with an XML document

**30 Min.
To Go**

Session 21 introduced cascading style sheets (CSS), which is one of two ways to format XML documents for display in a Web browser. The other way, XML Transformation Language (XSLT), enables you to convert your XML documents to HTML.

In this session, you're going to take a more in-depth look at the rules and syntax of CSS, so that you can better understand its capabilities and use it to display your XML documents.

This session does not cover all of CSS. We concentrate on the most useful CSS properties, and limit our coverage to CSS properties supported by Internet Explorer Version 5.5 for XML documents.

Note

Understanding Why XML Needs CSS

Why do you need CSS to display an XML file in a browser? Why can't you open an XML file, just like you do an HTML file, and have it display correctly?

The answer is simple. HTML is a *vocabulary* — a fixed set of tags that comprise a language for displaying Web pages. Because there is a fixed set of HTML tags, browsers have built-in rules for displaying each HTML element. A browser knows to render the contents of a <p> tag as a normal paragraph, to make the text within an <h1> tag bold and larger than the surrounding text, that an <img> tag contains an image, and that an <a> tag contains a link.

XML, however, is not a vocabulary, but rather a *syntax* for creating vocabularies. It's impossible to have XML formatting rules built into browsers, because a browser manufacturer couldn't know what XML elements the browser might display, let alone how each element should be displayed.

You may have heard of XHMTL, which is a version of HTML specified using XML syntax. Because XHTML is a fixed vocabulary like HTML, it can be rendered in a browser with no additional style sheet mechanism. You can learn more about XHTML in Session 26.

When displaying XML in a browser, you have two choices for formatting the XML document:

- Convert the XML to HTML via the XSLT language
- Use CSS to specify how each XML element should be rendered by the browser

You already know about the XSLT language. Now let's focus on CSS.

CSS Syntax

Session 21 introduced the CSS syntax. A CSS style sheet consists of a series of *rules*. Each rule specifies the formatting for an XML element or a set of elements. CSS rules apply to an element and all of that element's descendants.

Each rule consists of a *selector* and a *declaration*. The selector specifies the element or elements to which the rule applies. The declaration consists of a formatting *property* and a *value*, separated by a colon.

A rule can set several formatting properties, separated by semicolons. A single CSS rule, then, has this form:

```
selector {property1: value1; property2: value2;}
```

Two simple CSS rules to set the formatting properties for XML elements called `<price>` and `<warning>` might look like this:

```
price {display: inline; font-size: 18; font-weight: bold;
font-color: black;}
warning {display: block; font-size: 24; font-weight: bold;
font-color: red}
```

Setting the display Property

The `display` property is one of the most basic, and most important, properties for displaying XML documents in a Web browser. If you're familiar with HTML, you know that some elements — `<p>`, `<h1>`, and `<h2>`, for example — appear set off from the rest of the text. Elements that create their own text block, and are set apart from other elements by white space, are called *block elements*.

Other elements — `<em>`, `<b>`, and `<a>`, for example — appear within a block of text. Elements that share the text block of the parent element are called *inline elements*.

You can specify whether an XML element appears as a block or an inline element with the CSS `display` property.

```
element {display: inline;}
element {display: block;}
```

You may, for example, have an XML element called `<partNumber>`, which labels part numbers that occur in inline text. You could then define a CSS rule for `<partNumber>` as follows:

```
partNumber {display: inline; }
```

The following CSS rule would cause your browser to render `<partNumber>` in its own text block:

```
partNumber {display: block; }
```

Another useful `display` property is `display: none`, which allows you to suppress the display of particular elements.

Setting the `display` property is particularly important when using CSS to render XML elements. Your browser has no built-in knowledge of whether the contents of each XML tag should be displayed as a block or inline element. Explicitly setting the `display` property for each XML element is safest.

**20 Min.
To Go**

Controlling Text Properties

CSS text properties set properties of the font used to render each element. Text properties enable you to specify the family, size, style, weight, and color of the font used to display a particular element. Table 22-1 outlines CSS text properties.

Table 22-1
CSS Text Properties

CSS Text Property	Example Values
font-family	Arial, Verdana, Times, serif, sans-serif
font-size	12px; 150%, small, medium, large
font-style	italic, oblique, normal
font-weight	bold, normal
font-color	Red, FFCC33, Black

Controlling Text Block Formatting

CSS text block properties (see Table 22-2) set properties of the text blocks in which block (and, of course, any child inline) elements are displayed. Text blocks in CSS mimic the properties of text blocks, such as width, height, margin, and alignment, on the printed page.

Table 22-2
CSS Text Block Properties

CSS Text Block Property	Example Values
width	70%, 100em, auto
height	100em, auto
margin-top, margin-right, margin-bottom, margin-left	10%, 10em, auto
text-align	left, right, center, justify
text-indent	10%, 3em

Other CSS Tricks

Want to change your cursor when you hover over an element? The following CSS rule sets your cursor to a crosshair:

```
element {cursor: crosshair}
```

This sets your cursor to a pointer:

```
element {cursor: pointer;}
```

Setting your cursor to a pointer is a useful trick when creating active XML documents — documents in which clicking an XML element activates a script and causes a change to the page. The cursor change provides a clue to the user that clicking the element will make something happen. You will use this trick when you find out about scripting XML documents in Session 25.

Using Context-Based Styles

XML provides an explicit hierarchical structure. All content is nested beneath the root element. Within XML content exist other nested elements, which frequently demonstrate implicit relationships. In your example document, for example, the <name> element nested within <team> holds the name of the team; the <name> element nested within <division_standing> holds the name of the division.

```
<division_standing>
  <name>National League Central</name>
  <team>
      <name>St. Louis Cardinals</name>
  </team>
</division_standing>
```

You may want to format element content based on its nesting relationship. If you want to format the contents of the <name> element, child of <division_standing>, differently than the contents of <name>, child of <team>, CSS provides contextual selectors for that purpose.

Child context

The greater-than symbol (>) in a CSS rule specifies a direct child relationship. The following rule, for example, will render the contents of an element <name> — child of <team> — in 24 point bold type:

```
team > name {font-size: 24; font-weight: bold;}
```

The code renders St. Louis Cardinals in 24 point bold type.

Ancestor context

If you omit the greater-than symbol from a multilevel rule, the rule specifies a descendant relationship. The following rule, for example, will render the contents of any element <name> that is a descendant of <team> (regardless of the number of levels below <team>) in 12 point italic type:

```
team name {font-size: 12; font-style: italic;}
```

The code renders St. Louis Cardinals in 12 point italic type.

Cascading Rules and Conflict Resolution

By now, you may have figured out that it's easy to create multiple rules that can apply to any given element. Consider the following important facets of CSS: cascading rules and conflict resolution.

When more than one rule applies to an element, all unique formatting property/value pairs are applied to the element. It's as though the style sheet combines all property/value pairs that apply to an element into one big CSS rule.

When more than one property/value pair applies to an element, the pair associated with the *most specific* rule wins.

The following CSS statement says "render the content of any <name> element that is a descendent of <division_standing> in 24 point bold serif font."

```
division_standing name { display: block; font-family: serif;
font-size: 24px; font-weight: bold;}
```

But wait — you also have a <name> element within each <team> element. To create a rule for <team> in this context, you would type the following:

```
team name { font-family: sans-serif; font-size: 36px; font-style:
italic;}
```

Both rules are descendent rules — they apply to <name> elements that are descendents of <division_standing> (per the first rule) and <team> (per the second rule). So what property/value pairs would apply to a <name> element child of <team>? Here's the logic:

1. Only the first rule contains a display property. Because both rules match the element, and only one rule specifies a display property, the display: block property/value pair is applied.

2. Both rules contain a font-family property. Because <name> is a direct child of <team>, but only a descendant of <division_standing>, team name is the more specific rule. Therefore, the property/value pair font-family: sans-serif applies.

3. Both rules contain a font-size property. For the same reason as in Step 2, font-size: 36 px applies.

4. Only the first rule contains a font-weight property. Because both rules match the element, and only one rule specifies a font-weight property, the font-weight: bold property/value pair applies.

5. Only the second rule contains a font-style property. Because both rules match the element, and only one rule specifies a font-style property, the font-style:italic property/value pair applies.

The end result is that the following "virtual" rule is applied to a <name> element that is a child of <team>:

```
name { display: block; font-family: sans-serif; font-size: 36px;
font-weight: bold; font-style: italic;}
```

The following example documents are provided in the folder examples/ch22, files `conflict.xml` **and** `conflict.css`**.**

Test your CSS conflict resolution rules on the following short XML document:

```
<?xml version="1.0" ?>
<?xml-stylesheet type='text/css' href='conflict.css'?>
<division_standing>
<name>National League Central</name>
<team>
<name>St. Louis Cardinals</name>
</team>
</division_standing>
```

Figure 22-1 shows the result. As expected, the <name> child of <team> is rendered in a block display, in bold italic font, in a sans-serif face, at a size of approximately 36 points.

Figure 22-1
Demonstration of CSS rules for conflict resolution

Associating CSS with Your XML Document

**10 Min.
To Go**

All that's left is to tell your browser which cascading style sheet to use to render your XML document. To associate CSS with your XML document, use the `xml-stylesheet` processing instruction. Be sure to set the `type` attribute to `text/css` — this will be the proper setting for all your CSS processing instructions. The `href` attribute specifies the file location or URL of your CSS file.

```
<?xml-stylesheet type='text/css' href='division_standings.css'?>
```

Reviewing What CSS Does Not Provide

CSS does not solve all problems when formatting XML documents. The following are several limitations of CSS:

- CSS does not support manipulating, sorting, selecting, or reordering elements. (XSLT is needed to do this.) You can only suppress XML elements from being displayed.

- CSS suffers from uneven implementation support. Internet Explorer version 5.5, for example, does not support CSS tables, generated text, or lists. The rendering of a document with a particular CSS file is highly dependent on the choice of browser or other rendering application.

- CSS does not provide any programming capability. Conditional execution, computational capabilities, and variables don't apply.

- CSS does not support the display of attribute values.

- Although the CSS specification provides for rules based on the presence and/or value of named attributes, currently available browsers (at the time of this writing) support this unevenly, if at all. You cannot reliably render an element based on the presence or value of an attribute on that element.

- Although the CSS specification provides for generated text, currently available browsers (at the time of this writing) support this unevenly, if at all. Constructs like automatically numbered lists and text prefixes are not available. This means that your XML file must include things such as list item numbers, which are generally not present in pure data files.

Reviewing What CSS Does Provide

With these limitations, why use CSS at all? Well, CSS provides a relatively simple way to render your XML content in a manner consistent with what you've experienced in real-world Web publishing. For certain types of XML documents, in which the document contains all that you need to see in the Web browser (no numbered lists, no text prefixes), it may be reasonable to render the document via a CSS style sheet.

The most powerful solution for rendering XML documents in a Web browser is to use CSS in combination with XSLT. XSLT provides the initial transformation to HTML. This transformation can rely on any and all of XSLT's rich capabilities for selecting and manipulating XML content. The final rendering, then, is specified by a CSS file. This solution has the advantage of segregating tasks — the XML document processing is handled by the XSLT file; while formatting of the final output is specified in a CSS file. We cover this solution in more detail in Session 24.

Done!

REVIEW

- A cascading style sheet consists of one or more rules. Each rule includes a selector and one or more property/value pairs.
- Property/value pairs specify formatting properties, with values for each property.
- In the event that more than one rule applies to a particular element, CSS uses built-in conflict resolution rules to determine the formatting of that element.
- CSS has many limitations with respect to displaying XML, but can be a reasonable solution in some cases for rendering XML documents.

QUIZ YOURSELF

1. What CSS property would you use to specify a bold font? (See "Controlling Text Properties.")
2. Why is the CSS display property so important when rendering XML documents? (See "Controlling Text Block Formatting.")
3. How does one specify a CSS rule for a direct child descendent of an element (See "Using Context-Based Styles.")
4. True or False: When multiple CSS rules match an element, the more general rule applies. (See "Cascading Rules and Conflict Resolution.")
5. True or False: CSS suffers from uneven implementation (browser) support. (See "Reviewing What CSS Does Not Provide.")

Building Web Sites with XSLT — Part I

Session Checklist

✔ Learning about server-side XML processing

✔ Learning about SAXON

✔ Understanding XSLT extension functions

✔ Building multiple HTML files from a single XML source file

**30 Min.
To Go**

In previous sessions, you used XSLT, the XML transformation language, to transform XML documents to HTML for viewing in a Web browser. Because Microsoft Internet Explorer version 5.0 and higher has this capability built-in, it has served as a convenience platform for our exercises. As you worked through the exercises, however, you may have felt that you weren't doing things that you would do in the real world.

If you're running a Web site, it's unlikely that all your viewers are running Microsoft Internet Explorer version 5.0 or better. Only in the most closed corporate environments can the users' browser configuration be controlled and depended upon.

It's going to take time before all Web browsers support the XSLT language for transforming XML documents to HTML. You can expect even longer delays before all the older browsers fall out of use. In the meantime, most processing and transformation of XML must occur on the Web server, not at the client browser. This ensures that the Web server can provide good, old HTML source files to its client browsers — HTML source files that any current or future Web browser can process.

Strategies for Server-Side XML Processing

You can use several strategies to create HTML from XML on the Web server. Two of the most popular are the following:

- Transforming XML to create HTML when a client requests a Web page. This is the dynamic processing model and is similar to other popular methods, such as Java Server Pages (JSP) and Active Server Pages (ASP), for creating Web content on the fly.

- Transforming XML to create HTML in a batch process. In this method, static HTML files live on the Web server and are created from XML source files. The XML source files are transformed to HTML source files in a single process, which can be run late at night when server load is low.

Although the first method is probably more popular for today's highly customized Web sites, the second method is easier to demonstrate and understand. You're going to work directly with the second method in this session.

 If you are a Web site administrator, see your Web server's documentation for details about its XML support.

One-to-Many Processing

In this session, you're going to work with an expanded version of the division standings file that you used in previous sessions. Instead of containing information about only a single division, the source file for this session includes standings information for all divisions in both leagues.

Rather than converting this XML document to a single HTML document, you're going to use XSLT to create a single HTML page for each division. You're also going to use XSLT to create a table of contents with links to each of the division standings pages. This will demonstrate the ability to actually create a Web site from XML source documents — even a single XML document!

The ability to create multiple output documents from a single XML source file is not part of the XSLT 1.0 Recommendation. But the XML user community considers this feature so important (and so useful) that virtually all XSLT processors provide this capability. This feature is expected to become part of the next version of XSLT when XSLT 2.0 is finalized. For updated information, visit http://www.w3.org/TR/xslt.

Using the SAXON XSLT Processor

SAXON is an XSLT processor that was written by Michael Kay and freely distributed. SAXON is available as both a Java application and Windows executable file. In this exercise, you will use the Windows executable file on a DOS command line.

Thus far, you have used Microsoft's MSXML parser within your browser to run your example transformations. We chose MSXML primarily because of its tight browser integration. If you open an XML file in Internet Explorer version 5.0 or higher, and the XML file has an associated XSLT style sheet, the browser will apply the XSLT transformation to the XML file automatically and display the result.

You're switching to the SAXON XSLT processor in this session for the following reasons:

- To demonstrate that many XSLT parsers exist
- To demonstrate XML transformation to XSLT on the command line
- To demonstrate writing multiple output files from a single XML source file

SAXON supports this last functionality, while the version of MSXML available at the time of this writing does not.

Instant Saxon is available on the book's CD-ROM, in the file instant-saxon.zip, **or at** http://users.iclway.co.uk/mhkay/saxon/.

Preparing for this exercise

The following steps will help you prepare to run the exercise in this session and the following session. Create a folder for this session's exercise on your system's hard drive and call it something like c:\wcc\session23. After choosing a folder location, follow these steps:

20 Min. To Go

1. Locate the file `instant-saxon.zip` on the book's CD-ROM, or download it from the SAXON Web site.

2. Unzip the zip archive into your just-created exercise folder. You should see the file `saxon.exe` in your exercise folder. That's the saxon executable.

To test Instant Saxon, follow these steps:

1. Create a DOS command window. If you're unfamiliar with this procedure, choose Start ➪ Run and type **Command**.

2. In the DOS command window, change your working folder to the exercise folder. (For example, `cd c:\ wcc\session23`.)

3. Ensure that SAXON is installed correctly by typing **saxon -?** at your DOS prompt. If SAXON is installed correctly, you should see something like the following result:

```
SAXON 5.3.1 from Michael Kay of ICL

Version 5.3.1

Usage: saxon [options] source-doc style-doc {param=value}...

Options:

  -a            Use xml-stylesheet PI, not style-doc argument

  -o filename   Send output to named file or directory

  -t            Display version and timing information

  -u            Names are URLs not filenames

  -x classname  Use specified SAX parser for source file

  -y classname  Use specified SAX parser for stylesheet

  -?            Display this message
```

Be sure to copy the files from the CD-ROM to your hard drive before you attempt the exercises in this and the following session. If you do not copy the files to your hard drive, SAXON will fail because it will try to write its result files to the book's CD-ROM, which is read-only.

Writing multiple result files from SAXON

The XSLT Recommendation permits designers of XSLT processors to include extension functions in those processors. These extension functions offer capabilities that are not part of the XSLT Recommendation, but may be useful to users of the particular XSLT processor.

To distinguish extension functions from standard XSLT statements in XSLT files, extension functions are prefixed by the namespace identifier for the XSLT processor that provides the extension function.

Does that sound complicated? It's not, really — it just means two things. First, the <xsl:stylesheet> root element of the style sheet includes an xmlns: parameter that defines the namespace of the XSLT processor. Second, the <xsl:stylesheet> element should also include an attribute extension-element-prefixes, set to a space-separated list of namespace prefixes for extension functions used in this style sheet. In this example, only saxon is used as an extension element prefix.

Remember that your XSLT processor expects a namespace identifier in your <xsl:stylesheet> element for the version of XSLT to which your style sheet conforms. The attribute xmlns:xsl="http://www.w3.org/1999/XSL/Transform" conforms to the XSLT processor that the style sheet is written to by using the XSLT version 1.0 Recommendation version of the language (unlike some XSLT processors, which support an older working draft version of the XSLT language). The following code is the start tag of your <xsl:stylesheet> element. This start tag includes namespace identifiers for both XSLT and SAXON:

```
<xsl:stylesheet version="1.0"
                xmlns:xsl="http://www.w3.org/1999/XSL/Transform"
                xmlns:saxon="http://icl.com/saxon"
                extension-element-prefixes="saxon">
```

Virtually all XSLT parsers provide some mechanism for writing multiple output files from a single XML source document. SAXON provides this capability through the <saxon:output> XSLT element. <saxon:output> takes two parameters: method and file. Legal values for the method parameter are text, xml, or html. Because you're writing an HMTL output file, set the method parameter to html.

The value of method **is not significant. Setting** method **to** html **will adjust some aspects of the output to conform better to the HTML specification.**
, <hr>, **and** <img> **tags, for example, will be written as empty elements, instead of as begin-tag/end-tag pairs.**

The second parameter, file, specifies the name and location of the output file to be written. The value of file can be a relative pathname, a full pathname, or a URL.

The following XSLT extension function will write its result as HTML to the file TOC.htm:

```
<saxon:output method="html" file="TOC.htm">
[code to generate results in file TOC.htm]
</saxon:output>
```

XSLT extension functions, like any other XSLT statements, are in the form of XML elements. As XML elements, XSLT extension functions must not break the well-formedness of the style sheet (which is itself an XML document). Specifically, XSLT extension functions must be properly nested within the style sheet.

An extension function applies to all other XSLT statements in the body of the extension function. The <saxon:output> extension function, for example, will write any results generated by its child elements to the specified output file. Consider the following XSLT fragment (assume that this is part of a full XSLT style sheet):

```
<saxon:output method="html" file="output.htm">
<xsl:text>Welcome to XML!</xsl:text>
</saxon:output>
```

This fragment will write the string Welcome to XML! to the file output.htm.

All legal XSLT statements and functions are also legal within an XSLT extension function. The contents of the <saxon:output> element may be trivial, as shown in the preceding example, or may encompass all of a single style sheet's transformation results.

Preparing your XML source document

The XML source document for this exercise is significantly longer than those you've worked with in earlier sessions. You don't see the entire source file here, but you can view a copy of it on your book's CD-ROM. Take a look at the structure of the source file, standings.xml, in Listing 23-1.

Listing 23-1
Fragment of example XML source file containing division standings

```
<?xml version="1.0" ?>

<division_standings>

  <league name="National">
    <division name="East">
```

```
  <team>
    <name>Philadelphia</name>
    <record>
      <wins>30</wins>
      <losses>18</losses>
    </record>
  </team>
  <team>
    <name>Atlanta</name>
    <record>
      <wins>24</wins>
      <losses>25</losses>
    </record>
  </team>
  <team>
    <name>Florida</name>
    <record>
      <wins>22</wins>
      <losses>26</losses>
    </record>
  </team>
  <team>
    <name>New York</name>
    <record>
      <wins>22</wins>
      <losses>28</losses>
    </record>
  </team>
  <team>
    <name>Montreal</name>
    <record>
      <wins>20</wins>
      <losses>30</losses>
    </record>
  </team>
</division>
<division name="Central">
...
</division>
```

Continued

Listing 23-1 *Continued*

```
</league>
<league name="American">
...
</league>
</division_standings>
```

The sample XML source document and XSLT style sheet are available in folder session23 on your CD-ROM.

**10 Min.
To Go**

Preparing your XSLT style sheet

For now, you're simply going to create a table of contents for your set of sports standings; one for each division. You won't generate the actual sports standings HTML pages until the next session. You're also going to work on a cascading style sheet (CSS) in the next session to render the output more professionally.

The style sheet in Listing 23-2 is fairly straightforward. Your root template sets up the HTML page header and then iterates through the `<league>` and `<division>` elements in your XML source file with `<xsl:for-each>`. Within the innermost `<xsl:for-each>` loop, you create an HTML anchor element (`<a>`) that will provide a link to an individual division standings page.

A couple of things are worth noting here:

- The `<saxon:output>` statement is an immediate child of the root template (`<xsl:template match="/">`). All results generated by the root template will be written to the file `TOC.html`.

- Setting the value for the `href` attribute, which specifies the target of your HTML link, is a bit tricky. You can't use `<xsl:value-of>` here, because angle brackets are illegal within XML attribute values. Instead, you use the `<xsl:attribute name="href">` element as a child of `<a>` to set the attribute value.

The style sheet in Listing 23-2 is available on the book's CD-ROM as session23/`standings_toc.xsl`**.**

Listing 23-2
XSLT style sheet for creating an HTML TOC from your XML source file

---

```
<xsl:stylesheet version="1.0"
                xmlns:xsl="http://www.w3.org/1999/XSL/Transform"
                xmlns:saxon="http://icl.com/saxon"
                extension-element-prefixes="saxon">

<xsl:template match="/">
<saxon:output method="html" file="TOC.htm">
  <html>
    <head>
      <title>Major League Standings by Division</title>
    </head>
    <body>

<xsl:for-each select="standings/league">
<xsl:for-each select="division">
<p>
<a>
<xsl:attribute name="href"><xsl:value-of select="../@name"/>
League <xsl:value-of select="@name"/>.html</xsl:attribute>
<xsl:value-of select="../@name"/> League <xsl:value-of
select="@name"/>
</a>
</p>
</xsl:for-each>
</xsl:for-each>

</body>
</html>
</saxon:output>
</xsl:template>

</xsl:stylesheet>
```

Performing the transformation

You're now going to run SAXON to perform the XSLT transformation. To do so, use the same DOS prompt in the same folder that you used for the earlier section, "Preparing for this exercise."

The SAXON command line will look like this:

```
saxon standings.xml standings_toc.xsl
```

After you run SAXON, you should have a newly written file called TOC.html in your exercises folder. If you open TOC.html in your Web browser, it should look something like Figure 23-1.

Figure 23-1
Output of XSLT style sheet to create Web site TOC

TOC.html is currently just a list of links. Because you haven't yet generated all the files for your Web site, you will get an error if you click any of these links. You will create the target files for these links, from the same XML source file, in the next session.

Done!

REVIEW

- You can transform XML to HTML on the fly (at the client browsers' requests) to build Web pages, or you can transform XML to HTML in a regular batch process.

- Until most deployed browsers support XML, HTML (or possibly XHTML) will continue to be the standard markup language for rendering Web pages on the browser. To provide HTML to Web browsers, most XML is transformed to HTML on the Web server.

- An extension function allows an XSLT processor to provide capabilities not specifically included in the XSLT Recommendation.

QUIZ YOURSELF

1. True or False: The following example uses the correct namespace prefix for an extension function: `<xsl-extension-function:output>`. (See "Writing multiple result files from SAXON.")

2. True or False: You can add extension functions to an XSLT style sheet without regard to whether the style sheet is well-formed. (See "Writing multiple result files from SAXON.")

3. True or False: The XSLT Recommendation, Version 1.0, provides the capability for creating multiple output files from a single XML file and XSLT style sheet. (See "One-to-Many Processing.")

4. True or False: One `<saxon:output>` statement is required for each line of the transformation result that you wish to direct to a different file. (See "Writing multiple result files from SAXON.")

5. True or False: Angle brackets (< and >) are not legal within XML attribute values. (See "Preparing your XSLT style sheet.")

Building Web Sites with XSLT — Part II

Session Checklist

✔ Building a small Web site from a single XML source document

✔ Learning about XSLT variables and functions

✔ Learning to use CSS classes to make your transformed XML easy to style

30 Min. To Go

In Session 23, you looked at several strategies for creating XML-based Web sites. You worked with SAXON, an XSLT processor, which could generate multiple result files from a single XML source document. You also created a table of contents document from an XML data file.

In this session, you're going to extend the XSLT style sheet you started in Session 23. From the same XML source document that you worked with in that session, you're going to generate several result documents that will form a small Web site. You're going to exercise several of XSLT's more powerful transformation and computational capabilities.

Creating the Scenario

You're a Web master for a sports information portal, and have been tasked with the job of generating standings pages for professional baseball. Your requirements for this task are as follows:

- Each day, you are to receive a single XML source file, organized by league and division, which contains each team and their respective win/loss records.

- You must generate a single HTML result file for each division in each league. Professional baseball has two leagues with three divisions each, for a total of six files. Each file will contain a table of teams in that division, sorted by standing.

- You must generate a single HTML table of contents file that includes links to each of the six HTML result files.

- The look and feel of the result files will be specified through a cascading style sheet. Anything that you can do to make this easier is a plus.

You completed the table of contents component in Session 23. You must now proceed to generating your six standings files. Based on the requirements, each of the six standings files should look something like Figure 24-1.

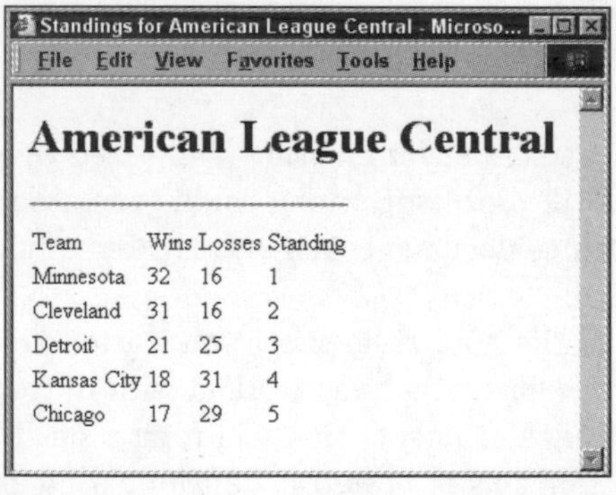

Figure 24-1
Sample league standing result document

Building the XML Source Document

Your source document is similar to the one you used in the last session, with one important difference. This time, the teams are not sorted by standing. Again, you can view the entire source document on this book's CD-ROM. Look at the structure of the source file, standings.xml, in Listing 24-1.

Listing 24-1
Fragment of example XML source file containing division standings

```xml
<?xml version="1.0" ?>
<standings>

  <league name="National">
    <division name="East">
    <team>
      <name>Atlanta</name>
      <record>
        <wins>24</wins>
        <losses>25</losses>
      </record>
    </team>
    <team>
      <name>Montreal</name>
      <record>
        <wins>20</wins>
        <losses>30</losses>
      </record>
    </team>
    <team>
      <name>Florida</name>
      <record>
        <wins>22</wins>
        <losses>26</losses>
      </record>
    </team>
    <team>
      <name>Philadelphia</name>
```

Continued

Listing 24-1 *Continued*

```
      <record>
        <wins>30</wins>
        <losses>18</losses>
      </record>
    </team>
    <team>
      <name>New York</name>
      <record>
        <wins>22</wins>
        <losses>28</losses>
      </record>
    </team>

    </division>
<division name="Central">
...
</division>
</league>
<league name="American">
...
</league>
</division_standings>
```

The sample XML source document and XSLT style sheet are available in folder session24 on the CD-ROM.

If you carefully compare your XML source document and your result document, you notice several things that you're going to have to take care of in your XSLT script:

- There are no explicit filenames in your XML data file, so you must generate the filename for each result file.

- You must generate the title of each HTML page (which appears in the top title bar).

- You must generate the heading of the page (which is the same as the generated title).

- You must sort the teams by number of wins.
- You must generate the value for the standings column (1, 2, 3, and so on).

**20 Min.
To Go**

Creating the XSLT File

Now you're going to create your XSLT file. By doing do so, you're going to learn about several XSLT capabilities, which you can directly apply to solving this problem.

Acquiring attribute values

You probably want to name the result files after each league name/division name combination (for example: `NationalEast.htm`). This ensures that each result file gets a unique name that describes the file's contents (which is always a bonus when you're trying to maintain a Web site). You also need the league and division names for the result file titles and headers.

If you examine your source file, you see that the league and division names are attributes on the elements `<league>` and `<division>`, respectively, as shown in the following code:

```
<league name="National">
  <division name="East">
```

You can use the XSLT longhand `attribute::name` to specify the name attribute on each of these elements or, perhaps better yet, the shorthand form, `@name`. You will use this syntax in `<xsl:value-of>` statements to acquire the values of these attributes when you build your filenames, titles, and page headers.

Because you need to acquire these values and reuse them several times (for the filename, title, and header), you're going to populate two XSLT variables. You do this by creating an `<xsl:variable>` element in your style sheet body and providing a name via the `name` attribute. The value of the variable is the contents of the `<xsl:variable>` element, in this case, the value of the name attribute for either the league or the division. Assuming that your context node is the current `<division>`, the following statements will do the trick:

```
<xsl:variable name="division_name">
  <xsl:value-of select="@name"/>
</xsl:variable>
```

```
<xsl:variable name="league_name">
  <xsl:value-of select="../@name"/>
</xsl:variable>
```

The string @name references the attribute named name on the current element. The string ../@name references the attribute named name on the current element's parent element. You use <xsl:value-of> to get the value of these attributes to populate the two variables that you create.

Building the result filename

Assuming that you've set the variables $league_name and $division_name, you must still build the result filename. You want the name to be in the form LeagueDivision.htm (AmericanEast.htm, NationalCentral.htm, for example). To build the filename, you must concatenate three strings: the league name, the division name, and the .htm suffix.

Fortunately, XSLT provides a function to do so. As in Session 23, you're using the <saxon:output> element to specify a result filename. Here, you set the value of the file by using the XSLT concat() function to build a filename from the league name, division name, and .htm suffix:

```
<saxon:output method="html"
file="{concat($league_name,$division_name,'.htm')}">
```

Building the title and header strings

Building the title and header strings is easier. You don't need to actually concatenate the league and division names; you can simply use <xsl:value-of> statements to select them within the <title> and <h1> elements:

```
<title>Standings for <xsl:value-of select="../@name"/> League <xsl:value-of
select="@name"/></title>
```

Sorting the teams by standing

You have no guarantee that your source XML document will contain teams in order of their current division standing. So, you must use your XSLT style sheet to sort the teams as you generate your result documents. Fortunately, this isn't too hard. The following XSLT statements will visit each <team> element in sorted order by the value of each team's <wins> element. Note that <xsl:sort> is an empty element, and that the entire contents of the <xsl:for-each> loop is not shown here.

```
<xsl:for-each select="team">
<xsl:sort select="record/wins" order="descending"/>
...
</xsl:for-each>
```

Have you noticed the order attribute? By default, <xsl:sort> will sort elements in ascending order. This would give you the teams with the fewest wins first. You want to sort teams in descending order, so that the teams with the most wins appear first in your results.

Computing the standing column

You may have noticed that the example result document (Figure 24-1) includes a column labeled Standing. You may have also noticed that your XML source file doesn't explicitly contain this information — in fact, your XML source file doesn't even present the teams in standing order. Not only do you need to sort the teams by the number of wins, you need to compute the value of each team's standing within the division.

In most *procedural* programming languages (such as C, C++, Fortran, and Perl), you simply set a counter inside the code that sorts your team output. For the first team, the counter would be set to 1. At each consecutive team, you would increment the counter — 2, 3, 4, 5, and so on. The value of the counter would provide the value of your Standings column for each team.

But XSLT is not a procedural language — it's a *declarative* language that consists of a set of template rules that, when matched by patterns in an XML source document, write information to a result document. XSLT does not directly support the concept of counters.

Fortunately, there's an XSLT function that can help you out. The XSLT position() function returns the numeric order of an element within a set of elements. Calling this function within your <xsl:for-each select="team"> loop will give you the number of the current team, in sorted order:

```
<xsl:value-of select="position()"/>
```

XSLT provides a rich set of functions to support general programming tasks within your style sheets. See the XSLT Recommendation at http://www.w3.org/TR/xslt **for information about all available XSLT functions.**

Using CSS Classes to Style Your Result

The example result document in Figure 24-1 looks rather, well, plain. You want to make sure that you design your XSLT transformation code to create HTML result documents that are as easy as possible to maintain in terms of style and presentation.

You're going to define several CSS classes for parts of the result document that you may want to format via a CSS. Based on the sample result document, here are some definitions for the following CSS classes:

- `.Header` — for the result page header
- `.TableTitle` — for the column headers (such as Team, Wins, Losses, Standing)
- `.TeamName` — for team names in the table
- `.TeamData` — for numeric data

In your XSLT transformation code, you're going to make sure to apply class attributes to the tags that wrap these elements. You can then create CSS formatting rules that apply to any element with a particular class attribute. Your page header, for example, will no longer be in an `<h1>` tag, but will be enclosed in a `<p class="Header">` tag. You can then create a CSS rule associated with the `.Header` class to choose the format of the page header.

Although you can create an external CSS file, for this exercise you will include your CSS rules directly in your XSLT style sheet. You're going to wrap the CSS rules in a CDATA section, so that the parser will pass this section through as-is to your result document. The following code fragment shows the CSS rules that you will include in your XSLT style sheet.

```
<![CDATA[
.Header {display: block; font-size: x-large;
         font-weight: bold; font-family: sans-serif;}
.TableTitle {display: block; font-size: large;
             font-weight: bold; font-family: sans-serif;}
.TeamName {display: block; font-size: medium;
           font-weight: bold; font-family: sans-serif;}
.TeamData {display: block; font-size: medium; font-weight: normal;
           text-align: right; padding-right: 20 px;}
]]>
```

Putting everything together

This sessions covers a lot of material. To put it together, copy the sample style sheet, standings.xsl, and the sample XML data file, standings.xml, to a folder on your hard drive. Follow the instructions from the Session 23 for running the SAXON XSLT processor to transform the XML data file into a set of HTML result files. From a DOS command line, type the following:

```
saxon standings.xml standings.xsl
```

The transformation should yield seven new files: one called TOC.htm, the others named after each league/division combination (NationalCentral.htm, AmericanWest.htm, and so on). Figure 24-2 shows the result file AmericanEast.htm.

The file TOC.htm should present a set of links for opening the remaining result files. We also provide a set of example result files on the CD-ROM in the folder session24/results.

Example files are available in folder session24 on this book's CD-ROM.

American League East

Team	Wins	Losses	Standing
New York	28	21	1
Boston	27	21	2
Toronto	25	24	3
Baltimore	24	24	4
Tampa Bay	14	35	5

Figure 24-2
Result file AmericanEast.htm

Done!

REVIEW

- Using an XSLT extension function provided by SAXON and most other XSLT processors, you can generate multiple result files from a single XML source file.

- XSLT provides a rich set of functions for computing values when the style sheet is processed.

- You can include CSS rules within an XSLT style sheet.

QUIZ YOURSELF

1. By default, the `<xsl:sort>` operation returns elements in ascending or descending order? (See "Sorting the teams by standing.")

2. Describe the function of the XSLT `position()` function. (See "Computing the standing column.")

3. What is the XSLT notation for an attribute on the current element? On the parent element? (See "Acquiring attribute values.")

4. Why should you include your CSS rules in a CDATA section within your XSLT style sheet? (See "Using CSS Classes to Style Your Result.")

5. What is CSS notation for a class rule? (See "Using CSS Classes to Style Your Result.")

Scripting XML

Session Checklist

✔ Creating and manipulating XML DOM objects with JavaScript

✔ Using dynamic HTML to manipulate XML data

✔ Modifying and reapplying XSLT style sheets automatically

✔ Creating interactive XML-based Web pages

**30 Min.
To Go**

Y ou have already learned about manipulating and displaying XML documents by using the XML transformation language (XSLT) and cascading style sheets (CSS). Although you used your browser's built-in XSLT engine to view your transformed documents immediately, the resulting documents were static — the result document wasn't interactive in the sense that you have come to expect from Web pages.

This session provides a brief introduction to manipulating XML documents on the fly by using the scripting technologies that are built into Microsoft Internet Explorer version 5.5. Using these scripting technologies, you can create XML documents that the reader can manipulate through controls in the Web browser.

Introducing the Document Object Model

Instead of processing your XML documents with XSLT style sheets, you're going to work with the World Wide Web Consortium's Document Object Model (DOM). The DOM is a platform- and language-independent interface for accessing and manipulating HTML and XML documents. The DOM is language independent, so you can use any programming language to manipulate your documents via the DOM. Because JavaScript is free, supported by all modern Web browsers, and is relatively simple, it is the language of choice in this session.

To use the DOM with XML documents, you must use an XML parser that supports the DOM. In this session, you're going to use the Microsoft XML Parser that is invoked by Internet Explorer version 5.5. As for all exercises in this book, you must install the Microsoft XML parser update, msxml3. A link to this update is provided on the book's CD.

Building an Interactive XML Document with the DOM

You've done plenty of work transforming XML documents with XSLT, and using XSLT and CSS to display documents. But this exercise is different — it's your first *interactive* Web page. Your DOM and XML-based Web page will do the following:

- Display your team standings in an HTML table
- Sort the table by standing
- Allow the user to re-sort the table by team name or by standing, by clicking the Team or Standing table header

Building an interactive Web page is going to be the most complex task you've done so far. You're going to draw on the tricks you've learned for using XSLT and CSS. This task is also going to require using the DOM and some JavaScript. So hang on, you have a lot to explore here.

Your source document again is division_standing.xml, which you have worked with for several sessions. This session's version of division_standing.xml is available on the book's CD-ROM in session25/division_standing.xml. You're also going to modify the style sheet that you have used, division_standing.xsl. The style sheet that you use in this session is also available on the CD-ROM as session25/division_standing.xsl.

You're going to use the same combination of XML source file and XSLT style sheet that you used previously. This time, your style sheet will pull a couple of different tricks. You're going to use the DOM (with the help of some JavaScript) to

- Modify the style sheet
- Retransform the source XML document with the modified style sheet
- Display the new result

Tour of the Building Blocks

Before proceeding, you need a quick lesson in the DOM and JavaScript — just enough for you to be comfortable with the technologies behind your style sheet.

Basics of the DOM

The DOM, or Document Object Model, enables you to manipulate objects that represent XML documents or components of XML documents. After you create an object that represents an XML document, you can manipulate that object in the same ways that you can manipulate an XML file; you can select components of that object, you can sort that object, you can manipulate, reorder, or transform that object.

Remember that an XSLT style sheet is also an XML document. You're going to create a DOM object that represents your XSLT style sheet. Through this DOM object, you will modify that style sheet before applying it again to your original XML document.

Basics of JavaScript

JavaScript is the glue that connects your DOM programming objects to your Web page. JavaScript is one of the oldest and most widely supported languages for scripting Web pages. Because JavaScript is relatively simple and is supported by your Web browser, you will use it in this session to manipulate your XML document and XSLT style sheet via the DOM.

Some excerpts from your style sheet

**20 Min.
To Go**

Before you look at the entire style sheet, you should take a tour of its components. Some of these components you've seen before, and some you haven't seen. What's important is to understand each component individually, and then understand how each works together to implement the completed page.

Creating and initializing DOM objects for your XML and XSLT documents

The following two lines from your style sheet, `division_standing.xsl`, initialize objects that represent your XML source file and your XSLT style sheet, respectively. The object names, `xmlSource` and `xslStylesheet`, are arbitrary variable names. To the right of the equal sign, you have DOM objects. `document.XMLDocument` represents the currently-loaded XML document; `document.XSLDocument` represents the currently-loaded XSLT document (your browser has already loaded the XML and XSLT files when this script is invoked).

```
xmlSource = document.XMLDocument;
xslStylesheet = document.XSLDocument;
```

Manipulating DOM objects

Not only can you create objects that represent your XML documents, but you can use those objects to manipulate your documents (after all, isn't programming mostly about manipulating things?). You manipulate these objects through methods that those objects make available. (*Method* is a term from object-oriented programming that is essentially similar to a *function*).

You can manipulate an object by invoking a method on that object. In your XSLT file, for example, you're going to allow the user to choose (by clicking a field) the `select` argument of an `<xsl:sort>` statement that you use to sort the team listing. Your `XSLDocument` object, which represents your XSLT style sheet, provides a method called `selectSingleNode`, which enables you to select a single element or attribute (or other XML node, such as a comment or processing instruction) from the XSLT style sheet. The `selectSingleNode` method takes a single argument — the location path of the node to be selected. The following statement selects the attribute named `select` of the `<xsl:sort>` statement from your style sheet. (The following is a general location path statement, which is okay because you know that your style sheet only contains one `<xsl:sort>` element.)

```
sortColumn = document.XSLDocument.selectSingleNode("//xsl:sort/@select");
```

Now that you have the `select` attribute of your `<xsl:sort>` element, you can change it. This line of code changes the `select` attribute of your `<xsl:sort>` element in the internal parsed copy of the XSLT style sheet.

Now you're going to create a Javascript function to update the value of the `select` attribute on `<xsl:sort>`, reapply the modified XSLT style sheet to the source XML document, and display the result.

Your JavaScript function display takes a single argument: `column`. Assume for now that `column` contains the value of `team` or `standings`, depending on which table column the user wishes to sort.

You just set `sortColumn` to the select attribute on `<xsl:sort>`. It just so happens that a method on `sortColumn` called `nodeValue` enables you change the value of `sortColumn`. You use this method to change the value of the sort key.

Next you need to reapply the XSLT style sheet and redisplay the results. You're going to use a single statement, with two pieces of magic, to do this. Your XML document object, `xmlSource.documentElement`, offers a method called `transformNode`. This method takes as an argument the name of the style sheet object. Your function invokes this method with `xslStylesheet`, to reapply the modified style sheet.

To display the result, you're going to use a bit of Microsoft Dynamic HTML in the form of the HTML DOM. You're putting your results in an HTML object called standings. The Microsoft HTML DOM offers a method called `innerHTML`, which enables you to change a chunk of HTML within an HTML page. Now the standings object holds your results.

```
function display(column)
{
sortColumn.nodeValue = column;

standings.innerHTML =
xmlSource.documentElement.transformNode(xslStylesheet);
}
```

All you need to do is insert the following marker in your HTML result file. The `innerHTML` method will replace this marker with the result of your XSLT transformation.

```
<div id="standings"/>
```

Invoking the display function

You may be wondering how you actually invoke the JavaScript display function? Once again, invoke the display function when the user clicks the "Team" or "Standings" headings in your result table by using a bit of JavaScript. When the user clicks the "Team" heading, you will invoke the display function with `team` as the sort column argument. When the user clicks the "Standings" heading, you will invoke the display function with `standing` as the sort column argument.

In previous sessions, your column headings looked like this:

```
<tr>
<th>Team</th>
<th>Wins</th>
<th>Losses</th>
<th>Standing</th>
</tr>
```

Not much is going on here — certainly nothing that would invoke a JavaScript function. You can take care of that by adding an `onclick` event handler to the "Team" and "Standing" headers, like this:

```
<tr>
<th onclick="display('name')">Team</th>
<th>Wins</th>
<th>Losses</th>
<th onclick="display('standing')">Standing</th>
</tr>
```

Now when the user clicks the "Team" header, it will invoke the display function with the `team` argument. When the user clicks the "Standing" header, it will invoke the display function with the `standing` argument.

Although the user can re-sort and redisplay the table by clicking two of the four table headings, nothing distinguishes those table headings to the reader — in other words, the reader has no clue that clicking the table headings will have any effect.

You can fix this with a bit of CSS magic. First, declare a CSS class to transform your cursor into a pointer. You can do this in an external CSS file, but you're going to insert the rule directly into your XSLT file, as follows:

```
<style>
.active {cursor:hand;}
</style>
```

10 Min. To Go

Now when you apply the `class="active"` attribute to an element, the cursor will change to a hand pointer when dragged over that element. Apply this CSS rule to your two active table headers, as follows:

```
<tr>
<th class="active" onclick="display('team')">Team</th>
<th>Wins</th>
<th>Losses</th>
<th class="active" onclick="display('standing')">Standing</th>
</tr>
```

Adding the finishing touches

You've covered the major components of your interactive Web page; now for some housekeeping details to tie everything together.

You're going to insert your JavaScript directly into your XSLT style sheet. Because you want to hide your JavaScript code from the parser and pass it through to the result file without modification, you're going to wrap it in a CDATA section.

You also want your JavaScript commented out in the result file. This is a trick that hides code from older browsers, yet it lets newer browsers recognize the code. You can't simply wrap the JavaScript in comment characters (<!--   -->) in your XSLT file; because these are also XML comment characters, their contents would be ignored! You need to tell the XSLT parser that you want to create a commented section in the result file. Fortunately, the XSLT statement, <xsl:comment>, will do that for you.

The script section of the XSLT file looks something like this:

```
<script>
<xsl:comment>
<![CDATA[
JavaScript code {...}
]]>
</xsl:comment>
</script>
```

This will create the following in the HTML result file. The <xsl:comment> statement creates a commented section, and the CDATA section ensures that the JavaScript code passes through to the result file unchanged by the XSLT processor.

```
<script>
<!--
Javascript code {...}
-->
</script>
```

Putting It All Together

Here's the entire listing of your style sheet, division_standings.xsl. Try to identify the parts in Listing 25-1 that have been described in this session, and see if you can figure out how everything works together.

Listing 25-1
The completed XSLT style sheet with embedded JavaScript

```
<xsl:stylesheet version="1.0"
                xmlns:xsl="http://www.w3.org/1999/XSL/Transform">


<xsl:template match="/">
  <html>
    <head>
      <title>Standings for <xsl:value-of
select="division_standing/name"/></title>
<style>
.active {cursor:hand;}
</style>
<script>
<xsl:comment>
<![CDATA[
                var xslStylesheet = null;
                var xmlSource = null;
                var sortColumn = null;

                function display(column)
                {
                    sortColumn.nodeValue = column;
                    standings.innerHTML =
xmlSource.documentElement.transformNode(xslStylesheet);
                }


]]>
</xsl:comment>
</script>
        <script for="window" event="onload">
            <xsl:comment>
                <![CDATA[
                xslStylesheet = document.XSLDocument;
                xmlSource = document.XMLDocument;
                sortColumn =
document.XSLDocument.selectSingleNode("//xsl:sort/@select");
                display('standing');
                ]]>
```

```
                    </xsl:comment>
              </script>
      </head>
      <body>
        <h2><xsl:value-of select="division_standing/name"/></h2>
        <div id="standings"/>
      </body>
   </html>
</xsl:template>

<xsl:template match="division_standing">

<font size="2">Click on <b>Team</b> or <b>Standing</b> to
sort</font>.
      <table>
      <tbody>
         <tr>
                <th class="active"
onclick="display('team')">Team</th>
                <th>Wins</th>
                <th>Losses</th>
                <th class="active"
onclick="display('standing')">Standing</th>
         </tr>
            <hr/>
         <xsl:for-each select="//team">
                <xsl:sort select="./standing"/>
            <tr>
             <td><xsl:apply-templates select="name"/></td>
             <td><xsl:apply-templates select="record/wins"/></td>
             <td><xsl:apply-templates
select="record/losses"/></td>
                <td><xsl:apply-templates select="standing"/></td>
            </tr>
         </xsl:for-each>
      </tbody>
        </table>
</xsl:template>

</xsl:stylesheet>
```

Trying It Out

Ah, you almost forgot to try it. You can rekey the XSLT file from this session (or, easier still, copy it from the session25 folder on the book's CD-ROM). As your data file, use `division_standing.xml`, also available in the session25 folder. If you use an earlier version of `division_standing.xml`, be sure to associate it with the proper style sheet, in this case `division_standing.xsl`.

Figure 25-1 shows the loaded XML file, with the cursor hovering over the `Team` heading. Clicking `Team` sorts the table by team name. Figure 25-2 shows the same file with the cursor hovering over the `Standing` heading. Clicking `Standing` sorts the table by team standing.

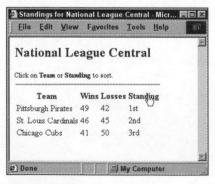

Figure 25-1
Dynamically generated XML file sorted by team name

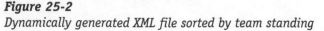

Figure 25-2
Dynamically generated XML file sorted by team standing

Done!

REVIEW

- The XML DOM provides a language and platform-neutral way to manipulate XML documents via programs.
- JavaScript provides a convenient interface for building programs within Web pages.
- DOM objects provide methods that support actions on those objects.
- You can use the DOM, JavaScript, CSS, and Dynamic HTML together to create interactive XML-based Web pages.

QUIZ YOURSELF

1. What is the role of the document.XSLDocument object of the XML DOM? (See "Creating and initializing DOM objects for your XML and XSLT documents.")

2. What is the function of the transformNode method on the document.XMLDocument object? (See "Manipulating DOM objects.")

3. What technology did you use to turn the cursor into a hand pointer? (See "Invoking the display function.")

4. True or False: You can include JavaScript code in your XSLT style sheet. (See "Adding the finishing touches.")

5. How can you create a commented section in your result document? (See "Adding the finishing touches.")

XHTML: An XML Vocabulary for the Web

Session Checklist

✔ Revisiting HTML limitations

✔ Learning about XHTML

✔ Understanding uses for XHTML

**30 Min.
To Go**

I n this session, you take a look at Extensible HyperText Markup Language (XHTML). XHTML, a W3C Recommendation, is basically HTML written to XML rules, without the sloppiness found in many HTML pages on the Web.

As discussed in the first session of this book, HTML documents work in a browser even if they're not put together exactly right. Browsers are forgiving of errors, which encourages posting of less-than-perfect Web pages. Even if tags are missing or a document is badly structured, Internet Explorer and other browsers try their best to display the content. XHTML, by using a more perfect structure, ensures quality documents are posted and will display as expected in the browsers.

Introducing XHTML

XHTML is a kind of transition-language you can use in preparation for creating XML. If you're creating HTML now, you can begin disciplining yourself for XML's strict rules by following the rules for XHTML. Documents still display in their HTML form, but they can be validated against the XHTML rules — which is good practice for your XML to come.

Essentially, XHTML is just HTML with a more perfect structure. Instead of putting together the minimum that the browser needs to display your Web page, you take more care with your tags.

Authoring XHTML

To write your XHTML documents, you follow the rules for XML documents, with the following additions:

- Start your XHTML documents with an XML declaration (optional).
- Include a DOCTYPE declaration to one of these document types: strict, transitional, or frameset.
- One root tag must surround the rest of the tags in your XHTML document. The <html> begin tag is above your first tag (though after the declaration if you have one), and the </html> end tag is after everything.
- Use HTML 4.0 tags but keep all begin and end tags lowercase (h2, not H2).
- Every begin tag has an end tag, and the begin and end tags match in name *and* are lowercase.
- Any empty tags must include an appropriate ending slash, as in <br />. You can alternatively replace the empty tag format with begin and end tags, thus
</br>.
- Attributes must have a name and value pair.
- Attribute values must be enclosed in quotes.

Follow these simple rules and your documents will conform to the XHTML standard. To test your XHTML, you can validate your document. To be able to validate your XHTML document, you must include the appropriate DOCTYPE declaration.

Reviewing HTML Documents

You're now going to take a look at an HTML document. This document is the typical form seen on the Web, where the HTML is not put together properly and includes structure errors.

```
<html>
<head>
<title>family tree</title>
</head>
<body>
This HTML document includes a list of family members.
<ul>
    <li>Joseph Q. Clark
    <li>Mary J. Clark
    <li>Jennifer Clark
    <li>Joseph Q. Clark II
    <li>Margaret M. Clark
    <li>Mark J. Clark
<ul>
<p>It displays in the browser despite numerous errors.
</body>
</html>
```

Type this code and save it in Notepad (or another text editor) as `family.html`. To save time, you may open this file from the session26 folder of the book's CD. Displayed in a browser, this HTML looks like Figure 26-1.

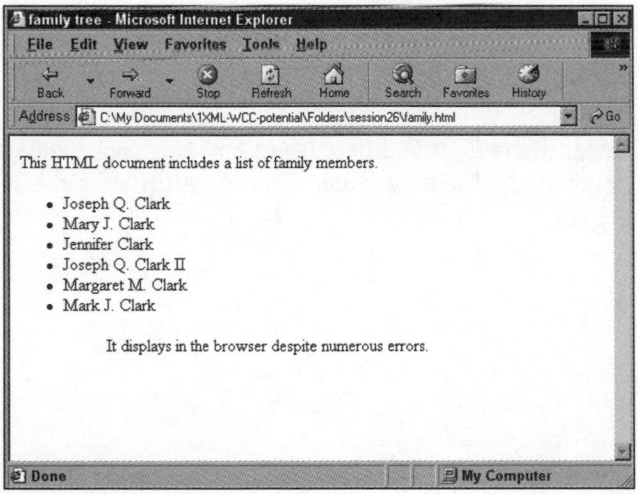

Figure 26-1
Sloppy HTML displayed in the browser

The first step in making this document comply with XHTML standards is to clean up the tag errors. XHTML requires all begin tags to have end tags, so you have to fill in all the </li> tags for your items and put in any other missing tags (such as the </ul> to close the nested list). You also need to add </p> end tags to your paragraphs. While these end tags are unnecessary for proper HTML display, they are required to conform to the more strict rules of XHTML.

```
<html>
<head>
<title>family tree</title>
</head>
<body>
<p>This HTML document includes a list of family members.</p>
<ul>
    <li>Joseph Q. Clark</li>
    <li>Mary J. Clark</li>
    <li>Jennifer Clark</li>
    <li>Joseph Q. Clark II</li>
    <li>Margaret M. Clark</li>
    <li>Mark J. Clark</li>
</ul>
<p>It displays in the browser despite numerous errors.</p>
</body>
</html>
```

Even with these changes, there is little difference in how this document views in your browser (see Figure 26-2). The only visible difference is that your last text line makes a shift to the left.

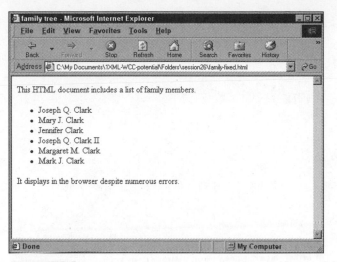

Figure 26-2
A cleaner HTML document displayed in the browser

Perfecting Attributes

**20 Min.
To Go**

HTML allows some leeway with attributes. If you forget the quotes around an attribute value, it works anyway. Perhaps you only type the attribute name if the name is the same as the value. To ensure that your document meets XHTML standards, you need to confirm that all attributes have a name/value pair and values are quoted.

Now you must adjust your document so that your <p> text items center instead of aligning left. To do so, you use an align attribute. First, intentionally leave out the quotes around the attribute value. You may wish to resave as family-attr.html.

```
<html>
<head>
<title>family tree</title>
</head>
<body>
```

```
<p align=center>This HTML document includes a list of family
members.</p>
<ul>
    <li>Joseph Q. Clark</li>
    <li>Mary J. Clark</li>
    <li>Jennifer Clark</li>
    <li>Joseph Q. Clark II</li>
    <li>Margaret M. Clark</li>
    <li>Mark J. Clark</li>
</ul>
<p align=center>It displays in the browser despite numerous
errors.</p>
</body>
</html>
```

When displayed in a browser, your <p> text is centered. This is despite the missing quotes around the attribute values.

Change the document above so that the lines that contain align are properly quoted.

```
<html>
<head>
<title>family tree</title>
</head>
<body>
<p align="center">This HTML document includes a list of family
members.</p>
<ul>
    <li>Joseph Q. Clark</li>
    <li>Mary J. Clark</li>
    <li>Jennifer Clark</li>
    <li>Joseph Q. Clark II</li>
    <li>Margaret M. Clark</li>
    <li>Mark J. Clark</li>
</ul>
<p align="center">It displays in the browser despite numerous
errors.</p>
</body>
</html>
```

You are improving this document and making it comply with the XHTML specifications. Continue with the rest of this session to finalize your XHTML document.

Using XHTML DOCTYPE Declarations

To continue moving your document toward XHTML compliance, you must add an XHTML DOCTYPE declaration. You can choose from three different XHTML declarations: strict, transitional, and frameset. You may want to go with transitional as a general rule — strict takes more time and effort in exchange for very little progress toward XML. Frameset is only used if your Web layout includes a frameset.

Strict

To follow strict XHTML structure, use the strict DTD that follows XHTML rules and does not use any soon-to-be-retired tags (deprecated tags).

```
<!DOCTYPE html PUBLIC "-//W3C//DTD XHTML 1.0 Strict//EN"
"http://www.w3.org/TR/xhtml1/DTD/xhtml1-strict.dtd">
```

Transitional

Another option is the transitional DTD, which allows use of some outgoing tags and can work with a style sheet or incorporated HTML formatting.

```
<!DOCTYPE html PUBLIC "-//W3C//DTD XHTML 1.0 Transitional //EN"
"http://www.w3.org/TR/xhtml1/DTD/xhtml1-transitional.dtd">
```

Frameset

Even a special XHTML document type for dealing with framesets exists. If your Web sites use framesets, this is the DTD you should reference.

```
<!DOCTYPE html PUBLIC "-//W3C//DTD XHTML 1.0 Frameset//EN"
"http://www.w3.org/TR/xhtml1/DTD/xhtml1-frameset.dtd">
```

Declaring the DTD

Place one of the DOCTYPE declarations mentioned above — strict, transitional, or frameset — at the start of all your XHTML documents. To continue the example, use the following transitional version:If you do not wish to type the changes, then open familyfin.html from your CD's session26 folder.

```
<!DOCTYPE html PUBLIC "-//W3C//DTD XHTML 1.0 Transitional //EN"
"http://www.w3.org/TR/xhtml1/DTD/xhtml1-transitional.dtd">
<html>
<head>
<title>family tree</title>
</head>
<body>
<p align="center">This HTML document includes a list of family
members.</p>
<ul>
    <li>Joseph Q. Clark</li>
    <li>Mary J. Clark</li>
    <li>Jennifer Clark</li>
    <li>Joseph Q. Clark II</li>
    <li>Margaret M. Clark</li>
    <li>Mark J. Clark</li>
</ul>
<p align="center">It displays in the browser despite numerous
errors.</p>
</body>
</html>
```

After adding the declaration, save your document as familyfin.html and redisplay in the browser (see Figure 26-3).

Your file extension is still .html**; there is no** .xhtml **extension.**

Notice that moving to XHTML does not improve anything in terms of display. While it doesn't compare to an XML document's descriptive tags, XHTML does require discipline on your part. Moving to XHTML's more strict code now will give you a solid base for moving to XML later.

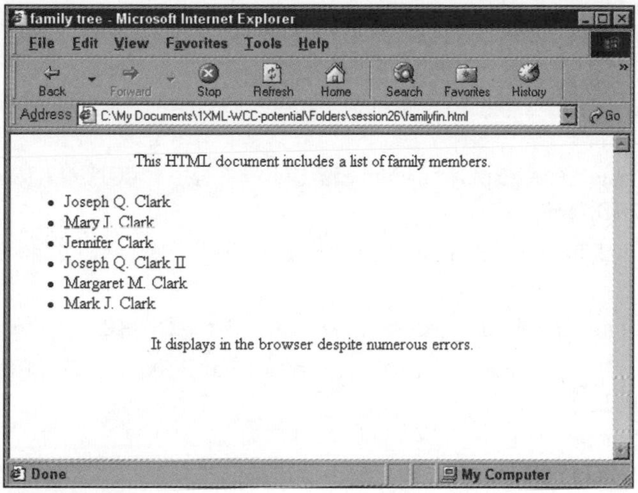

Figure 26-3
Your XHTML document

Validating XHTML

After you add a declaration to your document, you can then validate your HTML document against the XHTML DTDs located on the W3C site. If it validates, you have XHTML!

The W3C provides a validation checker for your XHTML code, which enables you to check your documents to ensure that they conform to XHTML rules.

If you would like to check this document for validity, visit `http://validator.` `w3.org/` and follow the instructions to "upload" your `familyfin.html` file. The validator, provided by the W3C, will let you know if your XHTML code is valid or not.

Done!

REVIEW

- HTML can be sloppy and still display in a browser.
- XHTML enables you to practice your structure skills and produce cleaner, validateable documents.
- XHTML fits in as a transition between HTML creation and XML creation.

Quiz Yourself

1. Is a declaration necessary for XHTML documents? (See "Introducing XHTML.")

2. Do browsers change your display if you adjust your HTML to XHTML? (See "Declaring the DTD.")

3. Do attribute values have to be quoted for XHTML? (See "Perfecting Attributes.")

4. Can you validate an XHTML document? (See "Validating XHTML.")

5. True or False: XHTML provides a transitional step from HTML to XML. (See "Validating XHTML.")

PART

V

Sunday Morning

1. Is it possible to publish XML information to multiple formats?
2. True or False: According to Session 21, HTML is considered easy to learn and easy to use.
3. What does CSS stand for?
4. Name the one major strength of CSS, as compared to XSLT/XPath.
5. Can CSS be used to adjust the formatting of an XML document?
6. True or False: CSS was originally developed for formatting XML documents in a Web browser.
7. True or False: XSLT was originally developed for formatting XML documents in a Web browser.
8. True or False: CSS enables you to sort and select XML data.
9. True or False: You must choose either XSLT or CSS for formatting XML documents on the Web, but not both.
10. True or False: XML documents can include scripts.
11. What does DOM stand for?
12. What is the purpose of the DOM when scripting XML documents?
13. True or False: To program with the DOM, you must use JavaScript or VBScript.
14. True or False: All modern browsers support the XML DOM.
15. List the general procedure for modifying a style sheet via the DOM.

16. True or False: It is helpful to embed your JavaScript code in a CDATA section within your XSLT style sheet, so that you don't have to escape all of the special characters.

17. True or False: XHTML does not support frames.

18. True or False: Closing tags for commonly-used elements like <p> are optional in XHTML.

19. True or False: XHTML is a W3C Recommendation.

20. Name the three XHTML DTDs.

PART

VI

*Sunday
Afternoon*

Introduction to XML Schemas — Part I

Session Checklist

✔ Introducing XML schemas

✔ Comparing and contrasting XML schemas with XML DTDs

✔ Understanding namespaces

✔ Learning about schema types

✔ Declaring elements and attributes in schemas

**30 Min.
To Go**

E arlier in this book, you learned about XML DTDs (Document Type Definitions) for specifying the vocabulary and structure of your XML documents. Through a DTD, you define the set of legal tags in your XML vocabulary, as well as the content of those tags. This content can include text, child elements, and attributes. You also learned to validate an XML document against a DTD — that is, to verify that the vocabulary and structure of the XML document conforms to the rules specified in the DTD.

But DTDs do have the following limitations:

● The ability to specify the type of content an element may contain is weak. A DTD, for example, can't specify that an element must be a number between 5 and 12, or that an attribute value must be a positive integer.

- The ability to specify occurrence rules is weak. A DTD, for example, cannot specify that an element must contain at least 3 and at most 6 of a given child element.

- A DTD is not expressed in XML syntax. Ideally, all your XML-related documents should use XML syntax, so that you can use the same set of tools (including programming interfaces like the DOM) to create and modify these documents.

These limitations are particularly egregious to people creating XML-based solutions for eBusiness and e-commerce. It's odd, for example, that a DTD for an invoice cannot specify that the contents of a `<price>` element must be a number!

You can think of a DTD or a schema as a *contract* that accompanies an XML document. A DTD would be a relatively weak contract — it can specify only the names and legal hierarchy of the elements within the document. An XML schema is a much stronger contract. A schema can specify the type of content (string, integer, decimal) that each element can contain and can provide stricter rules about the number and order of elements within an XML document.

Schema History

The designers of XML originally wanted to keep XML as compatible as possible with its much more complex predecessor, Standard Generalized Markup Language (SGML). Because of this goal, the XML Version 1.0 Recommendation specifies a simplified version of the SGML document type definition (DTD) for creating XML vocabularies and validating XML documents.

As the use of XML grew, however, the limitations of DTDs became more apparent. DTDs don't offer the strong data type verification and improved content modeling required by many XML-based applications.

The XML Schema Recommendation was finalized in May 2001 — more than three years after the XML Version 1.0 Recommendation. During that time, several companies, organizations, and individual XML experts developed their own schema mechanisms. Now that the XML Schema Recommendation is finalized, it's expected to quickly become more widely used in XML applications and more widely supported by XML tools.

Understanding Namespaces

Before discussing XML schemas, you must devote some time to another important XML concept: namespaces. Namespaces were not included in the XML Version 1.0 Recommendation. But it quickly became clear that some mechanism was necessary for associating specific element names with specific XML vocabularies. This is particularly important when combining several XML vocabularies within a single XML document. When your XML documents can contain your own customized vocabulary, plus industry-standard vocabularies like SVG (Scalable Vector Graphics), MathML (Mathematics Markup Language), and SMIL (Synchronized Multimedia Integration Language), the possibility of having a tag with the same name specified in more than one vocabulary increases significantly.

Namespaces provide a way to bind element names to a particular XML vocabulary. A namespace is essentially a prefix that is associated with some sort of identifier (the namespace) for that vocabulary. Namespace identifiers for industry-standard vocabularies are typically agreed upon. The XSLT vocabulary, for example uses the namespace `xmlns:xsl="http://www.w3.org/1999/XSL/Transform"`. The following root tag in an XSLT style sheet tells XSLT processors that any element that begins with the prefix `xsl:` is an XSLT element:

```
<xsl:stylesheet version="1.0"
        xmlns:xsl="http://www.w3.org/1999/XSL/Transform">
```

A common misconception is that the XML processor actually checks the URL provided as the namespace value. This is not correct — the namespace value is simply a string that identifies a set of elements. Using a URL that points to a specification or Web site is a convenient way to label a namespace.

Choosing Between XML Schemas and DTDs

**20 Min.
To Go**

Both XML DTDs and XML schemas are likely to be around for some time. XML DTDs are defined in the XML Version 1.0 Recommendation, so applications that fully support the XML Recommendation must support DTDs. During the more than three years that transpired between the XML Version 1.0 Recommendation and the XML Schema Recommendation, XML DTDs were the only official mechanism for validating XML documents.

If you or your organization is working on an XML application, you must decide whether to base the validation component of your application on DTDs or schemas. The next two sections look at some of the advantages and disadvantages of each.

Advantages of XML schemas

XML schemas provide the following advantages over XML DTDs:

- XML schemas support rich data typing, which enables you to constrain element contents to specific values or types of data.

- XML schemas support XML namespaces, which allow you to combine different XML vocabularies within a document.

- XML schemas are expressed in XML syntax, so that you can create and modify your XML schemas with the tools you use to create and modify your other XML documents.

Advantages of XML DTDs

XML DTDs offer the following advantages over XML schemas:

- XML DTDs use a much simpler (although much less feature-rich) syntax.
- XML DTDs are far less verbose than XML schemas. Most DTD files are far fewer lines than an equivalent XML schema file.
- At least initially, XML DTDs are more widely supported by tools that create, process, and validate XML documents (because XML DTDs have been around longer than XML schemas).

Consider the needs of your validation process and the capabilities of your tools when choosing between XML DTDs and XML schemas. If your tools support XML schemas, and you need the richer content rules that XML schemas provide, then XML schemas are probably a good choice for you. If your tools do not support XML schemas, you don't need the richer content models that schemas permit, your XML instances don't use namespaces, or you want to work with the simplest format, XML DTDs are probably for you.

Remember that, with the exception of namespace usage, your choice of schemas or DTDs in no way affects the content or structure of the XML documents that you create. You can create exactly the same XML documents whether you validate your documents against a DTD or a schema. The schema, however, provides the possibility of much stricter validation based on the contents of your elements.

Schema Concepts

Before you build your own XML schemas, you need to understand some of the concepts that form the basis of the XML Schema Recommendation.

Predefined types

Perhaps the largest advantage of schemas over DTDs is that schemas provide a rich set of types for constraining both element and attribute content. An XML schema, for example, can specify that the content of any element must be a number; a DTD cannot. This type checking greatly improves the ability for a schema-based validation to verify that the contents of an XML document are appropriate.

Table 27-1 lists several predefined types that are available for specifying the type of character content an element or attribute may contain. This is not a complete list; for all available predefined types see the W3C XML Schema Recommendation, Version 1.0, at http://www.w3.org/TR/2001/REC-xmlschema-0-20010502/ or on this book's CD-ROM.

Table 27-1
Sample of XML Schema Predefined Types

Simple Type	Examples (separated by comma)
string	Mary had a little lamb.
integer	1, 5, 1939
positiveInteger	2, 9, 214
negativeInteger	-5, -7, -123
nonNegativeInteger	0, 2, 9, 214
nonPositiveInteger	0, -5, -7, -123
decimal	3.14159, 98.6
float	-INF (negative infinity), INF (positive infinity), 0, 5, 8.97, 2E6, NaN (not a number)
Boolean	true, false, 1, 0
date	2001-07-11

Derived types

You can create new types from the set of schema predefined types. These types are called *derived* types. You may define a derived type for the following reasons:

- To specify that an element contain a number within a certain range
- To specify that an element contain one of a set of strings
- To specify that an element contain a string with a particular format, such as a telephone number (412-555-1212) or a postal Zip Code (15206-1500).

Schema elements: simple and complex types

XML schemas distinguish between two types of elements:

- Elements of simple type can contain only character content. These characters may be constrained to be of a particular type, such as a schema predefined type or a derived type. The schema, for example, can specify that the content of a simple element must be a date, an integer, a string, or any other type that is simply a character or sequence of characters.
- Complex type elements are those elements that contain child element content and/or attributes.

Because complex type and simple type elements are defined differently in an XML schema, the distinction between these types is important when you actually create your own XML schema.

**10 Min.
To Go**

Schema Building Blocks

The next few sections guide you through defining the basic XML building blocks — elements, empty elements, and attributes — in your XML schema.

Defining your schema's namespace

An XML schema must have the root element <schema>, with a namespace prefix xsd: set to the namespace http://www.w3.org/2001/XMLSchema, as follows:

```
<xsd:schema xmlns:xsd="http://www.w3.org/2001/XMLSchema">
[...schema content...]
</xsd:schema>
```

Because the XML Schema Recommendation was recently finalized, tools for authoring XML schemas may support an older draft version of the Recommendation. These tools may provide a different namespace — most likely `http://www.w3.org/2000/10/XMLSchema` **— for generated schemas.**

With this namespace declaration, elements within the schema that are prefixed with `xsd:` belong to the schema namespace.

An XML schema can also define a target namespace — that is, a namespace for the vocabulary defined by the schema. This is done by setting the value of the `targetNamespace` attribute on the root `<schema>` element:

```
<schema xmlns="http://www.w3.org/2001/XMLSchema"
     targetNamespace="http://xmlWCC.hungryminds.com/Schema"
     xmlns:target="http://xmlWCC.hungryminds.com/Schema">
```

Defining elements

Your schema describes the structure of your XML documents, much like your DTDs. To build your DTDs, you created elements and attributes. You defined a content model for each element, which specified the contents of that element. In this sequence of examples, you will build a schema for recipes in XML.

Begin by defining an element of simple type. Simple type elements cannot have child element content, nor can they have attributes. The following XML schema fragment defines an element named `<yield/>` whose type is the predefined simple type `xsd:string`. (Refer to Table 27-1 for a string example.)

```
<xsd:element name="yield" type="xsd:string"/>
```

Complex type elements can have element content and attributes. The following XML schema fragment defines a complex element named `<item/>`. The content of `<item>` is defined by the `<xsd:sequence/>` schema element to always be `<measure/>`, `<quantity/>`, and `<itemname/>`, with each child element occurring once and in that order.

```
<xsd:element name="item">
    <xsd:complexType>
        <xsd:sequence>
            <xsd:element ref="measure"/>
            <xsd:element ref="quantity"/>
            <xsd:element ref="itemname"/>
```

```
          </xsd:sequence>
      </xsd:complexType>
  </xsd:element>
```

Defining attributes

Because XML attributes cannot contain child elements or other attributes, they are by definition a simple type. An attribute type can be any of the predefined simple types from the W3C Schema Recommendation, or you can create your own simple type from one of the predefined simple types. You can define an attribute by using the `<xsd:attribute>` element, as follows:

```
<xsd:attribute name="attributeName" type="attributeType"/>
```

This is typically done as a child of the `<xsd:element>` that defines the element in which the attribute is defined. The following XML schema fragment, for example, defines a complex type element recipe, which has a required attribute meal. The attribute meal is of simple type xsd:NMTOKEN, whose value can be "breakfast", "lunch", "dinner", "dessert", "appetizer", or "party":

```
<xsd:element name="recipe">
  <xsd:complexType>
    <xsd:attribute name="meal" use="required"
      <xsd:simpleType>
        <xsd:restriction base="xsd:NMTOKEN">
          <xsd:enumeration value="breakfast, lunch, dinner, dessert,
            appetizer, party"/>
        </xsd:restriction>
      </xsd:simpleType>
    </xsd:attribute>
  </xsd:complexType>
</xsd:element>
```

Defining empty elements

You may want to create elements that have no text or child element content. These elements are typically placeholders or markers. The XHTML element `<hr />`, for example, marks the location of a rule, while a `<br />` marks the location of a hard line break.

Do you notice the space between the element names hr **and** br **and the closing slash? This is intentional; the space ensures that older browsers can recognize and properly interpret the empty XHTML tags. The space is legal per the XML Recommendation.**

You may want to mark the location of a photo or graphic in your XML document. You can use an element called `<image>` to do this. Because you can't actually include the binary image file in your XML document (because the binary data would break the rules of well-formedness), you need to provide the external location of the image file. You can do that through an empty element with a single attribute, like this:

```
<image href="filename"/>
```

Even though this element has no content, it does have an attribute, so you need to define a `complexType` with a single attribute, `href`. Since `href` is a filename, you can declare it to be of the schema simple type `string`. Finally, because an `<image>` tag with no filename location is meaningless, the `href` attribute is required. The resulting schema fragment looks like this:

```
<xsd:element name="image">
  <xsd:complexType>
   <xsd:attribute name="href" type="xsd:string"
    use="required"/>
  </xsd:complexType></xsd:element>
```

Going further

You continue with XML schemas in the next session, where you look at creating customized types and building content models for your elements. You also look at several example schema fragments, and take a quick look at tools that can assist you in creating your own XML schemas.

Done!

REVIEW

- Schemas provide an alternative to DTDs for specifying an XML vocabulary and validating XML documents.
- Schemas provide stronger data typing and stricter content modeling capabilities than DTDs.
- Schemas support XML namespaces, while DTDs do not.
- Schemas provide several predefined types, and enable you to define your own types.

QUIZ YOURSELF

1. True or False: If given a choice, you should always use a schema over a DTD. (See "Choosing Between XML Schemas and DTDs.")

2. True or False: XML Schemas are defined in the XML Version 1.0 Recommendation. (See "Schema History.")

3. True or False: Integer is a schema predefined type. (See "Predefined types.")

4. Name the important characteristics of a simple type element. (See "Schema elements: simple and complex types.")

5. Name the important characteristics of a complex type element. (See "Schema elements: simple and complex types.")

Introduction to XML Schemas — Part II

Session Checklist

✔ Learning about more complex schema content models

✔ Walking through a simple schema example

✔ Understanding tools for building schemas

**30 Min.
To Go**

Session 27 introduced you to XML schemas, which are a relatively new way to specify XML vocabularies and validate XML documents. You learned the distinctions between XML schemas and XML DTDs, about namespaces and schema data types, and how to define elements and attributes in an XML schema.

In this session, you're going to learn about defining content models in your schemas. You may remember from your DTD sessions that a content model is simply an expression of an element's legal content — either text, child elements, or both. Schemas enable you to create more tightly constrained content models than were possible with DTDs. Although we won't cover all there is to know about schema content models, we will certainly cover the most important features.

Using Occurrence Rules

You may recall the occurrence indicators in XML DTDs. Using the symbols ?, +, or * in a content model, you can specify whether an element is optional or required, and whether you can repeat the element.

XML schemas go further, allowing you to specify a minimum and maximum number of times an element may appear. This is done through two attributes on `<xsd:element>`, minOccurs and maxOccurs. The default value for both is one. A special string value for MaxOccurs — unbounded — means that the element can occur any number of times.

Restricting Element Value

XML schemas enable you to restrict the value of an element to a certain range, certain set of values, or even to a certain number of characters. The XML schema defines a set of *facets*, which are predefined properties by which simple types can be constrained. Facets are set via attributes on `<xsl:element>`.

You can, for example, set a minimum and maximum value for a number by specifying values for the minInclusive and maxInclusive facets. Likewise, you can constrain a string to a minimum and/or maximum number of characters by setting the minLength and maxLength parameters. You can find a complete list of facets and the simple types to which they apply in the XML Schema Recommendation.

Specifying Sequences of Elements

In real-world documents, elements typically appear in a certain sequence. A book chapter, for example, consists of a chapter title, followed by an introduction, followed by a heading, followed by paragraphs (and possibly more headings and more paragraphs). A recipe consists of a title, an ingredients list, and a procedure. This is certainly true of XML documents as well.

XML schemas enable you to specify a sequence of elements via (as you might guess), the `<xsd:sequence>` element. Within an XML schema sequence, you can define the following kinds of element groups:

- `<xsd:sequence>` defines a series of elements that must appear in the specified order (although some elements may be optional).

- <xsd:choice> defines a series of elements, of which only one may appear.
- <xsd:all> defines a series of elements, all of which may appear, but in any order. (You cannot specify this in an XML DTD.)

The XML Schema Recommendation specifies that all elements that contain child element content be of complex type. Therefore, these sequences are defined as children of a complex type definition (via <xsd:complextype>).

Using regular expressions

You can also use *regular expressions* to define schema types. A regular expression is a pattern, written in a special regular expression syntax, that matches sequences of letters, numbers, text strings, punctuation, or any other character.

Your XML vocabulary, for example, may have a tag called <zipCode>. You want the validation of your documents to ensure that this element's content is of the form of the U.S. nine-digit zip code — five digits, a separating dash, followed by four digits (for example, 15206-1700). You can define a type called USzipCode that will handle this as follows:

```
<xsd:simpleType name="USzipCode">
    <xsd:restriction base="xsd:string">
        <xsd:length value="10"/>
        <xsd:pattern value="\d{5}-\d{4}"/>
    </xsd:restriction>
</xsd:simpleType>
```

\d{5} means "match a string of five digits"; \d{4} means "match a string of four digits". The intervening dash is a literal character; it matches the dash in the zip code. \d is just one example of pattern-matching metacharacters that are available in XML schema's regular expression syntax.

Regular expressions can be a complex yet powerful tool for schemas and for solving other general programming tasks. The XML Schema Recommendation borrows its regular expression syntax from the Perl programming language. Consult virtually any Perl manual to learn more about regular expressions.

Now you can use this in your schema's element declaration for <zipCode>. Note that you're using the name of the simpleType that is defined in the preceding code in the value of the type attribute on xsd:element.

```
<xsd:element name="zipCode" type="USzipCode"/>
```

**20 Min.
To Go**

Walking Through an Example Schema

Enough with the book and theory learning. The following sections take a look at a real example schema!

Workflow for building a schema

The following workflow may help you as you create your own XML schemas:

1. Examine the implicit structure of your documents to determine appropriate element names and possible element hierarchies. You may want to sketch this out on paper first.

2. Define the simple elements that you will need. Simple elements have no attributes and contain content of one of the predefined simple types.

3. Define the complex elements. Complex elements have child elements as content, have content whose type is not predefined, or have attributes.

4. Within the complex elements, define sequence and occurrence rules. The XML schema recommendation provides several ways to do this.

5. Define any complex types that you might need. You can create a complex type from a combination of simple types and element content (typically with sequence or occurrence rules).

Getting started with a schema example

Imagine the ingredients list in a cookbook recipe. A typical ingredients list might look like this:

```
1 cup flour
2 cups sugar
1 teaspoon salt
```

Imagine representing this ingredients list as an XML document shown in Listing 28-1.

Listing 28-1
Example XML document for XML schema exercise

```
<?xml version="1.0"?>
<ingredientslist>
```

```
<item>
    <amount>1</amount>
    <unit>cup</unit>
    <ingredient>flour</ingredient>
</item>
<item>
    <amount>2</amount>
    <unit>cup</unit>
    <ingredient>sugar</ingredient>
</item>
<item>
    <amount>1</amount>
    <unit>teaspoon</unit>
    <ingredient>salt</ingredient>
</item>
</ingredientslist>
```

Building an XML DTD

First, consider an XML DTD that describes your ingredients list. This DTD would look something like the following:

```
<!ELEMENT ingredientslist (item+)>
<!ELEMENT item (amount, unit, ingredient)>
<!ELEMENT amount (#PCDATA)>
<!ELEMENT unit (#PCDATA)>
<!ELEMENT ingredient (#PCDATA)>
```

Nothing is particularly wrong with this DTD. But it does not specify that the contents of <amount> must be a number, nor does it specify any legal values for <unit>. The following document would validate just fine against your DTD:

```
<?xml version="1.0"?>
<ingredientslist>
    <item>
        <amount>fizzblop</amount>
        <unit>pooldish</unit>
        <ingredient>salt</ingredient>
    </item>
</ingredientslist>
```

Not specifying a type for the contents of <amount> and <unit> could cause trouble, particularly if you're a major cookbook publisher, and you're counting on the validation process to catch egregious errors. Now see if you can build something better with an XML schema.

Building an equivalent XML schema

An XML schema enables you to more tightly constrain the contents of your ingredients list. It is, however, a bit more complicated to create. Start by declaring your simple element types — elements that have no child elements or attributes, and whose content is one of the simple types defined by the XML Schema Recommendation. From your ingredients list, two elements fit the bill: <amount> and <ingredient>. <amount> will be a decimal number, while <ingredient> will be a string. You can define these elements as follows:

```
<xsd:element name="amount" type="xsd:decimal">
<xsl:element name="ingredient" type="xsd:string">
```

Defining the units element Things start to get more interesting with your <units> element. You can define <units> to be a simple element of type string. But because there are only a handful of possible measurement units, you want to constrain the value of <units> to be a legal measure. Just assume that all measures in your ingredients list will be cup, teaspoon, tablespoon, or none. (Use none for a pure number of items, with no unit; for example, 5 carrots.)

```
<xsd:simpleType name="unit">
  <xsd:restriction base="xsd:string">
    <xsd:enumeration value="cup"/>
    <xsd:enumeration value="teaspoon"/>
    <xsd:enumeration value="tablespoon"/>
    <xsd:enumeration value="none"/>
  </xsd:restriction>
</xsd:simpleType>
```

This schema fragment uses the <xsd:restriction> constraint to specify that element <unit> is of type xsd:string. The value of <unit> is further constrained by the *facets* (an XML schema term) defined by the <xsd:enumeration> elements. Each of these elements contains an attribute named value, which lists one of the legal string values for the <unit> element.

Defining your complex elements You have defined three of the five elements in your recipe list fragment. Because the remaining two elements, <item> and <ingredientslist>, have child elements as content, these are, by definition, complex elements.

Go ahead and start with <item>. This element must contain one or more of the triplet <amount>, <unit>, <ingredient>, in that order. You can set up the order of elements by declaring an element <item> of complex type, whose content is constrained by the <xsd:sequence> element.

```
<xsd:element name="item">
    <xsd:complexType>
     <xsd:sequence>
      <xsd:element name="amount"/>
      <xsd:element name="unit"/>
      <xsd:element name="ingredient"/>
     </xsd:sequence>
    </xsd:complexType>
</xsd:element>
```

That leaves only one item to go — <ingredientslist>. This element consists simply of a sequence of <item> elements. You can define it as follows:

```
<xsd:element name="ingredientslist">
   <xsd:complexType>
      <xsd:element name="item" minOccurs="1"
maxOccurs="unbounded"/>
   </xsd:complexType>
</xsd:element>
```

This schema fragment specifies that your <ingredientslist> element has only one child, <item>. The attribute minOccurs="1" specifies that at least one <item> instance must exist; while the attribute maxOccurs="unbounded" specifies that any number of <item> instances are allowed.

Associating a schema with your XML document After you have built your XML schema, all that remains is to associate your schema with your XML document. You will do this by adding a few schema-related attributes to the root element of your XML document.

Let's look again at Listing 28-1. The example document that we've been working with has root element called <ingredientslist>. We want to associate the <ingredientslist> element with the schema that defines the element

and its child elements. We do this by adding two namespace attributes to
`<ingredientslist>`. The first, `xmlns:xsi`, always has a value of `http://
www.w3.org/2001/XMLSchema-instance`. This attribute specifies that the
document is defined by an XML Schema. The second attribute, `xsi:
noNamespaceSchemaLocation`, provides a path to the schema document.

```
<ingredientslist xmlns:xsi="http://www.w3.org/2001/XMLSchema-
instance"
xsi:noNamespaceSchemaLocation="C:ingredientslist.xsd">
```

The namespace prefix `xsi` **in the attribute xmlns:xsi is not
mandatory.** `xsi` **is used by convention, although you may use any
namespace prefix string. Its value, however, must be**
`http://www.w3.org/2001/XMLSchema-instance`.

**Folder session28 in this book's CD-ROM includes a sample XML
recipe file (ingredient_list.xml), XML DTD (ingredient_list.dtd),
and equivalent XML schema (ingredient_list.xsd).**

**10 Min.
To Go**

Understanding the tools for building schemas

We've covered a lot of rules in the last two sessions, and we've only presented the
main points of the XML schema representation — many details remain to be
learned. If you think that XML schemas are difficult to learn and difficult to create, you're certainly not alone.

Fortunately, an alternative exists to hand-coding your XML schemas. Several
applications are available that provide a graphical user interface for creating XML
schemas. These applications use pop-up lists to write your schema content models
and present a graphical representation of your schema (or, if you want, your DTD)
to help you to visualize the structure of your XML documents. These applications
can also create schemas from XML instances (an XML instance is a fancy term for
XML document), and will create a sample XML instance from a DTD or schema.
An example interface from one such tool, TIBCO's XML Authority, is shown in
Figure 28-1.

**A 30-day trial version of Tibco's XML Authority is included on
this book's CD-ROM as part of the Tibco Turbo XML installation.**

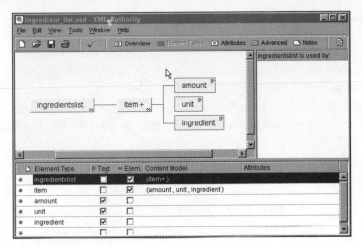

Figure 28-1
Example screen from TIBCO's XML Authority Schema Authoring Tool

Done!

REVIEW

- XML schemas enable you to further constrain the value of simple types through several methods, including facets and regular expressions.
- XML schemas support several types of sequence rules.
- Tools are available that allow you to create XML schemas without learning lots of schema syntax.

QUIZ YOURSELF

1. True or False: You can apply XML schema sequence operators to both simple and complex type elements. (See "Specifying Sequences of Elements.")

2. What sequence operator element specifies a group of elements that must appear, but can appear in any order? (See "Specifying Sequences of Elements.")

3. What is the default value of minOccurs and maxOccurs — the two attributes that enable you to specify the number of times an element may appear? (See "Using Occurrence Rules.")

4. What is the appropriate value for maxOccurs if an element can appear any number of times? (See "Using Occurrence Rules.")

5. True or False: Tools for creating XML schemas can create a schema from an example XML document. (See "Understanding the tools for building schemas.")

Using Industry-Standard XML Vocabularies

Session Checklist

✔ Learning about DTDs available via the Web

✔ Exploring advantages and disadvantages of ready-made DTDs

✔ Exploring advantages and disadvantages of creating your own DTD

✔ Creating a sample document using a ready-made DTD

If your plans for XML include valid XML, you will need to have a DTD to validate your documents against. This may mean using an existing DTD or creating your own. In this session, you review some available DTDs.

**30 Min.
To Go**

Exploring Industry-Standard Vocabularies

DTDs are available through the W3C. You can use these DTDs as they are or edit them to fit your needs. Using prepared vocabularies has its advantages. Refining a vocabulary can take months in man-hours, so using an industry DTD saves you all that time. You may use a standard vocabulary because of the application support for that vocabulary. Kay's Graphics Language, for example, wouldn't be very useful because no viewers are likely to support it.

MathML (Mathematical Markup Language)

The scientific community, long unable to display equations and chemical symbols on the Web, guided part of the drive toward XML. MathML (Mathematical Markup Language), one of the earlier XML applications, allows representation and display of complex equations. No major browsers (Internet Explorer, Netscape Navigator) support MathML directly at this time.

WML (XML for wireless data exchange)

WML allows presentation of data to a wireless device, such as a cellular telephone. You can create an XML document by using WML, and then have that data display on the small screen of a cell phone.

On the CD-ROM in the back of this book, you will find a link to download a cell phone simulation package by Openwave (see Figure 29-1). This simulator enables you to test the display of your data to ensure easy viewing.

Figure 29-1
The Openwave simulator

RDF: Resource Description Framework

RDF enables you to move beyond tags to associations between tags. In the long run, RDF should improve search hits on the Web by allowing you to search for several items and have them be related, rather than doing a Boolean search that returns thousands of inappropriate hits.

Suppose that you do an Internet search for a computer monitor. If you search for the word *monitor,* you may receive hits for computer monitors, hall monitors, and monitor lizards. With RDF, you can explain to the search engine the exact type of monitor that you want. The search engine can then intelligently determine which monitor hits are appropriate and return those that are applicable.

In the future, RDF may also be able to implement home appliance management. It's not beyond reason to imagine your alarm clock interacting with the Web to calculate an update for Daylight Savings Time.

HRXML (Human Resources Markup Language)

HRXML is the result of years of effort in the human resource area. This language is geared toward producing resumes in XML for easier sorting and referencing. With the HRXML vocabulary, you can also access style sheets and other related items to save time creating them.

SMIL (Synchronized Multimedia Integration Language)

This XML application enables you to design documents that play music, display movies, and display information in a browser. Some of the tags provide a way of timing when each multimedia piece will begin or end.

DocBook XML

A more recent creation, the DocBook XML vocabulary is a variation on the old DocBook DTD. DocBook has long been a standard for creating documentation in SGML (standard generalized markup language).

SVG (Scalable Vector Graphics)

SVG is a language for representing graphics in XML. Because SVG is made of XML, the graphics integrate well with XML documents. To view SVG graphics, use a viewer such as Adobe's SVG viewer. To create SVG graphics, use a creation program, such as Adobe's Illustrator 9.0 SVG export plug-in.

Because SVG graphics are XML, it becomes easy to cross-reference information in an XML document with information in an SVG graphic. This is discussed further at the end of this session.

Determining Whether to Use a Standard DTD or Write Your Own

20 Min. To Go

How do you decide if an industry-standard DTD will work for you, or if you need to write your own? First and foremost, you need to consider what you want XML to do for you.

If you plan to transmit information to wireless devices, certainly the WML is a good starting point. It will save you from reinventing the wheel when countless others have invested time and money to perfect this markup language. Because WML is supported by so many in the wireless industry, you need to use WML to move into that space — that's what the devices support.

If, however, you have a custom corporate database that you hope to link to specific corporate documents, you may be served better by creating your own.

Or, if your application of XML is simple, you may be better off creating your own. Some of the industry-standard vocabularies are very complex, with hundreds of available tags. You may be able to more easily create the needed dozen or so tags, rather than weed through and delete those available in a standard vocabulary.

Before you begin creating your DTD, you should do a thorough analysis and sketch out the potentials on paper. It can be helpful to see the tree structure for your documents and adjust on paper first. Visualizing the XML elements and content models may bring problems to light before you create an entire DTD, thus saving time adjusting later on.

Working with an Available DTD

In the next section, you review an existing DTD that is specifically defined for SVG. Then, you may follow this book to create simple graphics and attach those graphics to XML text. Refer to the SVG specifications, available through the W3C Web site, at http://www.w3.org, for clarification of the code and other coding options.

Reviewing an existing SVG graphic

Because SVG graphics are XML documents, it's easy to cross-reference information in an XML document with information in an SVG graphic (see Figure 29-2). This can then allow you to modify the graphic's display in a browser by activating an XML area.

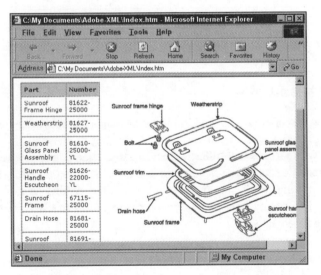

Figure 29-2
An XML document and SVG graphic from an Adobe file

If the mouse is moved over the XML document or the SVG graphic, information lights up both in the table and in the graphic (see Figure 29-3).

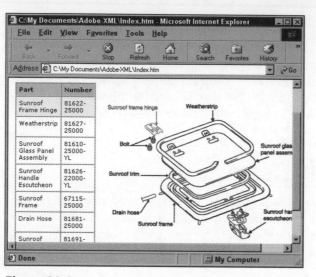

Figure 29-3
The same Adobe XML document with a hinge component highlighted
(in table and graphic)

Building your own SVG graphic

The SVG file for the graphic in Figure 29-3 is too large to display here. You're going to create a smaller graphic that you can manipulate yet still fit in these pages.

**10 Min.
To Go**

To begin, you need to create a small SVG graphic. Because time does not allow you to review all the specifications, you're going to use a few simple pieces of the SVG vocabulary to create some small graphics. We will explain each line as you move forward. To save time typing, feel free to open the person.svg file from the session29 folder on the CD-ROM.

```
<?xml version="1.0" standalone="no"?>
<!DOCTYPE svg PUBLIC "-//W3C//DTD SVG 20001102//EN"
"http://www.w3.org/TR/2000/CR-SVG-20001102/DTD/svg-20001102.dtd">
```

The preceding lines start the document. You may recognize the XML declaration. Because an SVG graphic is an XML document, it starts the same as your other XML documents. The XML declaration is followed by the DOCTYPE, in this case the W3C DTD for SVG graphics.

Now continue with your graphic creation. The content below describes the graphic and includes text. Note that SVG graphics can include images that you reference, text that you type, and graphics defined in SVG XML.

```
<svg width="300mm" height="300mm"    viewBox="0 0 2448 3168"
preserveAspectRatio="xMidYMid"
   xml:space="preserve"    style="fill-rule:evenodd; stroke-
linecap:round; stroke-linejoin:round">
```

The preceding code defines the graphic's size and provides some of its main attributes. After you finish typing and viewing your file, you may want to come back and adjust the width and height to see how your graphic is affected.

```
<g id="PageView">
<path style="fill:#000000;stroke:#000000;stroke-width:1"
d="M 1508,410 l 11,0 0,184 -11,0 0,-184 z"/>
<path style="fill:#ffffff;stroke:none"
d="M 860,399 l 648,0 0,184 -648,0 0,-184 z"/>
<path style="fill:none;stroke:#000000;stroke-width:3"
d="M 860,399 l 648,0 0,184 -648,0 0,-184 z"/>
<text class="t2"><tspan x="881" y="448">Joseph
Clark</tspan></text>
<text class="t3"><tspan x="881" y="483">b: February 1, 1985 in
Pennsylvania</tspan><tspan x="881" y="519">m: 2005</tspan><tspan
x="881" y="555">d:</tspan></text>
</g>
```

The preceding code defines the rectangle and its attributes, and it includes the actual text.

```
<style type="text/css"><![CDATA[
text.t1 {font-family:'Times New Roman',serif;font-
size:56;fill:#000000;font-weight:700;font-style:italic}
text.t2 {font-family:'Times New Roman',serif;font-
size:64;fill:#000000;font-weight:700}
text.t3 {font-family:'Times New Roman',serif;font-
size:32;fill:#000000}
]]></style>
</svg>
```

The preceding code defines the look for your text and ends the file with </svg>. After viewing your SVG file, you should modify the settings for the font family and size and review your document in the browser (don't forget to refresh your view).

After you save the code as a file and display it in the browser, you see a small square containing information on a family member, as shown in Figure 29-4.

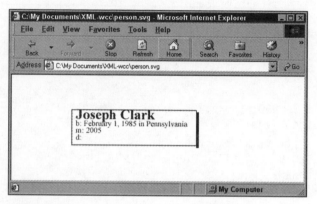

Figure 29-4
Your SVG graphic displayed in Internet Explorer (with Adobe SVG Viewer Plug-in)

Now that you have viewed your graphic, experiment by changing the code as previously suggested. Redisplay your graphic in the browser each time and check the results against the original.

Done!

REVIEW

- Many industry-standard and public vocabularies can give you a jump start toward creating XML documents.

- Industry groups have spent years developing quality vocabularies; in fact, XML and the need for industry consistency is driving collaborative efforts.

- To produce XML within certain industries, you may need to conform to existing vocabularies (such as WML in wireless devices).

- You may — due to unique needs or simplicity's sake — need to create your own vocabulary.

- SVG is one of many ready-to-use vocabularies; SVG allows creation of graphics by using an XML framework.

QUIZ YOURSELF

1. Is it necessary to create your own DTD? (See "Exploring Industry-Standard Vocabularies.")

2. What are the advantages of using a prepared vocabulary? (See "Exploring Industry-Standard Vocabularies.")

3. Are there any advantages to creating your own DTD? (See "Determining Whether to Use a Standard DTD or Write Your Own.")

4. True or False: "MathML" is the name of a DTD. (See "MathML (Mathematical Markup Language).")

5. True or False: An SVG graphic is an XML document. (See "SVG (Scalable Vector Graphics).")

Linking and Querying XML Documents

Session Checklist

✔ Learning about XML linking with XLink

✔ Using XPointer to address fragments of external XML documents

✔ Understanding the XML Query language for querying XML documents

**30 Min.
To Go**

The XML Version 1.0 Recommendation is a short document with a relatively simple purpose — to specify a syntax for creating markup languages, along with rules that documents must follow to be well-formed or valid XML Version 1.0 documents. By following these rules, you can write powerful documents that include metadata about their content and are easy to process with standard tools.

In this session, you're going to look at several specifications that increase the value of your XML documents by allowing you to create rich XML link structures, point to specific locations in external XML documents, and query XML documents on the Web like you query databases.

XLink for Creating Rich Link Structures

The ability to easily create hypertext documents — documents linked to other documents — was the force behind the explosive popularity of the Web. By now, you've probably used HTML links many times without really thinking about how they work. This section takes a closer look at HTML links, as you prepare to learn about XML links.

An HTML link consists of an `<a>` (anchor) tag with an `href` attribute. The value of the `href` attribute specifies the target location or document to be opened when the link is activated. A typical HTML, for example, link looks like the following:

```
<a href="target.htm">Click here to open the target</a>
```

These links have served the Web well, but there are many other possibilities for linking documents that HTML doesn't support. The designers of the XLink specification have attempted to specify a rich set of linking functionality that will expand upon what HTML linking provides.

At the time of this writing, the XLink Recommendation was not yet finalized. Watch the W3C Web site at `http://www.w3.org` **for information about the status of the XLink Recommendation.**

In part because the XLink Recommendation is not yet finalized, only a few applications support XLink. Watch for applications that support XLink so that you can use what you learn in this session.

Understanding limitations of HTML links

HTML links have the following limitations:

- HTML links are unidirectional (one way).
- HTML links can only link to an entire document, or to a predefined anchor location within the document.
- HTML only supports one link element (`<a>`).
- HTML links are always manually activated. You must click an HTML link to jump to the linked document.
- HTML links can only link to other documents or locations within HTML documents.

Some of these limitations may not make sense now, but they will after you examine the capabilities of XML links.

Learning features of XML links

The XLink specification provides a syntax for creating links in XML documents. Unlike HTML, any XML element can serve as a link element. An XML `<chapter>` element, for example, can be a link element to other supporting information about the chapter content (in addition to containing chapter content).

Also unlike HTML, XML links are not limited to pointing to other documents — XML links point to *resources*, which can be other files, documents, fragments of other documents, or images. A resource can also consist of things that you don't normally think of as documents, such as sets of links or programs that provide services.

The technical term for the string that identifies a resource is a Uniform Resource Identifier. These identifiers include things such as filenames and Uniform Resource Locators (URLs) and are extensible to include resources, such as Web services, to which you may want to refer to in the future.

XLink supports far richer link constructs than HTML. Here's a summary of the types of links that XLink provides:

- XLinks provide links to resources. A resource can be (as in HTML) a document. But a resource can be anything else, such as a group of links.

- An XLink can link to an element or range of elements in the target document.

- Any XML element can be a link.

- XLinks can be manually or automatically activated.

- XLinks can be multidirectional.

Creating XLink simple links

Even with all the capabilities of XLink, often a simple, HTML-style link is sufficient. For these cases, XLink provides simple links. (We discuss the second type of XLink, the extended link, later in this session.) An XLink simple link consists of

- A link element, which can be either `<xlink:simple/>` or an element of your choice. If you're defining your own link element, it must have an `xlink:type` attribute of value `simple`.

- An `xlink:href` attribute that specifies the target resource.

- Optional content of the link element. This is analogous to the link text in an HTML link. But an XLink element can have both text and element content. Because you can create arbitrary link elements, those link elements can have nested children.

You will need to declare the XLink namespace within documents that use the `xlink:` namespace prefix. You can do this by defining the following attribute on your document's root element:

```
<mydocument xmlns:xlink="http://www.w3.org/1999/xlink">
[rest of document content, which includes Xlinks]
</mydocument>
```

The string `http://www.w3.org/1999/xlink` **is the URI for the December 2000 Proposed Recommendation of XLink. Although unlikely, the final or future versions of the XLink Recommendation may specify a different namespace URI. Check the most recent XLink Recommendation at the W3C Web site, or the documentation for the application that is processing your XLinks, for verification of the correct namespace to use.**

The XML link element can be an XLink element, `<xlink:simple/>`, with one mandatory attribute, `href`. The following is an example of an XLink simple link element:

```
<xlink:simple href="target.xml">Link to target.xml.</xlink:simple>
```

**20 Min.
To Go**

Defining your own XLink elements

The XLink recommendation provides a specific set of attributes that define an XLink element. Any XML element can be an XLink element. This allows your XML link elements to serve multiple purposes — they can be containers for text and other elements, as well as links to other resources. All you must do to create an XLink element is define some XLink attributes on that element.

An XLink element requires, at minimum, the following attributes:

- xlink:type
- xlink:href

If you're validating your XML document against a DTD, you must include these in your DTD. The declaration of an XLink simple link element in your DTD, for example, would look like this:

```
<!ELEMENT TaskHead (#PCDATA)* >
<!ATTLIST TaskHead
  xlink:type    (simple)      #FIXED "simple"
  xlink:href    CDATA         #REQUIRED
>
```

This DTD creates an element called TaskHead. TaskHead must have two attributes: xlink:type, whose value must be simple, and xlink:href, which can have a string value. This DTD fragment declares that TaskHead is a simple XLink element, similar to an HTML <a> element.

A TaskHead element in an XML document would look like this:

```
<TaskHead xlink:type="simple" xlink:href="TaskHelp.xml">This is a
task heading</TaskHead>
```

Elements that you declare as XML links can have other attributes, in addition to XLink attributes. Unlike HTML link elements, XML link elements can serve other roles in an XML document.

Annotating XLinks with role and title

XLink provides two attributes for attaching annotation information to links. xlink:role is a string to be interpreted by the processing application. Although the specification does not define how xlink:role is to be used, it is expected to provide some information about the purpose of the link.

xlink:title is a human-readable string that describes the link. This string will be rendered and displayed by the processing application.

Specifying XLink behavior with show and actuate

XLink provides two attributes that specify the behavior of the link element. Behavior is defined around the following two characteristics:

- Whether the link should be activated *automatically* (when the document that contains the link is loaded) or *manually* (by clicking the link text).

Note

Why do you want yout links to be automatically activated? Remember that not just people process your XML documents. An automatically activated link may be appropriate if your document is going to be processed by a computer application.

- Where the contents of the link target should appear.

The xlink:actuate attribute specifies how the link should be activated. A value of onLoad means that the link should be activated when the document that contains the link is loaded. A value of onRequest means that the link should be activated by a manual request, such as a mouse click.

The xlink:show attribute specifies where the contents of the link target should appear. A value of new means that the link content should appear in a new window or frame. A value of replace means that the link content should replace the current content (this is the default HTML link behavior). A value of embed means that the link content should appear at the link location in the current content.

Both xlink:actuate and xlink:show support values of other and none. A value of other means that the application processing the XLink should look for other clues about how the link should behave; a value of none tells the processing application that no information is provided about the desired link behavior.

Using XLink extended links

XLink extended links provide a rich set of capabilities beyond those provided by HTML links. XLink extended links provide support for bidirectional linking (in which link resources refer back to each other), out-of-line links (in which links are maintained outside the current document), and link databases (sets of links). These capabilities are enabled through the following elements and attributes that define extended links:

- xlink:locator is a child of an extended link element that specifies the resources that are members of the extended link.

- xlink:arc is a child of an extended link element that specifies the connections between resources that are members of the extended link.

- xlink:from is an attribute on xlink:locator or xlink:arc that defines the starting resource of a link.

- xlink:to is an attribute on xlink:locator or xlink:arc that defines the ending resource of a link.

- `xlink:resource` is a child of an extended link element that specifies only local resources (within the current document) that are members of the extended link.

**10 Min.
To Go**

XPointer for Addressing External Documents

XPointer provides a way to address sections of external XML documents. To understand why this is important, you need to understand how HTML supports linking to external documents:

HTML linking to documents

HTML supports linking to entire documents, or to specific, predefined locations within a document. HTML supports linking to entire documents, like this:

```
<a href="target.doc">Link to target document</a>
```

HTML also supports links to specific locations within an external document, like this:

```
<a href="target.doc#location">Link to location within target
document</a>
```

The `#location` string refers to an anchor point within the target document. Anchor points must be explicitly inserted into a target document, via the following HTML statement:

```
<a name="location"></a>
```

What happens if you want to link to a specific location within a document that you do not own? Unless the author has already inserted anchor points, or you can contact the author to insert anchor points for you (which is, of course, not always feasible), you're out of luck. You can link to the entire document, or not link at all.

Identifying XML fragments via XPointer

What you really need is a mechanism to address fragments of external XML documents without the need to write explicit anchor points in those documents.

Because you've worked with XPath to address specific components within an XML document, it seems reasonable that you can figure out how to address specific components of external XML documents.

XPointer provides a syntax for specifying, in a URL or link target, a specific location or range within a target document. You can add an XPointer fragment identifier to a URL or link target by appending #xpointer() to the URL or link target. Within the parentheses, you will insert the actual XPointer identifier. The first occurrence of the string Mary had a Little Lamb within an element named title, for example, would look like this:

```
xpointer(string-range(//title, "Mary had a Little Lamb")[])
```

The first occurrence of the string Edgar Allen Poe within an element named author would look like this:

```
xpointer(string-range(//author, "Edgar Allen Poe")[])
```

The second occurrence of an element named chapter would be:

```
xpointer((//chapter)[2])
```

The first occurrence of an element with an id attribute whose value is tutorial would be:

```
xpointer(id("tutorial"))
```

Much of XPointer's syntax is borrowed from the XPath specification, which you have already used in your XSLT scripts to manipulate and transform XML documents. In addition to XPath's support for selecting elements in a document (by name or by hierarchical relation), XPointer adds support for specifying points and ranges. Not only can XPointer select external document fragments based on document structure, it can also select specific elements, elements with particular attribute values, or specific text content. XPointer also supports relative position expressions (for example, "the 5th element after the 1st element named 'title'").

XML Query for Searching XML Documents

The metadata within your XML documents provides a key advantage: Applications that process your XML documents can use that metadata to select and publish appropriate content. Applications can treat XML documents as databases — selecting and sorting the appropriate content for the task at hand.

Imagine being able to leverage the metadata information in all XML documents that are available on the Web. Suppose that you could use XML metadata to improve your Web searches, in effect treating the entire Web as a searchable, indexed database. This is what the XML Query activity promises to enable.

The XQuery language is being developed by the XML Query group of the World Wide Web Consortium (W3C). XQuery borrows elements from XPath and XPointer and adds facilities for supporting general query languages, including an algebra for constructing queries, support for binding preliminary results to variables, conditional expressions, and filtering of results.

> **At the time of this writing, the XQuery specification is still in early stages of development. Watch the W3C Web site at** `http:www.w3.org` **for information about XQuery's progress.**

Done!

REVIEW

- XLink was designed to improve upon the capabilities of HTML linking, and make fully available the power of hypertext links.
- XPointer enables you to link to specific fragments of external XML documents.
- The XQuery language will enable you to query XML documents just as you query databases.

QUIZ YOURSELF

1. Name the two required XLink attributes. (See "Creating XLink simple links.")
2. Name the two available XLink types. (See "Creating XLink simple links.")
3. Name three types of objects that an XLink can point to. (See "Learning features of XML Links.")
4. What is the syntax for an XPointer fragment identifier? (See "Identifying XML fragments via XPointer.")
5. True or False: XPath is the language for querying XML documents. (See "XML Query for Searching XML Documents.")

Sunday Afternoon

1. What does SVG stand for?

2. True or False: An SVG graphic is designed to display best at a specific resolution.

3. True or False: An SVG file is an XML document.

4. True or False: Using a readily-available DTD is frowned upon in the XML community.

5. What does WML stand for?

6. Why isn't it practical to send HTML documents to wireless telephone displays?

7. True or False: DocBook is designed for creating medical journals.

8. Name two benefits that XML schemas provide over XML DTDs.

9. Name a disadvantage of XML schemas over XML DTDs.

10. True or False: Using an XML schema, you can specify that an element contain only a number.

11. True or False: Using an XML DTD, you can specify that an element contain only a number.

12. How do you declare an entity reference in an XML schema?

13. True or False: You cannot create XML and post it to the Web unless it conforms to an industry-standard DTD.

14. Name three limitations of HTML linking.

15. Name the two types of XLinks.

16. True or False: XLink and XPointer provide all that is needed for a general XML query language.

17. Describe the behavior of an XLink whose `xlink:actuate` attribute is set to `onLoad`.

18. Describe the behavior of an XLink whose `xlink:show` attribute is set to `embed`.

19. True or False: XPointer uses much of the XPath language for identifying parts of an XML document.

20. True or False: XLink and XPointer require application support to be useful.

A

Answers to Part Reviews

Friday Evening Review Answers

1. Extensible Markup Language

2. Yes.

3. Binary

4. Ease of reuse, ease of publishing to different output devices, ease of changing formatting, ease of extracting only the appropriate information.

5. True.

6. World Wide Web Consortium or W3C

7. False. HTML was designed for easy presentation, not easy data exchange. XML is designed to support data exchange.

8. There isn't a limit on the number of tags you may create.

9. Limited number of tags and limited ability to reuse information.

10. XML. These tags are not part of the HTML vocabulary.

11. A small, manageable pilot project.

12. If it appears, it must appear at the top of the document.

13. Improper nesting. Because the <b> tag comes before the <i> tag, the <i> tag needs to close before the <b> tag closes.

14. True.

15. Any of the following: use an XML declaration, nest elements properly, include an end tag for every start tag, end empty elements with />.

16. Data about data.

17. False. Web browsers only have built-in support for displaying HTML tags. <child> is not an HTML tag.

18. Yes, as can XSLT style sheets.

19. Absolutely true.

20. Database publishing, e-commerce, document publishing, and many more!

Saturday Morning Review Answers

1. The formats and markup rules for a language, such as XML or HTML.

2. No. XML syntax is much stricter.

3. Hand coding in a text editor, outputting from an application, producing from other XML documents, outputting from a database, and more.

4. The first one is correct. The second does not have a proper close tag, and the third has an empty element in front of the data.

5. An underscore and the letter q.

6. True. HTML is forgiving on this, but not XML.

7. 1.0

8. Comments may be inserted in XML and in HTML.

9. True.

10. Any of the following: apostrophe, double quote, single quote, left angle bracket, and right angle bracket.

11. Entities.

12. True.

13. All start tags have end tags, optional XML declaration, empty tags end with />, proper nesting of tags, attribute values in quotation marks.

14. Yes.

15. No. You can work with XML without a DTD.

16. `<!ELEMENT`
17. Yes.
18. An asterisk.
19. No; it depends on your application.
20. False. Notepad is a text editor.

Saturday Afternoon Review Answers

1. Yes.
2. Yes.
3. True.
4. Yes.
5. The XML processor guarantees that the ID attribute is a unique value. This is useful for linking and other processing that requires a unique ID.
6. Yes.
7. True.
8. Yes.
9. True.
10. True.
11. Yes.
12. Yes.
13. False. XML provides NOTATION declarations for including references to graphics and other binary files in XML documents.
14. False. Through NOTATION declarations, XML supports any binary file format.
15. True.
16. Either.
17. Yes.
18. Yes, or to other XML vocabularies.
19. True.
20. Yes.

Saturday Evening Review Answers

1. False. XSLT and CSS are two different style sheet languages.
2. `<xsl:value-of select="location path"/>` or `<xsl:for-each select="location path"/>`
3. Yes.
4. Replace.
5. Yes.
6. False. XSLT is a feature-rich and complex programming language.
7. True.
8. Yes.
9. Yes.
10. Yes.
11. The current node visited by the XSLT processor as it processes the XML document.
12. Yes. Location path expressions are resolved with respect to the current context node.
13. True.
14. Yes.
15. Use XSLT to populate an HTML template with element content from an XML file.
16. Yes.
17. True.
18. `<xsl:value-of select="."/>`
19. `<xsl:value-of select="child_element_name"/>`
20. `<xsl:sort>`

Sunday Morning Review Answers

1. Yes.
2. True.

3. Cascading style sheet.

4. CSS is simple and can directly specify the formatting of an XML element.

5. Yes, in a browser that supports XML and CSS.

6. False. CSS was developed for formatting HTML documents.

7. True.

8. False. CSS does not support selecting, sorting, or manipulating XML data. You must use XSLT to do this.

9. False. You can combine XSLT and CSS.

10. True.

11. Document Object Model.

12. The DOM allows you to represent and manipulate XML documents as variables.

13. False. The DOM is language-independent.

14. False. Not all browsers support the DOM.

15. Load the style sheet into a DOM variable, select the element (node) you wish to modify, modify the node.

16. True.

17. False. The Frameset XHTML DTD supports frames.

18. False.

19. True.

20. Strict, Transitional, Frameset.

Sunday Afternoon Review Answers

1. Simple Vector Graphics.

2. False. Simple Vector Graphics are resolution-independent.

3. True.

4. False.

5. Wireless Markup Language.

6. Screen size limitations, user interface limitations.

7. False. DocBook is for general computer and technical documentation.

8. Strong data typing, stricter content models, inheritance, and schema is expressed as an XML document.

9. Schemas are more complex than DTDs, schemas were more recently developed and may not be as widely supported.

10. True.

11. False. An XML DTD can only specify that an element contain text content, child elements, or both. It cannot specify that an element must contain a number.

12. Declaration of entity references is not supported by XML schemas.

13. False. Using an industry-standard DTD is optional.

14. Unidirectional, cannot link within a document unless an anchor is present, always manually activated, can only link to other documents, only supports a single link element.

15. Simple and extended.

16. False. XLink and XPointer lack several elements of a query language, such as a query algebra and the ability to operate over result sets.

17. Link is traversed when document is loaded.

18. Content of link target is inserted in current document at point of link.

19. True.

20. True.

B

What's on the CD-ROM

This appendix provides you with information on the contents of the CD-ROM that accompanies this book.

The CD-ROM contains a variety of XML-related tools and many sample files, including the following:

- TIBCO Turbo XML
- Adobe FrameMaker+SGML
- Adobe SVG Viewer
- XML Spy
- Instant SAXON
- WorX for Word
- Microsoft Internet Explorer
- Adobe Acrobat Reader

We have also included the World Wide Web Consortium's XML Version 1.0 Recommendation, XSLT Version 1.0 Recommendation, XPath Version 1.0 Recommendation, and XML Schema Version 1.0 Recommendation. You can find updated versions of these at http://www.w3c.org.

Also included are source code examples from the book. Any time that we instruct you to type information, if you prefer, you can open the pretyped files. These are located in folders named for the corresponding chapter. If we ask you to save a file as family.xml in Session 2, for example, in the session02 folder you will find family.xml pre-made for you. Feel free, though, to practice by typing it yourself.

Finally, an electronic, searchable PDF version of *XML Weekend Crash Course* is included on the CD-ROM if you prefer to read online or electronically "carry" the book with you. Plus, the book PDF allows Boolean searches; this capability extends far above and beyond the capabilities of the book's index.

You can view the PDF with Adobe Acrobat Reader — the latest version is included on the CD-ROM.

System Requirements

Make sure that your computer meets the minimum system requirements listed in this section. If your computer doesn't match up to most of these requirements, you may have a problem using the contents of the CD.

For Microsoft Windows 95/98/NT/ME and Windows 2000, you need the following:

- PC with a Pentium processor running at 120 Mhz or faster
- At least 64MB of RAM
- Ethernet network interface card (NIC) or modem with a speed of at least 28,800 bps
- A CD-ROM drive — double-speed (2x) or faster

You will need free drive space to install the software from this CD. Some of the programs are small and only require a few MB of free space. Other installations, such as Adobe FrameMaker+SGML, may take close to 100 MB.

Using the CD-ROM with Microsoft Windows

To install the items from the CD to your hard drive, follow these steps:

1. Insert the CD into your computer's CD-ROM drive.
2. A window will appear with the following options: Install, Explore, eBook, Links and Exit.

   Install: Gives you the option to install the supplied software and/or the author-created samples on the CD-ROM.

   Explore: Allows you to view the contents of the CD-ROM in its directory structure.

eBook: Allows you to view an electronic version of the book.

Links: Opens a hyperlinked page of web sites.

Exit: Closes the autorun window.

If you do not have autorun enabled or if the autorun window does not appear, follow the steps below to access the CD.

1. Click Start ➪ Run.

2. In the dialog box that appears, type **d:\setup.exe**, where *d* is the letter of your CD-ROM drive. This will bring up the autorun window described above.

3. Choose the Install, Explore, eBook, Links, or Exit option from the menu. (See Step 2 in the preceding list for a description of these options.)

CD Contents

Following is a summary of the tools available on the CD-ROM. Note that some are full installs, while others are limited or trial versions.

Self-assessment test

The CD-ROM contains a 60-question self-assessment test. You can complete these questions before starting a chapter to see what you know, or after you read a chapter to ensure that you picked up the important points.

Applications

The CD-ROM includes the applications described in the following sections.

TIBCO Turbo XML

Turbo XML includes three separate XML-related tools. You can install all the tools or select what you like and install. This suite of tools includes the following: XML Console, XML Authority, and XML Instance.

You can install these from the CD as a 30-day trial version. A temporary registration number is available from http://www.extensibility.com. Use this number to start your trials of all TIBCO products.

You can find more information about these tools at http://www. extensibility.com. Related add-ins and test files are available at http://www.xmlschema.com.

Adobe FrameMaker+SGML

This unique publishing tool from Adobe enables you to create documents within a word-processing and page-layout environment. Because of the organized, structured setup of FrameMaker documents, you can easily output to paper, and then send the same files to XML (not to mention PDF, HTML, and online help!). You have control of the formatting through either internal reference pages or an external product called Quadralay WebWorks Publisher (trial version http://www.webworks.com).

The CD-ROM includes a demonstration version of Adobe FrameMaker+SGML. The CD version has no time limit, although save and print are disabled.

If you plan to create documentation, large volumes of published materials, or even materials that will be output to paper (printing), PDF, and XML, FrameMaker+SGML provides a user-friendly interface and validation tools.

Adobe SVG Viewer

This plug-in from Adobe enables you to view Scalable Vector Graphics. You may install this plug-in and it works within Internet Explorer to allow SVG viewing in the browser. Updates are available from http://www.adobe.com/svg/.

XML Spy

XML Spy provides an integrated development environment for XML. Its features include XML editing, XML validation, schema/DTD editing, schema/DTD validation, XSL editing, and XSL transformation. The CD includes a 30-day demonstration version. More information is available at http://www.xmlspy.com.

Instant SAXON

Instant SAXON is a freeware XSLT processor that runs as a Windows executable file for ease-of-use. Details on Instant SAXON and the Java-based SAXON are available at http://users.iclway.co.uk/mhkay/saxon/.

WorX for Word

WorX by HyperVision Ltd. is made of three tools that interact: WorX(tm) for Word, WorX(tm) Information Retriever, and the WorX(tm) Administrator. WorX for Word operates with Microsoft Word 2000. WorX allows non-technical authors to create well-formed XML. This WorX for Word tool is included on the book's CD.

For the other tools, visit `http://www.hvltd.com`. Note that the WorX Retriever module allows XML to be imported to a WorX document from almost any source. WorX Retriever preserves the XML markup and structure of the imported fragments. The third tool, WorX Administrator, is for use by IT staffers. It allows them to set up, map and maintain DTDs for a WorX workgroup.

Microsoft Internet Explorer

This latest freeware version of Internet Explorer enables you to view XML documents, validate XML documents, and run XSLT transformations in the browser. If your copy of Microsoft Internet Explorer is older than version 5.0, you should install this version.

To run the examples in this book, you must install the MSXML 3.0 update to the Microsoft XML parser and the `xmlinst` utility, available from `http://msdn.microsoft.com/xml`. Search for MSXML Parser 3.0 or visit the key topics Microsoft XML area.

Finally, you may wish to install Microsoft's Internet Explorer Tools for Validating XML and Viewing XSLT Output, downloadable from the same Microsoft XML area. This add-on provides some useful tools for viewing and debugging XSLT transformations in the browser.

Adobe Acrobat Reader

Adobe's free PDF Reader software allows you to view and print portable document format (PDF) files. You can view these files through a browser or directly in the Reader window.

You will need to install Acrobat Reader to be able to read the PDF version of this book; both the Reader and the book PDF are located on the CD.

Acrobat Reader will be useful the next time you receive a PDF via e-mail or locate a PDF on a Web site. Install this in place of any prior version of the Reader that you have; prior Reader versions cannot read all versions of PDF.

Troubleshooting

If you have difficulty installing or using the CD-ROM programs, try the following solutions:

- **Be sure that you are running the correct version of the Microsoft XML parser.** You must install the MSXML 3.0 update to the Microsoft XML parser to run the examples in this book. You must also run Microsoft's xmlinst utility to properly configure your Microsoft XML parser. These tools are available from the XML area on the Microsoft Web site, at `http://msdn.microsoft.com/xml`. A Web-based tool, called the MSXML Sniffer, will verify that your MSXML installation is correct. The MSXML Sniffer is available at `http://www.bayes.co.uk/xml/`. The MSXML Sniffer should report that you are running "Version 3 of MSXML2 in Replace mode".

- **Turn off any anti-virus software that you may have running.** Installers sometimes mimic virus activity and can make your computer incorrectly believe that a virus is infecting it. (Be sure to turn the anti-virus software back on later.)

- **Close all running programs.** The more programs you're running, the less memory is available to other programs. Installers also typically update files and programs; if you keep other programs running, installation may not work properly.

If you still have trouble with the CD, please call the Hungry Minds Customer Care phone number: (800) 762-2974. Outside the United States, call 1 (317) 572-3994. You can also contact Hungry Minds Customer Service by e-mail at `techsupdum@hungryminds.com`. Hungry Minds will provide technical support only for installation and other general quality control items; for technical support on the applications themselves, consult the program's vendor or author.

Index

A

Acrobat Reader (Adobe), 331–332
Adobe
    Acrobat Reader, 331–332
    FrameMaker+SGML, 330
    SVG Viewer, 330
aligning text (CSS), 225
*American National Standards
    Institute (ANSI), 14*
annotations, 136–137, 313
*ANSI (American National Standards
    Institute), 14*
answer key to part reviews, 321–326
applications, 36–38, 46–47, 213
ASCII data, 10
associating
    CSS with XML documents, 228
    schemas with XML documents,
      295–296
attaching XSLT style sheets, 161, 204
attributes
    comparison to elements, 58
    definition, 57–58

DTD (Document Type Definition),
    103–104, 106–108
elements, 106–107, 109–110
empty elements, 58
guidelines for using, 58, 60
handling, 109
HTML, 269–270
ID attributes, 113
IDREF links, 114–115, 118–119
names, 58
naming, 104
purpose, 108–109
rules, 58
schemas, 286
values, 58, 104–105, 189
XHTML, 269–270
XLink, 312–314
XSLT, 247

B

behavior of links, 313–314
binary data, 10
block elements, 223

X

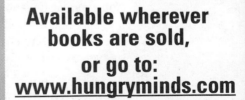

HUNGRY MINDS, INC.
END-USER LICENSE AGREEMENT

READ THIS. You should carefully read these terms and conditions before opening the software packet(s) included with this book ("Book"). This is a license agreement ("Agreement") between you and Hungry Minds, Inc. ("HMI"). By opening the accompanying software packet(s), you acknowledge that you have read and accept the following terms and conditions. If you do not agree and do not want to be bound by such terms and conditions, promptly return the Book and the unopened software packet(s) to the place you obtained them for a full refund.

1. **License Grant.** HMI grants to you (either an individual or entity) a nonexclusive license to use one copy of the enclosed software program(s) (collectively, the "Software") solely for your own personal or business purposes on a single computer (whether a standard computer or a workstation component of a multi-user network). The Software is in use on a computer when it is loaded into temporary memory (RAM) or installed into permanent memory (hard disk, CD-ROM, or other storage device). HMI reserves all rights not expressly granted herein.

2. **Ownership.** HMI is the owner of all right, title, and interest, including copyright, in and to the compilation of the Software recorded on the disk(s) or CD-ROM ("Software Media"). Copyright to the individual programs recorded on the Software Media is owned by the author or other authorized copyright owner of each program. Ownership of the Software and all proprietary rights relating thereto remain with HMI and its licensers.

3. **Restrictions On Use and Transfer.**

   (a) You may only (i) make one copy of the Software for backup or archival purposes, or (ii) transfer the Software to a single hard disk, provided that you keep the original for backup or archival purposes. You may not (i) rent or lease the Software, (ii) copy or reproduce the Software through a LAN or other network system or through any computer subscriber system or bulletin-board system, or (iii) modify, adapt, or create derivative works based on the Software.

   (b) You may not reverse engineer, decompile, or disassemble the Software. You may transfer the Software and user documentation on a permanent basis, provided that the transferee agrees to accept the terms and conditions of this Agreement and you retain no copies. If the Software is an update or has been updated, any transfer must include the most recent update and all prior versions.

4. **Restrictions on Use of Individual Programs.** You must follow the individual requirements and restrictions detailed for each individual program in Appendix B of this Book. These limitations are also contained in the individual license agreements recorded on the Software Media. These limitations may include a requirement that after using the program for a specified period of time, the user must pay a registration fee or discontinue use. By opening the Software packet(s), you will be agreeing to abide by the licenses and restrictions for these individual programs that are detailed in Appendix B and on the Software Media. None of the material on this Software Media or listed in this Book may ever be redistributed, in original or modified form, for commercial purposes.

5. **Limited Warranty.**

   (a) HMI warrants that the Software and Software Media are free from defects in materials and workmanship under normal use for a period of sixty (60) days from the date of purchase of this Book. If HMI receives notification within the warranty period of defects in materials or workmanship, HMI will replace the defective Software Media.

   (b) **HMI AND THE AUTHOR OF THE BOOK DISCLAIM ALL OTHER WARRANTIES, EXPRESS OR IMPLIED, INCLUDING WITHOUT LIMITATION IMPLIED WARRANTIES OF MERCHANTABILITY AND FITNESS FOR A PARTICULAR PURPOSE, WITH RESPECT TO THE SOFTWARE, THE PROGRAMS, THE SOURCE CODE CONTAINED THEREIN, AND/OR THE TECHNIQUES DESCRIBED IN THIS BOOK. HMI DOES NOT WARRANT THAT THE FUNCTIONS CONTAINED IN THE SOFTWARE WILL MEET YOUR REQUIREMENTS OR THAT THE OPERATION OF THE SOFTWARE WILL BE ERROR FREE.**

   (c) This limited warranty gives you specific legal rights, and you may have other rights that vary from jurisdiction to jurisdiction.

6. **Remedies.**

   (a) HMI's entire liability and your exclusive remedy for defects in materials and workmanship shall be limited to replacement of the Software Media, which may be returned to HMI with a copy of your receipt at the following address: Software Media Fulfillment Department, Attn.: *XML Weekend Crash Course*, Hungry Minds, Inc., 10475 Crosspoint Blvd., Indianapolis, IN 46256, or call 1-800-762-2974. Please allow four to six weeks for delivery. This Limited Warranty is void if failure of the Software Media has resulted from accident, abuse, or misapplication. Any replacement Software

Media will be warranted for the remainder of the original warranty period or thirty (30) days, whichever is longer.

(b) In no event shall HMI or the author be liable for any damages whatsoever (including without limitation damages for loss of business profits, business interruption, loss of business information, or any other pecuniary loss) arising from the use of or inability to use the Book or the Software, even if HMI has been advised of the possibility of such damages.

(c) Because some jurisdictions do not allow the exclusion or limitation of liability for consequential or incidental damages, the above limitation or exclusion may not apply to you.

7. **U.S. Government Restricted Rights.** Use, duplication, or disclosure of the Software for or on behalf of the United States of America, its agencies and/or instrumentalities (the "U.S. Government") is subject to restrictions as stated in paragraph (c)(1)(ii) of the Rights in Technical Data and Computer Software clause of DFARS 252.227-7013, or subparagraphs (c) (1) and (2) of the Commercial Computer Software - Restricted Rights clause at FAR 52.227-19, and in similar clauses in the NASA FAR supplement, as applicable.

8. **General.** This Agreement constitutes the entire understanding of the parties and revokes and supersedes all prior agreements, oral or written, between them and may not be modified or amended except in a writing signed by both parties hereto that specifically refers to this Agreement. This Agreement shall take precedence over any other documents that may be in conflict herewith. If any one or more provisions contained in this Agreement are held by any court or tribunal to be invalid, illegal, or otherwise unenforceable, each and every other provision shall remain in full force and effect.

CD-ROM Installation Instructions

The CD-ROM includes any XML files, XSLT style sheets, XML DTDs, XML schemas, and exercise result files that were presented in each session. These are included in the folder named Source Code. In this folder, programs and examples are organized in sub- folders named after each session number. Files from Session 1 are included in folder session1, Session 2 files are included in session2, and so on.

Although you can view files directly from your CD-ROM, we recommend that you copy all of the book's sample files to your hard drive. Any exercise that generates result files from an XML source file will fail if you run it from the CD-ROM.

Each third-party program is included in a separate folder. Appendix B provides information about installing these third-party programs.

The CD-ROM also includes a self-assessment test with which you can test and reinforce your knowledge of the material covered in the book. The folder named Self-Assessment Test contains the installation program Setup_st.exe. With the book's CD-ROM in the drive, open the Self-Assessment Test directory and double-click on the program icon for Setup_st.exe (your system might not display the .exe extension) to install the self-assessment software and run the tests. The self-assessment software requires that the CD-ROM remain in the drive while the test is running.